T0318179

ROUTLEDGE LIBRARY EDITIONS:
LABOUR ECONOMICS

Volume 13

PATTERNS OF LABOUR

PATTERNS OF LABOUR
Work and Social Change in the Pottery Industry

RICHARD WHIPP

Routledge
Taylor & Francis Group

LONDON AND NEW YORK

First published in 1990 by Routledge

This edition first published in 2019
by Routledge
2 Park Square, Milton Park, Abingdon, Oxon OX14 4RN

and by Routledge
52 Vanderbilt Avenue, New York, NY 10017

Routledge is an imprint of the Taylor & Francis Group, an informa business

British Library Cataloguing in Publication Data
A catalogue record for this book is available from the British Library

ISBN: 978-0-367-02458-1 (Set)
ISBN: 978-0-429-02526-6 (Set) (ebk)
ISBN: 978-0-367-02627-1 (Volume 13) (hbk)
ISBN: 978-0-367-02629-5 (Volume 13) (pbk)
ISBN: 978-0-429-39863-6 (Volume 13) (ebk)

Publisher's Note
The publisher has gone to great lengths to ensure the quality of this reprint but points out that some imperfections in the original copies may be apparent.

Disclaimer
The publisher has made every effort to trace copyright holders and would welcome correspondence from those they have been unable to trace.

PATTERNS OF LABOUR

Work and social change in
the pottery industry

RICHARD WHIPP

London and New York

For
Jesse, Sam,
Peggy and Arthur

First published 1990
by Routledge
11 New Fetter Lane, London EC4P 4EE

Simultaneously published in the USA and Canada
by Routledge
a division of Routledge, Chapman and Hall, Inc.
29 West 35th Street, New York, NY 10001

Typeset by LaserScript Ltd, Mitcham, Surrey
Printed and bound in Great Britain by
Biddles Ltd, Guildford and King's Lynn

British Library Cataloguing in Publication Data
Whipp, Richard, *1954–*
Patterns of labour: work and social change in the pottery industry.
1. Pottery industries, history
I. Title
338.4'76664

Library of Congress Cataloging in Publication Data
Whipp, Richard.
Patterns of labour: work and social change in the
industry/Richard Whipp.
p. cm.
Includes bibliographical references.
1. Potters—Great Britain—History. 2. Potters—United
States—History. 3. Trade-unions—Potters—Great Britain—History.
4. Trade-unions—Potters—United states—History. 5. Pottery
industry—Great Britain—History. 6. Pottery industry—United
States—History. I. Title.
HD8039.P82G78 1990
331.76663941—dc20 89-70147
CIP
ISBN 0-415-03076-5

CONTENTS

FIGURES AND TABLES

ABBREVIATIONS

CATU Coll   Ceramic and Allied Trade Union Collection, Hanley
     D (followed by number) – Document from CATU Coll
     L (followed by number)– Letter from CATU Coll

HBL   Horace Barks Reference Library, Hanley

1910 Lead C^{ee}   *Report of the Departmental Committee on the use of Lead in the Manufacture of Earthenware and China 1910*   Q – Question

L. Gazette   *Labour Gazette of the Board of Trade*

MRC   Modern Records Centre, University of Warwick

NCPI   National Council of the Pottery Industry

NAS   National Amalgamated Society of Male and Female Pottery Workers, the potters' union title from 1906-1917

NSJFS   *North Staffordshire Journal of Field Studies*

NSPW   National Society of Pottery Workers, the potters' union title from May 1917

P. Gazette   *The Pottery Gazette*

PRO   Public Records Office, Kew

S. Advertizer   *The Staffordshire Advertizer*

SRO   Staffordshire Record Office

S. Sentinel   *The Staffordshire Sentinel*

Times I.F.T.S.   *The Times Imperial and Foreign Trade Supplement*

US Report 1915   *Department of Commerce. Bureau of Foreign and Domestic Commerce. Misc. Series No. 21. The Pottery Industry* (Washington 1915)

PREFACE

I have incurred many debts of gratitude during my research, which I must repay. My thanks go to the staff of the university libraries of Warwick, Cambridge and Oxford; Birmingham Central Library; the British Museum; the British Library of Political and Economic Science; the Horace Barks Library; and the William Salt Library. The Gladstone Pottery Museum, the Dyson Perrins Museum, the Modern Records Centre, the Staffordshire Record Office, the Public Records Office and their directors and staff have also been extremely helpful.

A number of individuals gave me valuable assistance. John Briggs, Dr Malcolm Nixon, Muffi Fox and Frank Botham shared their knowledge of the pottery industry and the Potteries with me. My discussions with Dr Liz Hart and Dr Margarite Dupree on our common field of research were particularly useful. I would also like to thank those who commented on my work at various stages of the project: Dr Patrick Joyce, Professor Royden Harrison, Professor Sidney Pollard, Dr John Cumbler, Dr Margaret Grieco, Professor Alice Kessler Harris, Dr Alan McKinley, Dr Peter Clark, Professor Richard Price, Dr Alastair Reid and Dr Dennis Smith. Above all I wish to express my gratitude to Dr Tony Mason, for the benefits of his wise advice, indestructible humour and robust common sense throughout my research.

I remain eternally grateful to the Ceramic and Allied Trades Union and their head office staff in Hanley. They provided me with every possible help during my period of study and lightened the long days spent in their basement. Moreover, they did so while they and their members were experiencing the effects of a recession similar in intensity to the one I was examining which occurred at the beginning of this century.

Part of Chapter 2 uses material which is discussed in my article in *Midland History*, XII,1 in 1987. The first section of Chapter 4 emanates from part of my article in the *International Review of Social History*, XXIX, 3, 1984. The author is grateful to the editors of these journals for permission to use this material.

The research was funded by the Economic and Social Research Council.

I warmly appreciate the care and attention given to the manuscript by Deirdre Hewitt and the maintenance of her own high standards throughout. My thanks also to Rosemary Nixon and Talia Rodgers of Routledge for all their help

Lastly, Anne Whipp alone knows best the contribution she made to my period of research. I remain in her debt.

INTRODUCTION

This is a study of the British pottery industry, the potters and their working lives. Work is a significant part of people's existence, yet how groups such as the potters experienced work and its changing form from the nineteenth to twentieth centuries has gone largely unchronicled. What follows is an attempt to remedy that neglect. The process of exploring the patterns of labour in one of Britain's staple industries will reveal much of direct relevance to how one may understand work and analyse its changes.

WORK

The importance of work to western societies has been sharply evident in the 1980s. Anxieties concerning its place in human life are manifested in a number of ways. Planned and unintended restructuring of national economies in the name of monetarism has forced those both in and out of paid employment to re-assess the place of work in their lives. The collision of demographic changes, micro-electronics and altered values towards enterprise point to apparently radical transformations in the shape and content of labour.

Predictions about the future of work abound. Some see immense possibilities for personal development within the application of computer technology to manufacturing and service sectors alike (Zuboff 1988). Others maintain that a so-called information-based society will result in a complete reformation of working lives. Work, it is argued, will be increasingly located in the home. Individuals will work on temporary contract bases for a

1

range of employers during their careers. The balance between employment and leisure will alter accordingly.

The scale and intensity of such projections into the future give cause for concern. Statements on the likely form of work in the 1990s rely heavily on judgements about the present and the past. The nature of work is seen to have evolved through the distinctive pre-industrial, industrial and now post-industrial eras taking on a clear set of characteristics at each stage (Kaplinsky 1984, Robertson 1985). Yet how secure are these assumptions of the sooth-sayers and policy makers of the late twentieth century? What is the extent of our empirical knowledge of the previous forms work has taken? How sound are the analytical tools which we use to understand work in the past?

A brief consideration of the growing body of academic research on work suggests that empirical coverage is by no means complete and above all that our understanding is still modest.

Patrick Joyce, in a comprehensive review (Joyce 1988) highlights the many limitations of current notions of pre-industrial and subsequent forms of work. The simple distinction between agricultural and industrial production in the eighteenth and nineteenth centuries, for example, is shown to be over-drawn. Almost one-third of the total adult male population of England was already engaged in manufacture and mining in 1701. Major structural shifts are readily identifiable in the process of industrial-isation. These included: the early eighteenth century phases based on textiles; the widening base of manufacturing industry into the nineteenth century, which were in turn supplemented by the expansion of the food, drink and tobacco industries in response to the development of a mass-consumer market; and the rise of the motor manufacture, consumer durable and electrical industries after 1918.

Although these alterations to the UK economy are by now well-catalogued (Pollard 1982, Joyce 1988) recent research on the character of work performed in its industries raises many issues. The picture of a transition from 'traditional' to 'modern', rural to urban involving the separation of work and home, the dominance of large-scale mechanisation and waged labour has been ques-tioned. Basic information is still required on: the precise extent and experience of women's work; the persistence of casual and non-waged work; the ordering of work and non-work time; the construction of authority at work; the growth of management; and the interior life of the workplace.

As such information is collected, an altogether more complicated and demanding portrait of industrialisation in the nineteenth and twentieth centuries has begun to emerge. The process appears to have varied widely according to industry and location (Massey 1984). Women's work now appears to have been under-recorded and its full significance for work and family relations misunderstood (Knights and Willmott 1986). Casual and non-waged work forms seem to have survived as a central part of the economy (Pahl 1984). Uniform, managerial control of work time has proved notoriously difficult to establish (Whipp 1987b). Authority at work has remained the subject of contest (Edwards and Scullion 1982, Price 1983). In spite of the growth of formal managerial hierarchies from the 1920s and the rise of large-scale corporations, management's position has often been ambiguous and fragile (Merkle 1980). The culture of the workplace has not been somehow streamlined during the transition to a mature capitalist economy. On the contrary, its richness has become even more apparent.

This expanded view of the historical unfolding of work has been informed by a resurgence in its study by students from different disciplinary backgrounds. Nowhere has this been more evident than among social historians. A productive fragmentation of interests has appeared in the 1980s. From the late 1960s, the influence of E.P. Thompson's (1968/1963) path-breaking work on the making of class was immense, only to be superseded, as the next decade progressed, by labour process theory (P. Thompson 1983). The powerful insights offered by both schools could not overcome their partiality with regard to the understanding of work. On the one hand E.P.Thompson's analysis was seen to rely too heavily on culture which became a privileged site for interpreting worker behaviour at the expense of attention to changes in production (Dobb 1963/1946). Conversely, writers following Braverman's (1974) interpretation of Marx suffered from their over-dependence on the labour process as a means of explaining class formation.

In the present decade historians have attempted to transcend the restrictions in the two schools by re-examining what work is and has been. The aim has been to discover more precisely what

3

constitutes production and social reproduction. In other words, what form has the act of labour taken, by what dynamic does it change and what relationships inform that process of transformation? As in earlier periods of interest in understanding work, social historians have not tackled these questions alone. The project has become much more a joint venture with those from other areas of the traditional academic division of labour.

The contribution from sociology and anthropology has been immense. Many of the hopes of Abrams (1980) and Tilly (1981) have been fulfilled in the sharing of data and concepts across previously impermeable boundaries. Labour market scholars, for example, have revealed the way internal labour markets can stratify workforces both economically and ideologically (Edwards 1979). Sociologists and historians alike have overturned the notion of the capitalist labour process involving the necessary degradation of work and homogenisation of labour. Instead the recomposition of skill across time is apparent and its complex formation means that its control can never be taken for granted (Penn 1985).

Many of the detailed, ethnographic examinations of work (Messenger 1975) have sought to re-introduce the issue of consciousness with respect to both capital and labour. The importance of the subjective in the character of work has been strongly re-established by those studying the question of gender (Alexander 1984) and race (Khan 1979). The image of an inexorable, unilinear establishment of capitalist dominance and worker acquiescence has been dissolved. In its place has appeared a welcome recognition of the agency of labour and capital, the relevance of the distinctive interpretations of market forms by those involved and the way ideological assumptions underpin their actions (Berg 1985: ch. 7, Randall 1987).

As Burawoy (1985) shows, work requires not only the production of objects, it also generates social relations. Production is saturated with ideas about such relations, ideas which have their own means of reproduction and exhibit identifiable processes of change. Students of work are therefore now obliged to explore in their own right the mixture of values and motivations which both employer and employed bring to the workplace. The ideological and political apparatus which regulates production cannot be assumed; the outcome of production relations do not tend

4

inevitably or uniformly to the antagonistic. This approach to industrialisation and the labour process has centred therefore on the production of meaning and the way meanings attributed to work come into being (Joyce 1987).

The most recent developments in the study of work have tackled the issue of meaning head-on. Notwithstanding the difficulties of rarefied technical jargon and the hybrid philosophical foundations of certain practitioners, the use of semiotics and theories of representation suggest much for our understanding of work. If work involves the construction of meaning then the codes and languages which both structure and express that meaning are critical (Stedman Jones 1983, Kaplan and Koepp 1986). The study of visual representations of work, explorations of myth and memory and examinations of the way power relations are integral to the construction of knowledge (Abercrombie 1980, Martin 1981, Giddens 1984, Simmons 1988) have increased markedly within the last few yea

Many of these innovations draw heavily on the links between British and European academics. Less is heard of Anglo-American collaboration. In particular the potential contribution of US specialists in industrial and management studies to the understanding of work in Europe has not been realised. Clearly the impact of North American labour process writers (Braverman 1974, Zimbalist 1979) for example has been immense. Yet the insights of, say, institutional economists, into the way work is regulated (Lewchuk 1987) or the long-term processes of industrial change (Abernathy 1978) have much to offer to the expanded analytical approach to work which has evolved on this side of the Atlantic.

The aim of this book is to develop an appreciation of work in two senses. First the study will try to add to the existing empirical coverage by exploring the changing form of work in one of Britain's major staple industries – pottery. Given the character of pottery manufacture the opportunity arises to help fill some of the important gaps in basic information about work which we have just identified in this overview, for example: the nature of mixed workforces, the ordering of work and non-work activities. the construction of authority and the role of management.

The second main objective is to mobilise the key analytical resources at our disposal for understanding the nature of work outlined in the previous pages. The intention is to develop and deepen that analysis in a number of ways. Above all, the volume will demonstrate: what constitutes production and social reproduction, what ensemble of relations informs that process, and how the meanings of work are constructed. This will be achieved by crafting an analytical structure which embraces not only the economic imperatives of the market but also shows how they in turn were shaped by cultural forces; how relations around work were generated from the values and beliefs of the family, the owner/employer and the collective aspirations seen in organised labour and capital.

The study will show the extensiveness of the grid of relations which explains the character of work in modern capitalist modes of production. Such a grid produces a number of surprises: the boundary between work and home emerges as much less clear than previously; women's position in and around work cannot be characterised as one of total subordination to male authority; the differences within labour appear to be as significant as those which separate employer and employed; union forms can rely as much on community as workplace structures in their operation. The evidence from the pottery industry, taken in conjunction with the experience of other sectors, results in a profile of industrial change which sees no inevitability in the establishment of an omnipotent capital, the homogenisation of workforces or the ineluctable degradation of work. On the contrary, the empirical and analytical patterns of labour will be revealed in all their richness.

In broad terms the book will analyse the structural influences on the potters as workers as well as their individual or collective historical experience. On the one hand we will examine the economic and social constraints on the potters: the structure of their industry; the technology and the nature of the production process; the organisation of the union and the forms of employer action. But the pottery workers consciously interpreted the situations derived from these structural features and they constructed their own definitions of work and collective action. Therefore the thoughts and actions of the pottery operative will be reconstructed as well as their attitudes and values to work. Social and economic relations moulded workers' actions yet workers had the ability in turn to influence, shape and create those relations.

Moreover, a dynamic was involved whereby the structural forces and the perceptions and actions of individuals continuously affected each other. Pottery workers constantly reacted to the changing limitations placed upon them by the organisation of their industry: as workers and trade unionists they sought to modify these constraints. For example, the individual's behaviour was clearly influenced by his location within the division of labour. However, as a member of a workgroup or family network he might well be able directly to alter his experience of toil and enhance his ability to control his job.

A prime concern is to uncover the informal activities of the pottery worker and the rank and file union member in this period. Workers, especially women, have left few records of their past and a reconstruction of their thoughts and actions has always proved difficult. In the potters' case certain sources make the task easier. The Potteries[1] was well served by the local newspapers and an exceptionally detailed trade journal. A large body of parliamentary papers and official statistics on the pottery industry was published from the 1890s onwards which provided both general and detailed information on work. Oral testimony yielded useful, personal insights into the shopfloor world of the potbank in the absence of alternative written records. The recent discovery of the union's correspondence, dispute files and miscellaneous records had a major bearing on the research. The collection of decaying paper and binders, after initial classification, included nearly 1,000 letters, documents, ledgers and notebooks. Many pieces were no more than scraps of papers, some written by single potters, others were produced by workgroups, yet they revealed many details of the small-scale social and industrial relations of the potbank. Whilst this collection has provided important material for our investigation care has been taken to relate and test it against alternative or complementary sources wherever possible.

The book is structured in the following way: it analyses work in relation to the range of relations in play. These relations included the industrial framework; the social relations of the workplace; the unions' origins, composition and organisation and the relationships between employers and workers. Work will also be examined in a wider setting by identifying the potters' participation in the community, their role in the labour movement and the industry's reply to action by the state or its officers.

The economic structure of the pottery industry provided the principal influence on the work of the potter. Chapter 1 will observe how the growth and development of pottery manufacture over two hundred years gave rise to durable traditions of production technique, company form and business strategy which conditioned the industry's response to the changes experienced in the early twentieth century. The arrangement of the sub-industries, the variety of their products and their differing market positions will be identified and their varying effects on workers' attitudes and management or union policy displayed. The uneven evolution of ceramic technology helped to create a complex pattern of work routines and led to the creation of highly differentiated levels of skill and job content.

Chapter 2 focusses on the organisation and experience of work. It will reconstruct the production process and the division of labour. The social groupings and customs which originated within the workplace will be observed as well as the building and operation of the potbank's payment system and its status and authority hierarchies. A detailed investigation of the process of pottery manufacture and how potters experienced work will facilitate an understanding of the social relations between not only workers and masters but also those within the workforce. The changes in technology, skills and working practices of the period critically affected the industrial relations of the industry and formed the essential background to union organisation and action. An industry with almost half its labour force made up of women provides an opportunity to study the historical role of the female worker and to explore the relevance of the home and the family to work and trade unions. Given that the potters were beset with the problems of industrial disease, how they coped with ill-health and its associated difficulties had a clear impact on worker priorities and union objectives.

Chapter 3 will explain the intricate configuration of union form and assess the relationship between the workplace and union organisation and action. The dominant characteristics of the craft unions of the nineteenth century will be related to the process of creating a single, amalgamated society which occupied almost the whole of the period from 1890 to the early 1920s. Workgroup or occupational strength, together with family or local loyalties formed the basis of the new union's structure and power. A distinction will be drawn between official and unofficial types of union action. This perspective enables one to find out how the society operated as an institution and to uncover the meaning of union membership for all sections of the workforce. By examining the preoccupations of leaders and officials along with the aspirations of the membership the tensions between the need for collective union strength and the pressure for autonomous action become apparent.

Management played a vital part in shaping the nature of work and the practice of trade unionism in the Potteries as Chapter 4 will show. Managerial attempts to control production involved an extensive repertoire of techniques ranging from the use of piece work to the more subtle forms of paternalism. However, workers, in isolation or combination, consistently challenged management's efforts to control labour. The industrial relations of the industry which derived from this process also reflected the differences within capital and labour as well as the divisions between them. Contrary to popular belief conflict was widespread in the pottery industry throughout the period. The received view that collective bargaining became progressively centralised and more formal in British industry will be tested against the potters' experience.

Social scientists have become increasingly aware that workers and trade unionists should be located in the community of which they were a part, since industry and community co-exist. Chapter 5 will try to discern to what extent local, customary codes of behaviour informed and modified potters' values and attitudes towards their work or union. We also need to know how employers related to that environment, how active they were in the community and what connection their position on the potbank had with their more public images. The social and class relations of the potbank and the community merit comparison. The growth of a local labour movement was rooted firmly in the Potteries' culture. Surveying the potters' actions inside and outside the potbank helps illuminate the part they played in the labour movement of the Six Towns. Given the past association of the potters with protective legislation and the continuing relevance of government policy to industrial life the chapter will also suggest how the state directly and indirectly influenced worker and union consciousness.

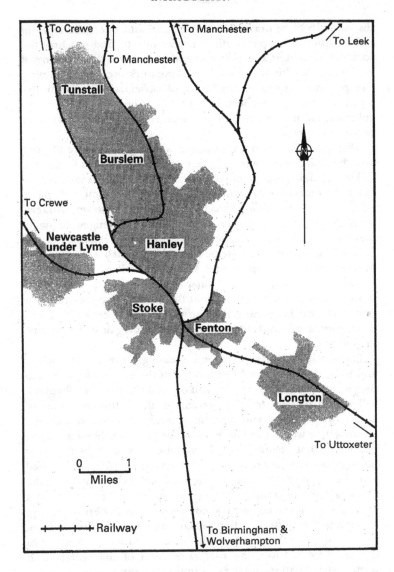

Figure 1 The Potteries 1900, showing the Six Towns
and Newcastle under Lyme

Source: 1" Ordnance Survey map, sheet 123, Stoke-on-Trent

10

THE POTTERY INDUSTRY

The concentration of six factory towns in the thirty square miles of North Staffordshire known as the Potteries (see Figure 1), was one of the notable products of Britain's industrialisation (Briggs 1980). The Potteries has remained an enduring feature of the area's manufacturing industry, social geography and modern industrial landscape. Much of what the outside world knows of North Staffordshire is based on generalised comments concentrating on its staple product, pottery. A number of dominant images and assumptions about potters and the Potteries have become established. Pottery manufacture is supposed to have been technologically backward and unchanging; managerial technique is thought of as unsophisticated; in the twentieth century the industry is said to have failed to respond to foreign competition leading to a period of long-term decline. Perhaps the most well known characteristics of the industry concern the apparently friendly relations of employer and worker, the 'absence' of trade unions and the basically peaceful industrial relations (Yeaman 1968). The success of Arnold Bennett, the locally born writer, and his novels based on the area have strengthened many of these images (Bennett 1902, 1907, 1912, 1916). Therefore, one of the tasks of this investigation into the pottery industry is to test these by now traditional assumptions. The Potteries in fact exhibited a rich diversity of industrial and social experience which the traditional views fail to capture. In 1924, Sydney Dodd, the manufacturer, concluded that 'the pottery trade is a peculiarly complicated industry' (CATU Coll 1924 Wage Inquiry).

Of the works on the pottery industry covering any part of this period, very few examine the potter's work experience in detail or attempt to explain the forms of associations. Charles Shaw's personal account of employment in the industry concentrates on the nineteenth century (Shaw 1903). Harold Owen's *The Staffordshire Potter* focusses on what he saw as the main events of the century; principally the strikes of 1834, 1836-37, 1881 and 1900, the emigration movement and the history of the arbitration board from 1868-1891 (Owen 1901). Warburton's analysis of trade union organisation is in many ways a minor classic of research (Warburton 1931). For the first time he mapped out a number of changes in trade, technology and skill in the potbank and connected them

11

to a clear narrative of craft union development. His period of inquiry ends in 1900. John Thomas, in a less well known piece, gives a broad overview of the historical development of trade unionism in the Potteries (Thomas 1971). He sketches the growth and changes in the union between 1900-21, including the formation of the National Amalgamated Society of Male and Female Pottery Workers in 1906, the expansion in membership during the First World War and the relative decline in the depressed trading of the 1920s. Burchill and Ross attempted to bring Warburton's history up to date (Burchill and Ross 1977). Unfortunately, they confine themselves largely to an institutional report of union evolution and official action. Most of the writers give little space to the important subjects of company form, female employment and the relations of the potters to their community. In contrast this analysis will pay direct attention to each of these subjects in order to understand the social relations of work.

The potters and the Potteries are worthy of study for a number of reasons. The North Staffordshire Potteries are an excellent example of what has been termed 'an isolatable case study which offers scope for intensive investigation' (Thistlethwaite 1958). The area's boundaries were well defined and the Six Towns remained relatively isolated. They were quite separate from the industries of Liverpool or Wolverhampton. In relation to the adjacent regions North Staffordshire would not be included with Manchester to the north or Birmingham and the Black Country to the south (Morgan 1942). Whilst the study remains localised it provides a clear case against which one may compare the general interpretations of industrial life. Second, in common with other regions the Potteries was an example of marked industrial concentration. In 1811, nine-tenths of the population of Burslem was employed in or connected with the pottery industry. This level of concentration continued into the twentieth century. In 1911, almost 47,000 of the area's total workforce of 111,806 were directly employed in the pottery industry. In 1918 it was said that 'the position of North Staffordshire depended largely upon the pottery trade, the people having no means of obtaining other work in the district' (*The Times*: 1.8.1918, Beaver 1964). The Potteries therefore provide an excellent opportunity to examine the overlap of work and community.

Third, one of the prevailing images of the Potteries is highly negative and has distorted the history of the potters. Outside observers in particular have concentrated on what they call the 'ugliness' of the industrial landscape, the monotony of the architecture and the 'squalor' which made up 'the total environmental image of a Victorian industrial city' (Manners 1980). Richard Crossman's opinion can be taken as an example of this negative view. He wrote in his diary in February 1965:

> Here is this huge, ghastly conurbation of five towns ... if one spent billions on this ghastly collection of slag heaps, pools of water, old potteries, deserted coal mines, there would be nothing to show for the money. There is nothing in Stoke except the worst of the industrial revolution and some of the nicest people in the world.
>
> (Crossman 1975: 151)

One of the aims of this study will be to show that previous authors have been far too sweeping in their judgements. Undoubtedly the Potteries suffered all the disadvantages of 'precocious urbanisation' yet that should not blind one to the richness of the potters' industrial culture and varieties of local communal life.

Fourth, the period of the late nineteenth century to the inter-war years has been chosen since it displays a range of events and features of especial concern to students of work (Hobsbawm 1987). Periodisation is an unnatural and arbitrary exercise: the historical experience of workers does not pay attention to these artificial limits. However, the period in question was arguably decisive for the history of labour in Britain and in the Potteries. Between 1880-1920 the modern British trade union movement was created. The middle years of the period have been described as 'one of crisis in the strict sense of marking a decisive juncture or pass, the outcome of which served as a turning point in the making of modern Britain' (Burgess 1980: 113). The first three decades of the twentieth century saw, for example, the introduction of new technology and methods of working, a sharp growth of union coverage and membership, and episodes of intense industrial conflict.

In the Potteries, the period was equally one of major change. During these years an amalgamated industrial union was established after almost 100 years of multiple craft unionism. A federation of manufacturers was created and industry-wide collective bargaining attempted. The formation of the National Council of the Pottery Industry in 1917 was described as 'epoch-making' (*P. Gazette*. 1.8.1917, 796). Key alterations in the organisation of work led to a series of disputes. Workforce and employers played an integral part in the development of an independent Labour party and the election of the first working potter to Parliament in 1924.

These were years when the 'labour question' became a national preoccupation. In the Webbs' view the trade unions became a scapegoat for the apparent failure of English manufacturers to hold their own against foreign competition. By 1917 a separate ministry had been created for labour issues (S. Webb and B. Webb 1902). In the Potteries in 1907, Noah Parkes, organiser in the potters' union and secretary of the North Staffordshire Labour Council, celebrated the council's highest membership to date which combined with the 'closest ever support and concerted actions of local unions for many years'. In April 1909, the major difficulty for pottery employers was said to be 'labour questions' and 1911 was described as a year of 'serious labour crisis' (*P. Gazette*. 1.4.1911).

During the crises of the period some of the main elements of pottery work were shaped and reinforced in forms which have remained in the industry ever since. For example, there are basic similarities between the 1977 'Wage Structure' and agreements and the results of the 1924 wage inquiry. Skill differentials, the high variability of piece work, waiting time, allowances and a range of trade customs are common to both. An examination of this key period in the past may aid our understanding of the pottery industry in the present. Together, they may shed new light on the nature of work more generally.

Chapter One

THE POTTERY INDUSTRY

In 1900 the Staffordshire Potteries formed the greatest geographical concentration of ceramic industry in the world. The region produced every article which had clay as its principal element. People spoke of the Potteries in international terms. Both masters and workers were 'admitted by everyone to be the most skilled potters in the world' (Remer, *Hansard*: 30.6.1927, Col. 631). The performance of those potters at the trade fairs of Brussels, Turin, Ghent, Paris or Leipzig demonstrated that Staffordshire 'set the standard for the whole world' (*Times* I.F.T.S.: 1.8.1917). Britain enjoyed supremacy not only in the quality but also in the variety and scale of its pottery production. At the turn of the century it accounted for almost one-third of the world's ceramic export market and boasted the world's largest pottery factories. By any standard the Potteries constituted 'the world's greatest pottery industry' (*US Report 1915*: 389).

In national terms the Potteries could justifiably be called 'a great industrial district'. Eighty per cent of the country's pottery workers lived within a five mile radius of Stoke Town Hall where they produced nine-tenths of Britain's pottery output in 1900. In 1911, 46,000 workers were employed directly, 80,000 indirectly, and almost the entire Potteries population of a quarter of a million people was supported by the staple industry (Owen 1901: 4, *Census of Staffordshire* 1911: Table 23). In the same year the pottery industry accounted for 0.3% of the national occupied workforce and 0.6% of the national industrial workforce (the mean percentage of the occupied workforce per industry was 4.17%). Though smaller than the coal, iron and steel or textile industries, relative to its size pottery made an important contribution to national

15

production. *The Times* regarded pottery as 'a great industry, valued at £7 million a year' during the First World War. Gross output began at £3 million worth in 1900, grew to £7 million during the 1907–1912 period and in the early 1920s went over £10 million. Gross pottery output made up between 0.3 and 0.4% of gross national output and between 0.3 and 0.6% of national net output during the entire 1890–1930 period. The export role of pottery was a strong one. In 1907 approximately a quarter of the goods in the UK went for export: pottery exported between 35 and 40% of its production and has continued to do so until the 1980s.

To understand the forms of work and trade unionism connected with pottery manufacture one must first come to terms with the economic structure of that industry. This chapter will try therefore to identify and explain the salient elements of that structure. Whilst located within a maturing capitalist economy the pottery industry exhibited a set of distinctive, almost unique features (cf Cannadine 1984) which provided a highly specific context for the labour process of potting.

First, it is necessary to explore the development of the industry during the preceding 200 years in order to appreciate how the main characteristics of pottery production were deeply embedded in the past. Second, the industry's sub-divisions will be highlighted thereby revealing the varieties of product and production. Third, a survey will follow of the market formation, its movements and the consequent changes in technology, work intensity and levels of employment. Fourth, it is imperative to investigate the shifts in the international ceramic industry which helped form local managerial strategy.

An assessment will be offered of the broad experience of the industry during these years. This will convey the range of economic rhythms, periods and levels of performance the industry contained and the implications of these contingencies for the organisations and actions of capital and labour (cf. Langlois 1983: 584). Each of these five structural facets of the pottery industry had important bearings on the content and changes in pottery work and its attendant social relations.

HISTORICAL DEVELOPMENT OF THE INDUSTRY

In spite of the pottery industry being one of the most notable products of Britain's early industrialisation, no general history of the industry exists. Nevertheless, if we seek to create that history many of the industry's main features in the early twentieth century became more intelligible.

Why was the industry concentrated in North Staffordshire? The original attractions were the good quality local clays and the region's coalfield which provided fuel particularly suited to the firing of ware. Both clay and coal, as well as lead for glazes were easily mined from the early eighteenth century. There was little local competition for the use of the coal. Pottery production remained on the coalfield, despite the discovery of high quality clays elsewhere, since the ratio of coal to clay use was 4:1 and it was therefore cheaper to import the new clays to Staffordshire. Infant pottery centres in the North-East and the East Midlands faced competition for labour and capital in a way that North Staffordshire never experienced (Gay and Smyth 1974: 14).

Once established, the concentration of the industry was reinforced by a cluster of factors. The region enjoyed a central national position in relation to its markets and its 'arrangement of freights'. The industry's late-eighteenth-century growth relied on displaced local agricultural workers for a pool of labour which ensured the development of a native workforce. In time the presence of an indigenous population experienced in ceramic production became a vital reason for the industry remaining in the area: no other region could supply the telling combination of raw materials and a skilled workforce. As happened in other areas, the concentration of the industry was intensified by the establishment of a group of ancillary traders including crate-makers, coopers, flint-grinders, colour-makers, brush-makers and paper-millers. By the early nineteenth century the forces making for concentration were so strong that firms began migrating to the Potteries from other areas (Allen 1937: 1, Moisley 1950: 95-97).

The industry which grew up in North Staffordshire in the seventeenth century was essentially a cottage industry. Red unglazed ware and salt-glazed pieces were the dominant products from 1690 onwards. It was not until the mid-eighteenth century that the first large-scale expansion of the industry occurred.

17

Between 1660 and 1760, on the supply side, improvements in production technique had proceeded slowly involving ovens, kilns, wheels and lathes. Plaster moulds were in use by the 1740s which facilitated the general making of irregular-shaped articles for the first time. In the 1750s new fluid lead glazes and double-firing were common, leading to the production of earthenware which superseded the risky and therefore expensive salt-glazed ware by the 1780s. White earthenware was a key departure in the growth of the industry since it became exceptionally popular for domestic and 'useful' purposes given its hard but smooth finish (Wedgwood 1913: 46, 67, 81, 84, Surrey-Dane 1950: 8ff). On the demand side, the period witnessed a social revolution in consumer taste as each stratum of society emulated its social superiors: tea drinking for example, changed from a luxury to a necessity in the second half of the eighteenth century.

Table 1.1 Pottery industry size 1710-1901

Date	Workers	Potbanks	Output p.a.
1710-1715	500	40-47	£6,417
1762	7,000	150	–
1769	10,000	124	–
1785	15,000	–	–
1801	–	146	–
1835	20,000	157	–
1841	24,724	–	–
1851	25,000	160	£2,000,000
1861	27,000	170	£2,210,000
1871	31,279	214	–
1881	36,230	297	–
1891	44,550	–	–
1901	46,451	400	£3,000,000

Sources: Wedgwood 1913: 48, Warburton 1931: 66, 53, E. Surrey-Dane, 1950: 8, 12, 19, 20, Thomas 1971: 6, 9-12

In response to the widespread demand for inexpensive decorated ware, advances followed in transfer printing between 1756-1760 and the perfection of painting, gilding and use of colours. Ornamental wares (often in new forms such as Basalt or

18

Jasper) were added to the range of pottery products on a large scale, stimulated by, *inter alia*, the neo-classical revival. By this time therefore, pottery manufacturers, with products suited to growing consumer expenditure and demand, broke through to a national and later international market. Innovations in production techniques and ware types were paralleled by new forms of factory organisation, increased division of labour and enhanced market and communications networks (McKendrick 1961). By 1800 British earthenware, as Bourry put it, ruled supreme, and all the countries of Europe paid tribute to the faience (earthenware) manufacturers of Staffordshire.

It was in the nineteenth century that the pottery industry diversified into its modern form of a group of related sub-industries. Between 1800-1850 there were no major innovations in production technique. Instead there was a gradual diffusion of the best practice which the trade leaders had established. Earthenware was still the foundation of the industry. Stoneware products based on the cheaper clays continued to be made. In the early nineteenth century Staffordshire took the lead in china production from the previous century's centres at London, Worcester and Derby. China or porcelain manufacture expanded with Longton specialising in the cheap mass market while an elite group, led by Mintons ('the first of European factories'), dominated the higher-priced sectors of Europe (Briggs 1980: 165). A variant of porcelain known as Parian was added to the range after mid-century to satisfy the increased demand for statuary porcelain in the 1870s and 1880s. The growth in output and sales of this initial product range arose primarily from serving the mass market. Design was always a weakness but Staffordshire possessed commanding advantages over incipient foreign manufacturers regarding its quality clays, cheap coal, good transport facilities, the benefits from concentration in a single region and above all the extreme dexterity of the English artisans (Wedgwood 1913: 188).

As the nineteenth century progressed one section of the industry expanded markedly and two entirely new branches were created. The demand for bricks and tiles increased with the growth of industry and towns. The two sections of the industry which were children of the late nineteenth century were the sanitary and electrical trades. Sanitary ware was in its infancy in the 1860s. New ware types were added in the 1880s and the 1890s saw high levels of production in response to the increasing needs of housing, hotels and public institutions. Twyford's earthenware pieces, with their greater adhesive qualities and polished finish, were replacing the enamelled metal products of Wolverhampton. Foreign potters were forced to imitate. Specialist electrical ware was made to serve the needs of the late-nineteenth-century electrical industry's growth (cf Landes 1969: 235). Porcelain had high-quality insulation properties and could assume an extensive variety of very small shapes. By 1900 almost half the world's supply of electrical insulators came from Bullers. At the start of the twentieth century the pottery industry was composed of seven sub-branches, the form it has retained down to the present day (Moisley 1950: 69, Landes 1969: 235).

The growth in the pottery industry's size mirrored the expansion of pot-making. The clear growth spurts were in the second halves of the eighteenth and nineteenth centuries and were based upon the demand for new sets of products in each case. Between 1760 and 1800 the workforce increased by 185%: from 1840 to 1900 the increase was a more modest 84% (Marx 1938/1889: 230).

During this growth three important features of the industry appeared: the uneven levels of mechanisation of the production process; the stratification of the industry by company type and the generation of a high density of work customs. Each characteristic which developed during this growth period will provide a key variable in the analysis of work at the start of the twentieth century.

Berg has suggested that technological development in the nineteenth century was not uniform and that in many industries mechanisation of basic production phases remained incomplete. Others show how the use of machinery in one part of the production process could often be accompanied by increased manual labour elsewhere. Mechanisation could also require, not necessarily displace, manual (often skilled) operation (Samuels 1977, Berg 1979: 5). The pottery industry is a good example.

In the late eighteenth century pottery was one of the leading industries in the application of steam power (mainly in flint and glaze milling). Yet by the early nineteenth century the dominant position of the kiln in the production process reduced the importance of mechanisation in other phases. The expansion of the industry also relied heavily on innovations in body or glaze composition and improvements in factory organisation. Certain mechanical devices had been improved, such as the potter's wheel and lathe, but never to the same extent as in textiles for example. These devices also were based on manual operation and with a large pool of local labour pottery remained a labour-intensive industry (Surrey-Dane 1950: 21, Thomas 1971: 11, Nixon 1976: 90). It was as late as 1864 that the effects of the Factory Extension Act produced the decisive turning point in the mechanisation of the industry before 1900. The restriction of work hours and the advent of half-time child labour produced a new need to concentrate production. In the late 1860s steam-power transmission was applied to grinders, blungers, pugging and later to parts of 'making' (Lamb 1971: 1-8).

Between 1870 and 1900 bouts of reduced demand coupled with nascent foreign competition increased the need to mechanise as profit margins fell. The levels of domestic and foreign competition meant that potters could not increase prices and therefore machines were used to try and economise on wage costs. It was in this relatively late period that the term 'revolution' was used in the industry to describe the introduction and spread of machinery which began to intensify and replace manual skills in certain areas of production (Warburton 1931: 191-197, Celoria 1973). The result of this uneven and partial mechanisation of pottery manufacture was that craft skills were of central importance to production down to 1900 and beyond.

The division of labour in the industry reflected the irregularity and lateness of mechanisation. There was a change from the two or three main operations of the seventeenth and early eighteenth centuries to the separation out of a range of skilled trades by the nineteenth. The growth in demand for a vastly increased range of products increased the spread of specialist craft occupations by 1850 to between 20 and 30. Yet given the relative lack of mechanisation the general division of labour was little altered between 1850 and 1900. The skilled firemen, pressers, printers or modellers may have had elements of their job refined or simplified by certain mechanical developments but they were not replaced. Pottery manufacture remained a hand-craft activity much longer than other industries. As a craft it did not slot easily into the 'age of manufacture' where the new machinery led to 'the equalisation of labour', dispensing thereby with the aptitudes of the 'self-willed and intractable' skilled workman (Dobb 1963/1946: 259, Marglin 1974). In pottery the opposite was true.

The second important feature to appear during the industry's growth was its stratification by company type. A model exists (Gordon, Edwards and Reich 1982) which explains capitalist development in terms of a core-periphery argument. The core of an industry consists of the largest, most efficient and techno-logically advanced companies who employ the more skilled and higher-paid workers. At the periphery there exists the smaller, least efficient, often transient units with relatively unskilled, low-paid labour. The pottery industry's growth does not fit this model. As demand increased from the late eighteenth century the traditional single master employing around ten workers could not cope. Production units grew in order to increase output (Warbur-ton 1931: 24). However, as Samuels points out the modes of production found in even the nineteenth century could take on a range of forms and these were not uniformly equated with the factory system (Samuels 1977).

So although the average size pottery firm had increased from 75 employees in 1785 to 155 in 1836 and 167 in 1862, the 1857 census shows that over 60% of pottery masters in earthenware still employed less than 20 men. What emerged by the mid-nineteenth century was a three-tier structure. At the base were the smallest units, employing up to 100 hands, with little capital, producing mainly cheap wares which were either imitations of larger manufacturers' designs or produced on sub-contract for them. At the top were the leading firms, highly capitalised, with world markets for their high-quality product ranges. In 1842 a group of 25 such factories existed, each employing between 500 and 1,000 workers (Burchill and Ross 1977: 24-25).

There was also a third, intermediate layer made up of firms employing between 100 and 500 people. The largest companies in the industry had multi-site plants and produced more than one of the seven ware types: a single ware type made on one site characterised the medium-sized potbanks. Unlike the smallest 'banks the firms in the middle layer could be specialists, as in the china trade, with high-quality output for specific markets. The simple distinction between core and periphery does not work in the case of pottery. One element which was common to all levels of the industry's structure was the family basis of the firm. In an intensely localised industry native families of potters supplied the capital and basic managerial skills necessary to run a majority of the firm types. In the smaller and intermediate firms especially, the social distance between master and worker could be very small (Wedgwood 1913: 193, Gay and Smyth 1974: 36, cf Marglin, 1974, Shaw 1903). The implications of the three-tier structure and pervasiveness of the family firm for the industry's labour market or the social relations of the potbank in the early twentieth century will be revealed when we look at these subjects in detail below.

The development of pottery manufacture included a third component: the work customs peculiar to pot-making. In the absence of guild regulations the pottery industry became saturated with trade customs and work practices. The dominant forms were as follows: the 'count' contract of the eighteenth-century craftsman evolved into the intricate piece-work system for all operatives. Embedded in the count and piece-work contracts were strong determinants of the social relations between potters. The contract hiring system confirmed the importance of the craft potter. His power was enhanced by the way he sub-employed his assistants. The craftsman alone decided the wages and work conditions of his sub-employers (*Potteries Examiner*: 19.12.1874). Sub-employment thrived as masters used it as a form of delegating supervision throughout the nineteenth century. The attempts to regain direct managerial control of production in the 1900s were therefore highly contentious.

Sub-employment also helped shape the form of gender relations at work. Male skilled potters often used women as assistants, sometimes from among their own kin. Relatively few women were skilled therefore, or earned wages higher than men. The use of family relations to form work groups meant that a close, traditional link was perpetuated between home and work. At the same time, *images* of male authority in the home reinforced male dominance in the workshop. As a result, direct female employment by masters was opposed by male potters and the impact of women on the potters' unions minimised (*Potteries Examiner*: 9.1.1875, 15.11.1879, *Morning Leader*: 11.12.1902, Shaw 1903: 46, 48, 67).

Between 1700 and 1900 the pottery industry exhibited both continuities and discontinuities. The industry's evolution produced a workforce and form of manufacture with singular traits.

To understand how these qualities were generated is to be better equipped to realise how they operated in the 1890-1930 period. The social relations of the latter era were the product of a set of forces specific to that period: there was no inevitable progression of events which produced those forces. However, the actions of workers at a given point in history are informed by their awareness of the traditions and customs of their industry and its region (Whipp 1987b: 223-229). The pottery industry's previous growth was evoked by potters, masters and workers in their construction of custom and practice. Potters reconstructed the past when choosing particular actions in the face of immediate, violent changes in their lives. The role of craft authority, the range of skills in the division of labour and the linkages of work and family will prove useful in assessing how and why potters used the past in the way they did in the early twentieth century. As will be clear the pottery industry displayed strong continuities of structure and practice.

The discontinuities that occurred were occasioned by growth in the late eighteenth and nineteenth centuries. In these phases additional products, techniques and even sub-industries were added. They did not supersede or destroy existing forms but were complementary to them. The result was an industry which enjoyed a relatively continuous growth. Its geographically concentrated location, the seven sub-industries and company strata were features which were not critically altered by trade or macro-economic fluctuations. That the potters and their industry were so embedded in the past helps explain why changes witnessed in the 1890-1930 period were regarded as profound and in many cases traumatic.

INDUSTRIAL STRUCTURE 1890-1930

During these years the pottery industry remained a composite group of sub-industries. The differences in product alone were sufficient to establish a variation of worker status, union strength, industrial relations style and even to affect the forms of community life. Certainly potters conceived of their industry as composed of a number of sections. This exchange during an inquiry in 1924 is indicative: *Wethered* (Chairman): 'You say china and earthenware. Is that the same as sanitary?' *Clowes* (Trade unionist): 'No, the china is one branch of the industry and the earthenware is another. The sanitary is again entirely separate' (*1910 Lead C* Vol. 1: 6).

Table 1.2 Distribution of pottery manufacture in the Six Towns 1907

	Stoke	*Hanley*	*Longton*	*Fenton*	Burslem	*Tunstall*
Earthenware	16	47	31	18	46	11
China	11	11	50	12	11	3
Jet & Rockingham	1	4	2	3	12	3
Sanitary ware	2	8	1	–	8	–
Tiles	14	14	–	1	13	10
Others	2	15	1	3	6	1
Total:	46	99	85	37	96	28: 391

Source: Reconstructed from the entries in *The Potteries, Newcastle and District Directory* (1907) Hanley: Cooper

In total there were seven sub-industries distinguished by their products: earthenware, china, jet and rockingham, sanitary ware, electrical ware, chemical ware and tiles. Only the larger firms consistently produced more than one type. Most pottery firms were firmly located in one sub-industry only.

As Table 1.2 shows, the distribution of the sub-industries amongst the Six Towns was not uniform. Earthenware was the most widely spread. At the other extreme, the concentration of china makers in Longton was very high, with more china works in the one town than in all the other five towns combined. The jet and rockingham trade was centred on Burslem whilst sanitary ware was made in the heart of the Potteries with 85% of the producers in Hanley and Burslem. The relative concentration of the sub-industries was important. In earthenware it was difficult for workers to consider themselves as part of a single sub-industry. Earthenware making was too diffused among the towns and the 169 firms. By contrast in Longton to be a potter was to be a china potter. Similarly the twelve 'jet and rock' or eight sanitary ware units in Burslem both formed recognisable groups united by production methods and location.

What were the results for collective action? It was impossible to organise the earthenware trade by reference to a unitary self-image when it did not exist. The differing levels of concentration and irregular distribution of trades also explains why the early craft unions mobilised craft groups related to single towns. Further, it shows why the union cohesion of the earthenware trade, and indeed the whole industry, proved so difficult. By contrast the solidarity of sanitary potters is more understandable given their distinctive product, status and geographical concentration.

The high density of firms in Hanley and Burslem (nearly half the industry was found there) also helps explain the strong propensity for trades unionism and political activity which this area showed. Hanley and Burslem witnessed the widest range of economic and technical changes and provided the means of comparing wages and conditions for the workers in those sub-industries. By contrast, Longton had a tradition and conscious-ness confined to china production. Longton was relatively isolated, given the communications of the Potteries and the low mobility of china workers. China workers were as susceptible, therefore, to the influence of other industrial groups (principally the miners) as they were to potters in other sub-industries, and this was reflected in the towns' political growth.

Table 1.3 Output by product type in the pottery industry 1907-1924

	1907		1912		1924	
	Value in £1,000s	%	Value in £1,000s	%	Value in £1,000s	%
Earthenware (incl. jet & rockingham)	4,277	55.11	4,492	53.59	9,031	54.75
China	1,025	13.21	1,221	14.57	2,021	12.25
Sanitary	1,035	16.81	1,464	17.47	2,495	15.13
Electrical & chemical	561	7.23	585	6.98	1,209	7.33
Tiles	593	7.64	620	7.40	1,738	10.54
Total:	7,761	100.00	8,382	100.00	16,494	100.00

Sources: Final Report on the First Census of Production 1907, Part I, Cd. 6320 1912: 750-751; Final Report on the Third Census of Production, 1924, Manufactures of Clay, Stone, etc. 1932: 209-213

In order to discover the influence of the variety of sub-industries within pottery manufacture on the forms of work experience and collective action one needs to look now at output levels and product types. From Table 1:3 it is clear that earthenware was by far the largest sector and the foundation of the industry. Contemporaries often spoke as if earthenware and the pottery industry were synonymous. Given that earthenware provided a base-line against which other sectors were compared it became as important as it was difficult for a mass union to organise it. China and sanitary ware accounted for between 12 and 17% of output respectively and were key sectors in output terms. Between them earthenware, china and sanitary ware were responsible for nearly 85% of pottery sold.

By contrast the remaining sectors were, in output terms, quite small in this period and did not dominate the potters' consciousness the way the earthenware, china and sanitary did. China's and sanitary's status was also enhanced by the nature of their output. China was low bulk but very high value as befitted the skilled china workers' image. Sanitary produced very large items, as the quantity by weight figures show, so that sanitary potters also enjoyed high prestige for the physical and mental skills their work involved.

The differences in product type were large both between and within the sub-industries. This range of products ensured a rich mixture of technological and work forms, as well as stark differences in the degree of technical change. Varying the ingredients, recipes[1] and the making, glazing, decorating and firing processes made the product range possible. Earthenware (Gay and Smyth 1974: 20) itself included general earthenware, majolica and stoneware. Some earthenware for the table almost rivalled porcelain while stoneware was made from more simple clays and had a very basic use. Such variety of product made uniform piece rates or the standardisation that industry-wide collective bargaining required very difficult (*1910 Lead Cᵐ* Vol 1: 5-6). The work intensity in making china plates in one firm could be quite different from the firm across the street making the same 9" plate simply because the bodies' working plasticity varied with the nuance of recipe. The problems inherent in the product type were therefore immense for union representations and negotiators (Machin 1973: 63).

The social distance between workers or among manufacturers in the industry was often great given the different products. China boasted of its production of 'the most beautifully manufactured porcelain in the world'. Earthenware's body was more suited to machine production given its simple recipe. China however had a more intricate recipe mix process and was less amenable to mechanical handling. As one ceramic expert put it 'the limits of composition are exceedingly wide'. The manufacture of china in 1919 was described as 'the province of the skilled craftsman and of the artist, and it is as true to-day as it ever was'. In comparison earthenware had a very different reputation. It was said that: 'the production of earthenware is a business; the making of porcelain an art and craft' (*Times I.F.T.S.* 1917: xii).

Sanitary, like china, had a self-image of being a world-leader in its product and yet possessing the unique skills needed to make the often large and heavy fireclay based bodies. Individual crafts in sanitary ware stood out from their counterparts elsewhere (*P. Gazette.* 1.1.1906). Firemen in stoneware fired their product once only while in sanitary some pieces required prolonged firing and specialised ovens and techniques. Sanitary workers were as proud of making a well-glazed, evenly balanced closet (toilet) as were china craftsmen of their bone-china services. Also, because of the differences in body type the industrial relations in china as opposed to sanitary ware were quite different. Casting hardly affected china; in sanitary the new process threatened the very existence of the highest paid craftsman.

The smaller electrical, chemical and tile sectors were far removed in character from the other sub-industries. In electrical and chemical use the industries they supplied required body qualities hitherto unheard of. For example, high voltages required special insulating properties and higher standards of pyrometry and firing operations. The technical control of production was here more firmly in the hands of management and ceramic specialists than in other sectors where craftsmen often determined design, translation and execution themselves. Also, the degree of change in chemical and electrical ware was far greater than in the other sub-industries. Between 1880 and 1918 a complete shift in product type occurred. Makers of china furniture nearly all went over to producing electrical switch gear through to insulators. During the First World War the first British hard-paste electrical porcelains and refractory ware were produced in response to demand from government, the explosives industry and the makers of engines. Worker control of production was therefore low given the unusually high involvement of ceramic specialists. The constant changes in output and techniques meant that collective action and traditions were inhibited. Production of tiles was differentiated by its use of clay powder, not liquid, for its bodies.

In all three sectors (electrical, chemical and tile) the use of machinery or the closer sub-divisions of labour led to comparatively simple tasks which were classed as unskilled. As a result, these sub-industries were distinguished by their labour markets as they employed large numbers of women. Low pay, the negative image of female labour held by craftsmen and the separate qualities of the electrical, chemical or tile sections meant that union levels were low. This differentiation in the tile section, for example, largely explains why an outside union, the Navvies and General Labourers, became so important in that area during this period.

It is therefore inappropriate to speak of the pottery industry as if it made a single product range by a uniform production process (cf Freeman 1982). The notions of 'the pottery industry' or 'the potter', if used without qualification, are entirely artificial constructs. Even the seven sub-industries we have delineated contained sub-sections. Frederick Parkin thought that even his small sub-industry, jet and rockingham 'presented something like a jig-saw puzzle' (Horace Barks Library, Parkin nd: xvi).

The pottery industry in 1900 was therefore an amalgam of sub-industries. Each sub-section revealed its own forms of product range, industrial process, labour market and consequently their own variants of unionism and capital/labour relations. This is not to argue that there were no common features or points of contact between sub-industries. What the following chapters will be exploring when they look at organisation and action in the industry, is a tension. The tension was between those striving for an industry-wide union, or industrial collective bargaining and the forces making for local diversity, prompted by the structure of industry.

PRODUCT MARKETS AND INDUSTRIAL PERFORMANCE

The segmentation of the pottery industry was well reflected in its product markets. In the broadest sense there was a two-fold division between those sub-industries which produced for personal demand (useful and decorated ware) and those which made for industry (tiles, electrical, chemical and sanitary). The potters in the first and largest group saw their market in very defensive terms. They regarded their product as less essential a commodity than say coal: the local axiom that pottery was first in and last out of a depression, mirrored their sense of muted national industrial power (Astor 1922: 301-302). However, one also needs to examine the home and export markets. The market performance of the industry strongly influenced not only the levels of employment in the Six Towns but also helps explain the work experience of the potter and the degree and timing of industrial conflict (cf Cronin 1979: 58, 101). One needs to know therefore: how important were the home and foreign markets for the whole industry and each sub-industry; how did these market relations change; and what effect did these shifts have on work in pottery?

The potters catered for an extensive home market. Between 60 and 65% of production was consumed in this country. British buyers purchased £1 million worth of china each year alone in the 1900s (*Times Eng. Supplement*: 21.4.1913). Home demand had a reputation for reliability, as a *Pottery Gazette* article observed in 1914 (*P. Gazette*: 1.4.1914):

> We are of the opinion that the home market provides the
> backbone of the business of the average [pottery]
> manufacturer ... The demand from the British public is steady
> and substantial, not being subject to violent fluctuations
> either as regards quantity or style.

For the manufacturer, home demand was comparatively 'steady' when put next to the foreign but for the operative the periodic fluctuations of the domestic market were of immediate significance. For example, the generally low employment of the early 1900s was broken by the sharp demand for coronation goods in 1902. Domestic demand was depressed in the 1900s and again in 1914. In 1906 a potter looked back on the years 1900-1905 and counted 'nearly forty factories void'. The first reason he gave was the state of the home market. The significance of the large home market was shown with force in late 1907. Despite expanding pottery exports, home demand remained low with the result that the newly-formed mass potters' union found it very difficult to attract the wide membership it required in these early years (*L. Gazette* 1902: July, *Times I.F.T.S.*: 2.7.1917).

For the sanitary trade the home market in housing was crucial. The poor performance of sanitary in the period 1911-1920 and the apparent quiescence of its workers compared to other potters is well correlated with the building cycle (*L. Gazette* 1911-20: pottery industry entries). Conversely the exceptional general home demand for pottery during and after the war made the main growth phase of the potters' union possible. Also, as pottery workers tried to move to companies producing for the home market at this time, conflict arose as masters attempted to prevent the labour flow. As these examples show, it was the fickleness, not the steadiness, of the home demand for pottery which made pottery workers so conscious of their industrial vulnerability.

The world market for British pottery was a wide one covering over thirty nations. How this market's composition changed and the variance in export performance within the industry are key contextual features of work and trade unionism in the pottery industry.

In a general sense the pottery export market composition would appear to have changed relatively little during the period. The USA, Australia, Canada and Argentina took around 50% of Britain's exported pottery throughout. The United States market had been a pillar of the industry. In 1900 potters said that 'it has always been the solid American trade which has made the fortunes of the Staffordshire potters' (Wedgwood 1913: 191-193, *The Times*: 21.1.1919). Eighty-two per cent of ware sent to the US was earthenware and the workers at Wedgwoods, Doultons, Copelands, Mintons, Meakins, Maddocks and Johnsons in particular relied heavily on American demand (*P. Gazette*: 1.9.1918). However, the US market was changing. Not only was America developing its own pottery industry but it was also beginning to compete with Staffordshire in Canada. In 1900 the US took 28.95% of British pottery exports; by 1925 America received only 14.97%. For the large firms (70% of ceramic exports to the US were made in 19 potteries) the dislocation in their trade and forms of employment was considerable (*P. Gazette*: 1.1.1926).

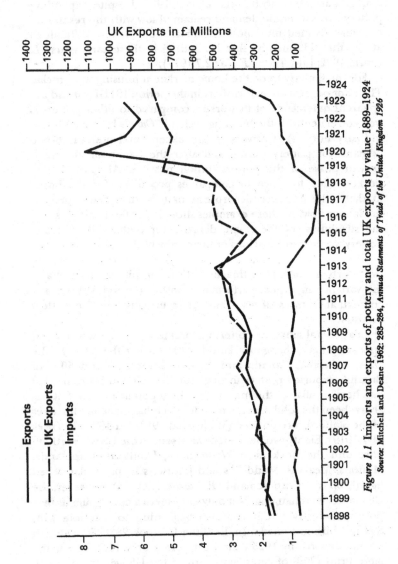

Figure 1.1 Imports and exports of pottery and total UK exports by value 1889–1924

Source: Mitchell and Deane 1962: 283–284, *Annual Statements of Trade of the United Kingdom 1926*

By contrast, exports to 'British Possessions', as opposed to 'Foreign Countries', was expanding. Exports of pottery to the empire increased from 32.3% of total pottery exports in 1900 to 51.44% by 1925. Pottery manufacturers were seen embarking on 'imperial tours' of their main markets. In 1917 a manufacturer, when asked to write on ceramic export markets stated that Staffordshire sent her products 'throughout the King's Dominion and wherever the British flag is flown on the Seven Seas' (*P. Gazette*: 12.12.1917). In common with other British staple industries the pottery industry emerged from the depressed trading of the 1870-1890 period heavily and increasingly reliant on traditional export outlets. In an increasingly hostile world ceramic market, Staffordshire clung to those markets which she could supply with existing products. As a potter admitted in 1909, his industry had been 'satisfied to maintain, not extend its sales' (*P. Gazette*: 1.11.1909). The result was that the existing production methods which accompanied these products for the traditional imperial markets continued in large sections of the industry (Pollard 1962: 22). When technological change was forced on the potters by the war or intense bouts of foreign competition in certain sectors of the industry, the impact on working methods, customs and union rules was immense.

A relationship between export performance and industrial relations in exporting industries has been suggested by Cronin (1979: 58). In the pottery industry the export profile for 1898-1924 (see Figure 1.1) does seem to run parallel with trade union organisation and action. The generally difficult period for unionism in pottery from 1870 to 1900 corresponds with an overall decline in exports of 1.68% (UK exports only increased by 5.4% in this period) (Landes 1969: 230). In our period export and union expansion seem linked. In particular, rises in export levels seem to coincide with the major bargaining and disputes phases. For example, the 1906-7 union formation, the 1906-8 and 1910-11 sanitary strikes, the large jump in membership from 1915 onwards and the 1923-24 conflict, all seem tied in with export growth periods. The leap in pottery exports during the war owed much to government prohibition of trading with German firms and the active help of the commercial research and consular departments. By 1916 it was declared that Germany and Austria had been 'shut out almost entirely from both home and overseas markets'.

Seventy-two porcelain factories alone closed in Germany (*P. Gazette*: 1.9.1914, 1.1.1916, 1.12.1917). Conversely, the periods of export decline are concurrent with union contraction and defensive, reactive dispute activity by potters, as in 1900-1902, 1908-10 and 1921. This relationship between export movements and industrial relations is strengthened since the larger companies dominated the export markets as well as supplying the principal union leaders (see Chapter 3 below).

Table 1.4 Proportion of pottery export production within each sub-industry by value, 1907-1924

	1907 %	1912 %	1924 %
Earthenware	48.24	41.31	51.83
		(incl. jet & rock.)	
China	18.99	14.42	15.34
Sanitary	21.07	36.24	51.75
Electrical & chemical	27.73	N/A	22.12
Tiles	24.28	37.25	31.18
Jet & rockingham	N/A	N/A	1.80

Source: Calculated from the *Census of Production* for 1907 and 1924, and the *Annual Statements of Trade* 1909, 1913 and 1925

In order to understand how the pottery's product markets added to the fragmentation of the industry, one must recognise the differing effect of exports on each sub-industry. Clearly earthenware and sanitary ware provided the bulk of pottery industry exports (between 75 and 85%). The contribution of china, electrical and chemical ware, tiles and jet and rockingham was very small. However, each sub-industry differed in the balance between its home and export market (see Table 1.4). Earthenware exported between 40 and 50% of output whilst china only sent 15-19% abroad. The main division was between china and jet and rockingham on the one hand and the other four sub-industries, which exported 20-50% of their output.

Yet the three *Census of Production* measurements do not capture the changing effect of exports within each sub-industry. China might be a generally low exporter but for individual firms such as Aynsleys virtually the entire output was exported and their industrial life bound up with foreign trade. Also there could occur short-term changes in export participation. In the First World War china suddenly exported 40% of its wares as Longton replaced German and Austrian suppliers. This period of prosperity for Longton not only led to strengthened union organisation in that town but the establishment of minimum, standard rates across the sub-industry for the first time ever. For the sanitary and tile sections the opposite held true. Sanitary's export role was growing steadily until 1914 but during the war the general interruption to national building programmes virtually shut the sub-industry. This was a huge blow for the potter's union. Whereas sanitary workers had formed the shock troops of the newly-formed union in the 1900s, during the vital war period they were disbanded (*Women in Ind. C* 1919: 122, 124, NSPW 1945: 14).

Pottery's product markets were significant for work and unionism therefore in three main ways. First, the split between crockery, a semi-luxury consumer good and other industrial products led to a relatively restrained sense of industrial power among potters. Second, the differing relationship between each sub-industry and its home/export market participation added to the differentiation within the industry as a whole. Third, the general composition of the industry's markets and the unchanging nature of demand which the imperial sectors maintained, helped perpetuate certain forms of technology, work and customs which made future changes difficult.

The industrial performance suggested by pottery's market figures is underwritten by the industry's output levels. Employers in 1918 asserted that 'the pottery industry had not been remunerative to the manufacturers for the last twenty-five years': Gay and Smyth speak of 'the long period of stagnation which had dominated the industry since the 1890s' (Gay and Smyth 1974: 11). These statements are over-simplified. Different sections of the industry varied in terms of output and profit just as they varied in market performance (cf Payne 1974: 48). By using a combination of contemporary reports and statistical series it is possible to track the continuing changes in demand, output and employment. In absolute terms the changes were often small but for the potters concerned these movements could represent considerable short-term dislocation.

Export and general output evidence reveals that the period breaks down into three main parts: 1900-1914, 1914-1920 and

1920-1930. For most manufacturers 1900-1914 contained a trend of gradually expanding demand, especially in exports, punctuated with important contractions in 1900-1902, 1904-1905, 1908-1909 and 1914. There was no single year in which every section of the industry performed well. 1912 might have qualified had it not been for the effects of the miners' strike (*Census of Production* 1907, 1924, *P. Gazette* monthly trade reports). 1908-1909 was the worst period. Home and foreign markets were depressed in every section and unemployment was widespread. This phase saw some of the most bitter disputes of the entire period and unemployment agitation at its strongest in the Potteries (*P. Gazette* 1.7.1908).

By contrast in 1906-1907 the industry was in 'a far more flourishing state than has been the case for a number of years'. From late 1910 until 1913 trade and output expanded strongly. In April 1911 it was stated that 'by common consent trade has never been so good'. £40,000 more was paid out in wages than 1908-1909 while 1912-1913 experienced the highest price and output levels in most potters' memories (*P. Gazette* 1.7.1911). However, after initial dislocation, 1914-1920 was an exceptional growth period for the majority of the industry. Home demand was 'greater than the manufacturers can supply' and firms also found new opportunities in foreign markets as enemy companies withdrew. One firm supplanted twenty-six German competitors in the South American market (*Times I.F.T.S.*: 1.5.1918). Except for the temporary closure of sanitary production 1916 was greeted with the claims that business 'was never better' (*P. Gazette* 1.11.1918, 1.3.1920).

For most pottery manufacturers the only problems caused by the war were shortages of raw materials and labour, whereas the third period, 1920-1930 could not have been more different. After the collapse of the 1920-1921 replacement boom demand was low as foreign competition grew and hostile tariffs were erected abroad. The large crowds of unemployed which formed in the market-place of the Six Towns in 1921 and 1922 were to be a feature of the region for the remainder of the decade. Demand recovered slightly in 1923-1924. Once more the sanitary and tile sections outputs were out of step as they benefited from re-opened foreign markets and renewed domestic building. In 1924 demand even exceeded supply in these sections (*P. Gazette* 1.2.1921, 1.1.1922, Board of Trade 1946: 3).

In general the economic performance of the pottery industry appears to have resembled the experience of the older staple industries of Britain during these three decades. Between 1900 and 1913 a broad recovery is apparent from the slow growth and low prices of the 1870-1900 period. During the war both general industrial and pottery output fell but this must be placed in the context of high demand, operation at full capacity and sharply rising prices. The available evidence indicates that the pottery industry participated in the rapid expansion of the post-war replacement boom and suffered from the contraction of demand which followed. In common with the older industries pottery found the contraction of markets and the rise of large-scale, direct foreign competition a serious problem in the 1920s (Pollard 1962: 124ff).

However, while the pottery industry's performance seems to have paralleled the development of the major sectors of British industry (Matthews, Feinstein and Odling-Smee 1982) this level of generality is of limited analytical use. The general picture conceals many details and divergences from the overall trend which are important in understanding the experience of the potters. First, Lomax describes the pottery industry in the twentieth century as a relatively stagnating industry comparable to mining, textiles, clothing or drink. Yet on closer inspection his index shows that for the years 1900-1924 pottery's annual average increase in productivity was 2.4%, the sixth highest of all industries and well above the national average of 1.6% per annum. These figures for pottery are entirely consistent with the evidence we have on reduced numbers of workers and the increased use of technology by certain sections of the industry.[2]

Second, as we have seen, the sub-industries of pottery manufacture performed very differently over the whole period and especially in terms of the short-term changes they experienced. The result was that in the same year or month different sub-industries could be enjoying entirely opposite trading, output or employment positions, as in the First World War. These detailed differences from the national economic trends are vital in appreciating the specific economic contexts within which pottery owners and workers acted. Also, by reconstructing the year-by-year profile we can begin to detect the seasonal rhythms of the industry which helped shape the potters' wider work experience and upon which management and union strategies were based (cf Turner, Clack and Roberts 1967).

FOREIGN INDUSTRY

The actions of foreign ceramic producers had both direct and indirect repercussions for the working lives of the Staffordshire potters. The direct effect came as German and Austrian manufacturers, for example, took away trade and therefore employment from the potter. The indirect consequence came via the intensified competitive environment which foreign pottery manufacturers helped to create, which in turn resulted in important changes in local managerial strategy and labour policies (Aldcroft 1968: 12-27, cf Hunt 1981: 107). It is necessary therefore to find out how real the impact of foreign producers was and how British masters perceived and reacted to the challenge.

Pottery manufacturers' public reaction was often one of alarm. A ceramic textbook published in 1898 opened with the warning that Britain's pottery industry 'should be roused to an appreciation of the fact that her commercial position is seriously assailed'. Successive trade journal editorials chronicled what they saw as the increasing grip of foreign potters on world markets. As one piece claimed: 'unhappily the lead which this country once held in the pottery markets of the world has in recent years been reduced very considerably by manufacturers in enemy countries' (*Times I.F.T.S.* August 1917). Yet while those views may have been genuinely held it is revealing how consistently manufacturers raised the spectre of foreign competition, during wage bargaining or inquiries on potters' health, as a reason for their inability to act on such issues. As unionists noted manufacturers over-played their hand by continuing to plead 'foreign competition' even in times of expanding Staffordshire exports and falling foreign imports. It was a tactic used from the 1870s at least. Manufacturers cut prices and wages rather than radically reorganise production (*Royal Commission on Trade* 1884: 107, *P. Gazette.* 2.4.1894). What is important is that masters and workers differed over what they each saw as the meaning of foreign competition and what the appropriate response should be. The issue forms a continuous theme from the wage disputes of the 1900s down to the argument over protective tariffs in the 1920s.

Without doubt some foreign pottery industries expanded and exported at higher rates than their British counterparts. However, examining the pottery industry in more detail it becomes clear how uneven the impact of foreign industry was on the domestic manufacturer and worker. For instance, Bernard Moore wrote an article in *Eclipse of Empire* in 1916 on the pottery industry. He clearly showed how 'the foreigner' had secured large parts of the cheaper trade but Britain 'still held first place in the higher end of the market'. Similarly certain manufacturers at the British Pottery Fair in February 1913 were intent on not just 'holding their own, but of gaining ground' in the world markets. Also as L.L. Grimwade noted in 1907, Germany was not competing directly with Britain, since she was producing and exporting very different products (*P. Gazette* 1.11.1907). This helps put in perspective the figures used by some manufacturers and commentators. The report of the Tariff Commission on pottery in 1907 reflected the varied effect of foreign industry (as quoted in *P. Gazette* 1.4.1907). In the early period, china bore the brunt of foreign competition while the sanitary section almost monopolised world trade. Great care is necessary therefore when using the available statistics on the world pottery market in this period.

Between 1895 and 1913 British pottery exports increased 70.64%, the United States increased 1,432.34%, the Germans 160.46%. British exports were expanding but not at as fast a rate as the US or Germany. Britain was still the producer and exporter of the largest range of pottery in the world. Indeed the competition from the US and Germany was highly localised and specific. America's infant sanitary and electrical industries were only beginning to compete for areas of the Canadian and her own American market. Germany's main role in world markets was as an exporter of very cheap ware which Britain did not even produce (*US Report 1915*: 650). Similarly, the effect of imports on the British market was very specialised. Although imports of pottery increased by 18% between 1900 and 1913 it was one section, the china trade, which bore the brunt of the competition. Yet china only accounted for one-tenth of the home market: the other nine-tenths were made up of mainly earthenware and sanitary ware. It was not until 1926 that earthenware began to be imported into Britain and the sanitary trade never saw an American lavatory sold in this country. There is no doubt that the results for the china section were serious. In 1906 of the £1½ million worth of china bought in Britain, Longton supplied only £500,000 worth. It was estimated that this competition resulted in a loss of £¼ million in wages per annum for china workers. Nearly 20% of Germany's exports were targeted at this one small section of the UK market.

A recognition of the localised effect of foreign competition enables us to unravel the contemporary debates and discourse. Manufacturers very skilfully tried to use china's experience as a reason for obtaining protective tariffs and lower wages in the huge earthenware trade which was largely free of foreign competition (Brown in *Hansard*: 30.6.1927, Cols 603-649). Also, the strength of foreign competition changed significantly. As Figure 1.1 indicates, imports were almost entirely shut out of the domestic market during the war and British manufacturers (including china) were even able to replace German ones in countries outside the Empire. In the 1920s foreign competition became very intense as Japan and Czechoslovakia began competing directly with British products in large areas of her overseas markets (*P. Gazette*: 1.5.1923, 1.1.1926).

An objective examination of why foreign potters were producing different ware types from Britain and why certain countries could compete very effectively with certain Staffordshire sub-industries does not exist. Such a task lies outside the aims of this study. What concerns us are the subjective arguments manufacturers used to explain their predicament. Their reasoning had a great influence on the course of industrial relations in pottery; their public pronouncements especially, helped shape the popular consciousness of the Potteries at certain moments in the period.

The three main strands of the pottery masters' case concerned technology, state aid and tariffs (*US Report 1915*: 24, 41, 54, 601, 621). As was noted at the time, manufacturers turned conflict over new technology and working methods into much wider, less focussed concerns regarding foreign competition. T.B. Johnston was clear that new technology would cheapen production and stated that 'it is not cheap labour and cheap materials only that are the greatest factors of cheap production, but it is quantity of production coupled with the efficient use of labour-saving machinery' (CATU Coll L612: 11.3.1911). During the 1908, 1911 and 1923/4 disputes, in particular, masters translated union resistance to new machinery into questions of national economic survival. The argument put to the public was that Germany or America could produce up to 133% more than Staffordshire on some machines. What the potters' union had to do was uncover the assumptions contained in these arguments. These included the facts that German wages were one third lower than Staffordshire's, their hours longer and their division of labour quite different. Similarly manufacturers contended that only state aid would enable the new technology to be developed. The campaign for state assistance looked to raise a unified industrial consciousness and ignored the real issues of what kind of technology and how to control it. In the same way industrialists in the Potteries argued for protective tariffs at the political level by conjuring up the demise of the Staffordshire pottery industry due to overwhelming foreign competition (*S. Advertizer.* 23.11.1907, *Times I.T.F.S.*: 3.6.1918).

Clearly the growth of the world pottery market in the early twentieth century was an event of great significance for Staffordshire's industry. Yet the distinction between rhetoric and reality is crucial to understanding that significance. Manufacturers' perception of foreign producers deeply coloured their stance on technical questions within the potbank. These stances contributed to wider managerial strategies: they also suggest ways of understanding manufacturers' relations with the community and local politics.

CONCLUSION

In this chapter we have analysed the changing structure of the pottery industry as an initial step to understanding its form of work. This industrial structure influenced work and collective action in four main ways. First, the industry's historical development revealed the reasons for pottery's concentrated location, the range of product, the stratification by company type and the high density of work custom. Second, the pottery industry of the early twentieth century was highly fragmented. This fragmentation by product and company produced a rich mosaic of employer and employment forms. Union organisation and industrial relations reflected that fragmentation. Third, the self-image of the potters in each sub-industry differed according to the status of their product and its market performance which affected workers' propensity for collective action. Fourth, Aldcroft's injunction to be wary of the generalisation regarding foreign competition was useful (Aldcroft 1968: 35). The impact of foreign pottery producion was highly localised. Foreign competition cannot be accepted as an explanation for all the problems of the industry: the meaning attributed to foreign competition was instead a controversial topic of debate. Moreover, the industry has been analysed using a dynamic perspective. Besides the dynamic of conflict generated by technological change and the struggle for control, the economic changes of the period also provided key contexts for the actions of all potters.

The main aim has been to identify the structure of the industry and its major influence on the activity of the people who worked there. This influence has been construed in two ways. First, the industry's structure has been presented as a set of objective features which influenced and constrained the potters' actions (Pfeffer 1987). Second, the subjective dimension has been fully recognised, whereby potters interpreted and reacted to the structure of their industry (cf Hodgson 1988: ch.8). An interpretation of the structure of the industry underlies the statements of all potters: an appreciation of that structure will enable a decoding of these assertions. As will become clear, manufacturers and workers developed their own constructions of their industry's main economic features: these in turn helped to frame their strategies towards change during this period.

This analysis of the pottery industry has provided an explanation of a major external influence on work and collective action; Chapter Two turns to the internal features of the potters' working lives and how these characteristics related to trade union organisation and action.

Chapter Two

WORK AND HOME

Social scientists have developed a number of analytical tools with which to understand the organisation and meaning of work. Some writers have suggested that the mode of production provides a kernel of human relationships from which all else grows. Others stress that the production process is not just about the production of objects but involves the creation of social relationships (Fox 1971: 2, Burawoy 1978: 268). Yet precisely how such social relations are created has, with a few notable exceptions (Messenger 1975, Hareven 1982, Thompson, P. 1987, Westwood 1984) not been extensively investigated and reconstructed. The potters provide an exciting opportunity to mount such an investigation and to uncover the full range of possible relations.

The main aim is to discover how potters behaved at work; what forms of consciousness were produced and what was the quality of their social relations? The experience of work is a social one. At the centre of this analysis of work therefore is the workgroup since it was the workgroup which bound workers together by their shared experiences. As Sayles points out (Sayles 1958: 3-6, 165, Parker *et al.* 1980: 101) the organisation of work contributes significantly to the behaviour of workgroups and in turn the workgroup helps shape the behaviour and beliefs of its members. The first task of this chapter is to show that the organisation and basic orientation of the potter's workgroup followed the lines of the production process but that the potter and the workgroup evolved means of adjusting their work environment. In other words, the way in which potters experienced and acted at work depended neither on the influence of technology nor on the potters' orientations to work alone: it depended on the interaction of the two (Beynon and Blackburn 1972: 4).

The second task is to find out what were the principles which underlay the pottery workers' attempts to make sense of their working lives. It will be necessary to uncover and assess the apparently rich forms of custom and practice which operated on the shopfloor. Third, the wage contract is one of the most important facets of work experience. The wage system of pottery manufacture was influenced by the organisation and customs of work yet also gave very clear expression to the skill and status divisions which arose from the division of labour. Fourth, the following sections will show that the range of social groups was extensive. Inside each potbank the combination of the organisational structure with the characteristics of the workers produced a wide variety of social groups. These features of work were reinforced by the actions of potters, by their codes of custom and by the industry's wage system. The interaction of the potters with these basic elements of production was responsible for both the marked stratification of the workforce and also resulted in the intense sectionalism which typified the social relations of the potbank.

THE PRODUCTION PROCESS AND THE DIVISION OF LABOUR

The starting point for analysing work in the pottery industry is the production process: the sequence whereby a clay mix was converted into a finished piece of ceramic ware.

In the period 1890-1930 the production process remained as complex as it had been in the nineteenth century. Experts in the 1900s concluded that work in the pottery industry was 'infinitely sub-divided' and that 'probably no more detailed and intricate manufacture exists today' (*Truck Acts C^ee* 1906: Q 17077). Any discussion of work in pottery must emphasise the intricacy of a production sequence composed of so many interdependent phases. The largest potbanks contained between 100 and 150 departments while even the smaller 'banks used over thirty separate phases. These sub-divisions are well documented in contemporary accounts of pottery making. Graham's *Cup and Saucer Land* (nd 1908?) reveals a potbank as a collection of functionally separate workshops, sheds, galleries, studios, ovens, kilns, cellars and warehouses (see Figure 2.1).

There were two main reasons for the complex sub-division of production. First, the product range of even one potbank was often extensive so that each firm had to carry a number of alternative manufacturing processes or sub-processes which could accommodate that variety. Second and more important, the generally low level of mechanisation meant that there were few machines which combined or simplified tasks and no machines were introduced which encompassed the work of a whole department. The result was a remarkably unstreamlined production process. Even where machinery was used the operation was still dependent on manual manipulation. Pottery was therefore a relatively small user of electrical, diesel or steam power. Power was not applied to 'making' equipment since any power source, other than the hand or foot, was irregular and difficult to standardise or control. A survey in 1920 showed that 21.2% of the respondents did not work with externally powered jigger-drives. By 1924 steam power use was still three times that of electric (*Production Census* 1924: 209, Lamb 1971).

However, there were changes in the use of ceramic technology during this period. The two major changes in the production process were in the pressing and firing departments although there were minor changes of technique elsewhere. Without doubt the greatest technological change was the introduction of casting. With the discovery of certain alkali mixtures, casting slips became viable at the turn of the century. Pressers traditionally worked with solid clay. Casting involved working with a simple, liquid clay and mould. Potters found they were working with a new material entirely. Complex shapes could now be made in a single operation whereas the hollow ware presser needed several stages to make such articles. Casting was slowly introduced down to 1914. During the war its use increased rapidly and by the 1920s, hand pressing and hollow-ware pressing in particular had been largely superseded. One expert in 1914 thought casting 'bids fair to revolutionise certain departments of the industry' (*P. Gazette* 1.6.1914).

The second type of change concerned oven design and firing techniques. A handful of firms pioneered gas firing in tunnel ovens. Less publicised yet more influential with regard to the

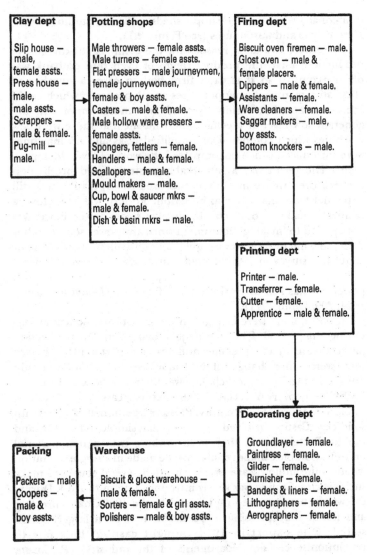

Figure 2.1 The production process and division of labour of pottery manufacture

Source: Times Engineering Supplement 2.4.1913, CATU Coll: 1924 Wage Inquiry, Accountant's Report

46

intensity of work was the increasing size of bottle ovens in order to fire larger batches of ware. Cauldons, for example, replaced a 17-foot diameter oven with a $21^{1}/_{2}$-foot model in February 1910 which gave an oven capacity of 6,000 dozen (*P. Gazette*: 1.2.1910). The large cost of making the saggars for the ovens (£60,000 p.a. was spent unnecessarily on this process in 1908) led to the use of machine presses to replace hand methods. This in turn resulted in new saggar sizes and shapes which held more ware and therefore involved more work (*Inquiry into Pottery Regulations* 1911: Q523).

In other departments of the production process, changes in technology were more gradual, less dramatic and involved the refining of methods or the increased application of existing machinery. In the mixing and clay preparation department mechanical grinders, blungers and mixers gradually ousted the older hand techniques. In decorating, improved transfer machines were developed. Liquid gold made gilding much easier. Aerography was a new method of colouring and glazing and litho transfers reduced the difficulty of some forms of painting. By the mid-1920s there were seven ceramic transfer companies in the Potteries who supplied potbanks with transfers ready made, thus doing away with the need to employ a printer on the 'bank (Amal. Society of Lithographers: 22.6.1928). In hand pressing William Boulton produced a steady stream of improved jiggers and jollys. In dipping, machines had proved to be failures. The sorting, warehouse and packing sections were without any form of mechanical assistance (*P. Gazette*: 1.4.1922).

There are therefore three major features of the production process which concern us in investigating the work experience of the potter. The complexity and multiple sub-divisions made for a spatially and physically fragmented work environment for the potter. Also, with manual operation dominating production the poor continuity of production flow ensured that the potential for conflict amongst workers as well as between worker and employer was high. Lastly, in spite of the low level of mechanisation, the isolated changes in ceramic technology were particularly important since they concerned strategic points within the production process. For key groups of potters the period was one of fundamental change.

The production process has provided a key analytical starting point. Having examined it in its phases together with the relation

47

between those phases it is now possible to map out the division of labour more clearly (see Figure 2.1). However, there is an important distinction to be made. The division of labour is not a direct outcome of the production process. Management or the formal owners of the production process do not have unlimited freedom to determine the configuration of tasks and jobs which serve that process. On the contrary, the formal owners may set certain important limits, but the attributes which workers individually or collectively bring to a job critically influences the division of labour (cf Kaplan and Koepp 1986). There exists a constant interplay between the abilities of owners and workers to define, demonstrate and control the nature of a job or task in detail and hence determine the character of the division of labour in general. Moreover the division of labour is constantly changing, even though for purposes of analysis one may artificially freeze it at certain points in time.

The first outstanding characteristic of the division of labour in the pottery industry is its very large number of separate occupations. Commentators at the time noted how pottery manufacture was 'subdivided to very fine limits' (*Times I.F.T.S.*: Aug.1917) compared to other industries. In 1913 a survey of a group of factories discovered 87 occupational groups within the production of earthenware. Nine years later an investigator noted 98 separate occupational groups amongst only the skilled workers of the industry (CATU Coll 1924 Wage Inquiry: Wage Tables). Figure 2.2 condenses the division of labour down to a basic list of 33 main occupations in pottery in 1922 and indicates the numbers employed in each. It is noticeable that there are no clear numerically dominant groups. Instead the potters were made up of a large collection of very small occupational groups. The three largest formed only 10% of the workforce: most groups amounted to between 1 and 4%.

Second, a wide range of skills was exhibited within pottery's division of labour. Conceptually, skill may be divided into two types: genuine skill, which is the alliance of a manual facility with knowledge useful to industry; or skill may be socially constructed and attributed to workers by themselves or by others. The label 'skilled worker' may derive from the technology a person uses, from an agreement between management and worker, from workshop custom, or from power relations at the workplace (More

48

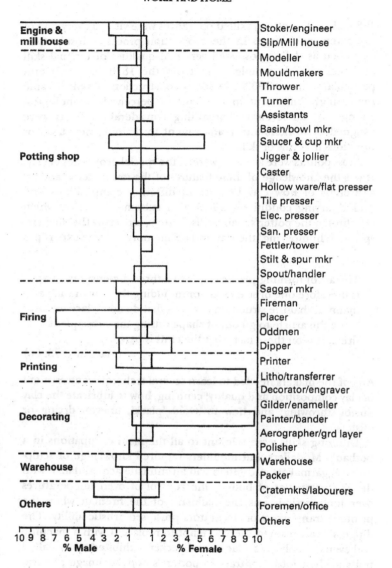

Figure 2.2 Size of occupational groups in the pottery industry 1922
Source: CATU Coll: *Census of employees in the pottery industry 1922*

1980: 15ff). In pottery, skilled operatives were vital to every one of the seven main stages in the production process. Most potters described as skilled possessed very real qualities of manual skill and technical knowledge. Yet from the 1870s onwards and particularly in the 1900s the social construction of skill became increasingly important in the light of perceived technological change. At all levels of bargaining considerable efforts were assigned by workers and management to defining new tasks or functions in terms of skill.

Most potters were acutely aware of the special properties of clay. It was the knowledge of these features of the raw material and an awareness of how clay behaves in differing compositions and under varying conditions, allied with extreme dexterity, which constituted the potter's main skills. Potters, especially the 'makers' spoke of 'humouring' the clay and its 'memory'. As one expert put it:

> The art of forming plastic clay into a three dimensional shape is therefore one of stretching or moulding the clay in such a manner, that the structural changes that do take place do not cause the article to go out of shape during the subsequent fire ... It is on these facts that the craft is based.
>
> (Machin 1973: 66)

Any of the makers needed to learn several techniques: assessment of clay composition and quality; centring; how to lubricate the clay during throwing; and how to avoid 'plack', uneven drying or blisters.

Differing skills were relevant to all the main occupations in a potbank. Modellers and moulders required knowledge of sculpture; saggarmakers and fitters had an intimate acquaintance with the characteristics of bodies; the control of oven temperatures over long periods was the hallmark of the fireman while the printers, transferrers or decorators possessed artistic ability. The dippers' craft resisted every attempt to replace it with a machine and even the polishers, placers and packers exhibited many skilled traits in their jobs. Contrary to pottery's popular image physical strength was a common requirement of many key occupations, especially in the firing department (*P. Gazette* 1.6.1916, Board of Trade 1946: 4).

Furthermore, the potter's self-image was usually one of a skilled worker and indeed a craftsman. Today, potters still speak of their 'craft occupation'. In the 1900s the tradition of the potter as a craft worker was immensely strong. Colin Sedgly, a potter's fitter, leaves us in no doubt regarding his skill when he described his work in the following terms in March 1919:

> I am not a polisher but a china or potters fitter which requires a lot of training and takes years to learn to become efficient in the business as figures, ewers, vases, bowls, &ctra are made in sections and I have to grind and fit them perpendicular and horizontally true then stick them together with a body composition and send them through the kiln and make them one whole piece, work that requires great care and skill besides mental capacity. There are about 5,000 shapes to remember how they have to be fixed and not put the wrong sizes or parts on one another and you are [also] expected to know if the potter has made any of the parts wrong.
>
> (CATU Coll L573: March 1919)

However, by identifying the components of skill within each task and the varying status different occupations enjoyed, it is clear that a hierarchy of skill existed within the industry. Figure 2.3 is an attempt to represent that hierarchy.

Figure 2.3 also tries to indicate that this hierarchy was not static during the years 1900-1924. Changes in both technology and attitudes had a strong impact on the skill and status of some potters. The impact was often very specific. The increased use of improved jiggers and jollys meant unemployment or the decimation of the ranks of the hand throwers and turners. With the need for greater precision and uniformity moulds were used, thereby relegating the thrower to a very limited product range. It was said of the thrower in 1905 that 'he has gradually been turned into a machine, and now the tool of steel (not the hand) is doing his work' (Barrett-Greene 1905: 68). Another effect of jigger and jolly use was that male pressers were restricted to work on particular, usually larger pieces of ware and women were introduced by manufacturers to do jigger and jolly work on the smaller sizes. Cup and saucer making in the 1880s was a skilled job on a par with flat-pressing. In the 1900s such work was entirely semi-skilled. In

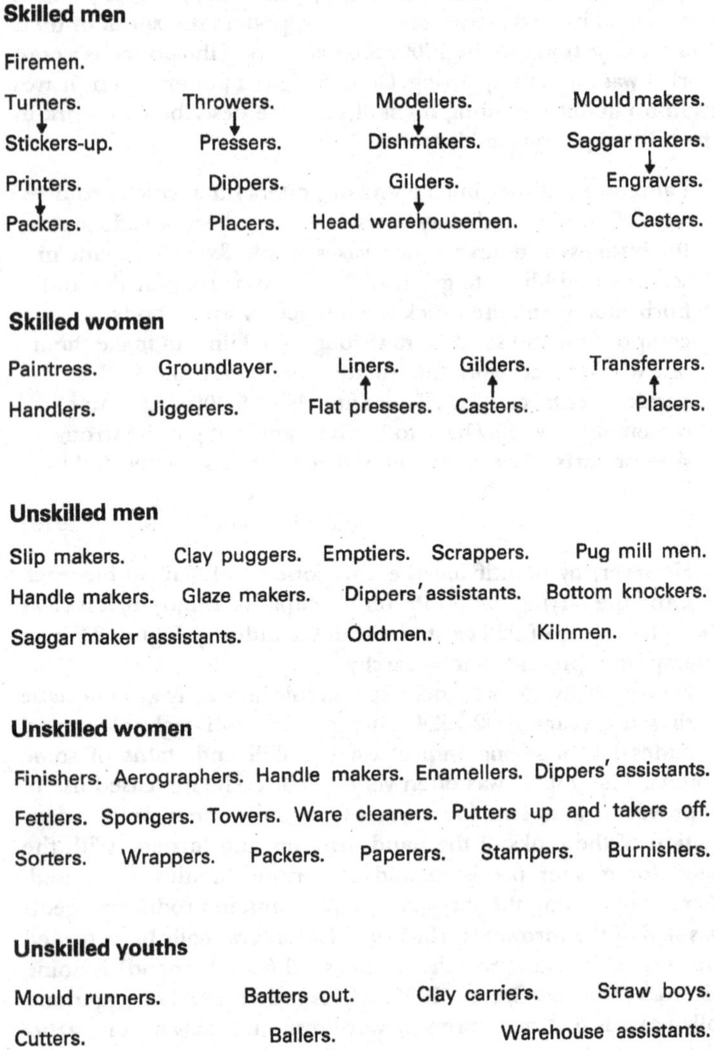

Skilled men

Firemen.

Turners.	Throwers.	Modellers.	Mould makers.
↓	↓	↓	↓
Stickers-up.	Pressers.	Dishmakers.	Saggar makers.
↓	↓	↓	↓
Printers.	Dippers.	Gilders.	Engravers.
↓	↓	↓	
Packers.	Placers.	Head warehousemen.	Casters.

Skilled women

Paintress.	Groundlayer.	Liners.	Gilders.	Transferrers.
		↑	↑	↑
Handlers.	Jiggerers.	Flat pressers.	Casters.	Placers.

Unskilled men

Slip makers. Clay puggers. Emptiers. Scrappers. Pug mill men.

Handle makers. Glaze makers. Dippers' assistants. Bottom knockers.

Saggar maker assistants. Oddmen. Kilnmen.

Unskilled women

Finishers. Aerographers. Handle makers. Enamellers. Dippers' assistants.

Fettlers. Spongers. Towers. Ware cleaners. Putters up and takers off.

Sorters. Wrappers. Packers. Paperers. Stampers. Burnishers.

Unskilled youths

Mould runners. Batters out. Clay carriers. Straw boys.

Cutters. Ballers. Warehouse assistants.

Figure 2.3 Skill hierarchy of pottery manufacture

decorating, liquid gold and the aerograph reduced the level of skill required by decorators in general. Casting's introduction was a major battle. Owners fought desperately hard to label casting as unskilled since casting replaced one of the strongest craft workers, the hollow-ware presser with unskilled, often female labour. Many hollow-ware pressers, with their specialist skills, high wages and militant reputation, were forced to find labouring jobs (*P. Gazette*: 1.9.1908, 1.9.1922).

It has been argued that the main thrust of technological change in general, and in Britain during 1880-1920 in particular, is that the division of labour increased and was accompanied by de-skilling (Hobsbawm 1968: 174, Landes 1969: 317, Braverman 1974). The experience of the pottery industry questions this conclusion. To portray the process of technological change as universally de-skilling in its effects is simply not true for pottery. Many of the skilled strata of the workforce were untouched by new machinery or methods: of those that were affected some still retained either a large measure of real hand skill or succeeded in maintaining their skilled status. Indeed in some cases the technical advance by using semi-automatic machinery was marginal. The maker could still provide a flexibility which accommodated variations in materials and temperature, a flexibility no machine could match (Machin 1973: 77).

Moreover, there is no *a priori* reason why increased mechanisation should necessarily involve further sub-division or decline of skill. New technology may enhance certain manual or skilled operations, lead to a higher-quality product and worker status or require more sophisticated knowledge and create an entirely novel skilled job (Rowe 1928: 90, Samuels 1977: 9-11, More 1980: 183). Also, as has already been pointed out, new technology and task content are the outcome of worker/management relations which vary greatly with the relative power of each side. This investigation of the social relations of the potbank is guided therefore by an awareness of the fluid, changing status of workers in this period, as their skill was enhanced or eroded. The movement of workers both up and down the skill hierarchy will be shown to have had important consequences for union composition, internal relations and policy.

The third major element of the division of labour in pottery arises from its organisation. The division of labour is in part a product of a social process: management and workers both seek to define, organise and control the nature of tasks. In the pottery industry workers had a large influence on the detailed forms of work via sub-employment. Sub-employment was as old as the industry. Employers or merchants in the eighteenth century contracted work with individual craft potters, who then brought their own workgroups to the factory to produce a 'count' of ware. As factories became the permanent location of production the total division of labour was organised around sub-employment and continued to be so down to the 1900s (Schloss 1907: 197). Inside the slip house, for example, the head slipman and pugman paid a group of scrappers, emptiers and labourers. In the potting shops, pressers sub-employed fettlers, towers, batters and ballers and clay carriers. The saggarmakers had their own bottom-knockers and frame-fillers. Firemen and head placers ran the ovens on a gang system. The printer and transferrer's team is a perfect example. The printer was paid by the owner to produce printed ware. The printer then sub-employed a team. He paid a transferrer; the transferrer paid a cutter; both printer and transferrer made up the wages for an assistant. The dipping house and the cratemaking and packing sheds also relied on the employment of worker by worker (NEC mins: 18.3.1918, CATU Coll Pressers and Attendants Agt: March 1919).

Sub-employment in the pottery industry is therefore a major corrective to any simple notion of direct control and organisation of work by employers. This form of work organisation was also a major influence on the social relations between workers in the industry. Though sub-employment remained a dominant feature in our period it was not left unchanged as manufacturers sought to win more direct control of the detailed form of work.

WORKSHOP CUSTOM AND PRACTICE

Customary behaviour in the workplace can tell us much about the human relationships which surround work (Thompson, P. 1988). Custom and practice are often indications of how workers make sense of a bewildering or problem-filled activity: via customs they can influence and regulate the nature of their daily toil. Montgomery shows how work practices are often 'group-enforced codes of ethical behaviour on the job' (Montgomery 1979: 113). This notion of custom has implications for our method. In order to discover how all types of potter, not just the dominant groups, governed their working lives we must be prepared to delve deeply into not only the craftsman's workshop but also the tiny work-groups of the unskilled in order to reveal the range of customary forms (cf Price 1980: 11).

The richness of workshop custom in the pottery industry is readily apparent. Each occupation generated its own commonly accepted working methods and rules. Potters consciously decided how they were to organise their work and legitimised their behaviour by reference to notions of accepted practice with nineteenth-century antecedents (Thistlethwaite 1958: 274). Outside observers found in 1912 that 'old customs and methods are difficult to displace ... The tenacity with which many persons still hold to this idea in spite of the evidence of scientific potters and others is really surprising' (HMI Factories Report 1912: 46).

There were sound reasons for those customs. Work sharing is an example. Given the irregular production flow orders would slow up in the pressing shop. Commonly, the pressers would meet and decide on how the work would be divided among themselves, each worker or team being given a stint (or stent) of articles to produce. Even during high demand it was noticeable how 'the equalisation of work between one team and another is arranged by the men' (Truck Acts Cee 1906: 778). Trade customs or 'usuages' as they were called included the appointment of senior workers to monitor the weekly 'counts'; the allowance and balance practices; and also the privilege of a second firing to 'make good' a worker's apparently defective piece. Management were not allowed to retain a piece of spoilt ware (it might be sold as a second without the worker's knowledge); instead it was smashed as 'shard'. In comparison with other industries factory inspectors thought of the potbanks as 'places by themselves, with hardly any supervision ... the ordinary discipline of a factory or machine shop is not brought to bear upon them' (Truck Acts Cee 1906: 778).

As management sought to increase control of the industrial process a reformation of shopfloor custom was considered necessary. Much of the turbulence in industrial relations of this period centres precisely on worker opposition to what they saw as unfair changes in ordinary work practices. Some workers never accepted that management had the *right* to change them. For instance,

55

Arthur Hollins had to tell an arbiter in 1917 that 'with regard to the flattening of foot battles, the pressers [in one firm's potting shop] maintain that it is not a question for the Arbiter as to whether a portion of the work should be given to another branch of the trade, as it is a violation of the trade privileges' (CATU Coll L532: 27.9.1917). In addition workers attempted to alter customs which had been constructed under different or outdated working conditions. Management derived certain cost advantages from these, such as good-from-oven or the allowance system and fought to retain them.

Perhaps two of the best examples of the centrality of custom to the potter's work experience lay in the area of apprenticeship and the internal labour market (More 1980: 41-45). Two main functions of apprenticeship, wage regulation and socialisation, together helped perpetuate the hierarchy of skill.

The internal labour market of a potbank shows how a set of working practices was the product of both worker and management attempts to determine customary forms (cf Marsden 1986). Workers did not drift between jobs or factories but generally progressed through accepted career sequences. Notions of social justice or the defence of skill were uppermost in the minds of potters. All the departments of a potbank had well-known patterns of career progression. In the potting shops a lad might begin as a clay-carrier, then be accepted for an apprenticeship and eventually become a journeyman making the smaller ware. As competence increased the young presser would move up to the larger, more difficult ware sizes. Eventually he could become the head presser with responsibility for the shop's general operation and its relation with the press shop and 'green house' (*Inquiry into Pottery Regulations* 1911: 3). Similar occupational progressions occurred in the firing and dipping departments.

With experience a few workers could hope to become foremen or in the larger works 'departmental managers'. A prize for head placers, firemen or very senior workers was to be put 'on the staff' where job tenure was more secure. In a world of daily or weekly pay, irregular employment and income, to become one of the staff was a considerable gain. George Burton, for example, entered Cauldons as a warehouse assistant progressing subsequently to warehouseman, head warehouseman, head of ordering and then to the office where he finally attained the position of confidential clerk (CATU Coll L103: 30.4.1929, cf Holden 1981: 22). Clearly it was impossible for all or even a majority of workers to follow such a path. The effect could be symbolic; potters could aspire to staff status as management realised. This added to the fragmentation of the division of labour in the potbank. Workers who were put on the staff routinely left the union. In some cases individual workers' support for unionism waned after their father or a close relative had become a member of staff and now 'spoke for them' (NSPW Collectors' Survey 1924: Area 12).

A significant outcome of the internal labour market of pottery firms was that many potters, especially the more skilled, remained in one occupation for most of their career. Variations in production technique coupled with the prevalence of traditional job progressions made movement between potbanks or trades difficult. A report in 1926 required for examination 'workers who had only been at one occupation and in particular those who had only been in one branch of the industry'. The investigators found 18,000 who satisfied that condition (*Report on Evidence of Silicosis* 1926).

Longevity of attachment to one firm was an outstanding trait of many potters' work experience. At Gibsons in 1905, 20% of the workforce had been employed there for over ten years. The personal testimony of potters suggests the almost permanent connection with an occupation and a company. Mrs Freally of Fenton was employed for twenty-five years by Radfords. Large companies such as Wedgwoods were noted for the length of attachment between them and their workers (*P. Gazette* 1.3.1907, 1.5.1910, 1.3.1913, 1.1.1916). As will become clear, manufacturers attempted to make use of this phenomenon in their strategies of control. Also the relations workers experienced with union officials and management was clearly influenced by the nature of individual potters' working careers. Union activists and managers, in different ways, were faced with attitudes and values which were the product often of years of effort invested in their particular trade or firm.

Custom was an essential ingredient of the potters' work experience and consciousness. Custom and practice were a means of rationalising and regulating work. The values implicit in these shopfloor codes influenced not only how workshop or occupational groups related to each other, inside a potbank or across the industry, but also how potters viewed other social groups in the community. It has been shown that a wide range of customs existed, that the customs involved were malleable, and subject to differing use. Therefore, the potters' union both gave an expression of the dominant customs and values of the workshop in its policy; yet at the same time it proved to be an arena for the competing interpretation of custom and practice made by the highly fragmented workforce.

WAGES

The wage contract has been shown to be the worker's most direct experience of the relationship between capital and labour. Writers such as Marx (1938/1889: 391), the Webbs (1902: x) and Blackburn (as quoted in Hyman 1972: 91) note how the productivity of labour is remunerated on an individual basis and that the labour contract is not an exchange of equivalents. However, the individual worker does not necessarily experience the labour contract in isolation (cf Cole 1924: 5). Potters have been aware of many related features of this contract. Furthermore, the precise form of the wage contract has clearly varied according to the nature of the industry and even the firm involved. The need therefore is to try to reconstruct not only the conditions of the wage contract in pottery but also the industry's wage structure, and how it changed.

Most industries' wage systems are complex but in the case of pottery a particularly large set of variables have influenced the final form (cf Rowe 1928: 10-12). The effect of the industry's wealth of custom has already been suggested. Why E. Burton's wages could vary from 8s. 4d. to £1. 2s. 8d. in one month or how two flat pressers in 1913 could receive wages differing by 15s. for the same work (CATU Coll D22: June 1913, L195: E. Burton 1921) is basically due to four main variables. The piece-rate system; the variation in mechanical operation; the influence of the allowance custom; and the fluctuations of employment associated with pottery manufacture. In terms of the potters' work experience, the wage system intensified the fragmentation of the workforce and its consciousness.

Many wage figures quoted for pottery are really gross wages. Net figures (what potters took home) resulted from the many deductions and 'allowances' which had grown up with each craft or job. In the craftsman's wage contract the manufacturer had supplied heat, light and machinery which the craftsman then 'allowed' so much per piece price in order to pay back the employer. The tradition remained and many manufacturers extended the practice to less skilled workers (*HMI Factories Report* 1909: 55). Lily Ash, a lithographer at Pearl Pottery wrote 'I worked 3 days, 24 hours for 13s. 5d. The money I had to draw when stoppages were off was 10s. 11d.' In 1920, out of 53 firms 61.35% made 'deductions' on their wages. 'Good-from-oven' was a notorious way of reducing wage costs and bitterly resented by workers who had no control over the firing process (CATU Coll D43: Saucer Making Price Inquiry 5.11.1915). These deductions became a *cause célèbre* of the union. Lastly, seasonal demand affected earnings as did the malfunction of the industrial process as the Royal Commission on the Poor Law's detailed study of pottery wages revealed in 1908 (*Royal Comm. on Poor Law* 1908 App. XVI: 371-373).

Reconstructing a wage structure for an individual firm is possible, the difficulties of recreating one for the whole industry are immense. The main problem lies in the differences between the sub-industries. Jet and rockingham rates were recognised as the lowest. The high levels of machinery and female labour also depressed electrical and chemical rates. China's wage levels were erratic in response to its changing market performance. Within earthenware the range of earnings within one occupation across the sub-industry was very large. By contrast sanitary work was universally known for its exceptionally high wage levels (CATU Coll NEC mins: 31.8.1916).

However, if one takes cross-sections of the sub-industries at different dates a broad wage hierarchy does emerge. The results of the combined wage determinants of skill, custom and the power relations between employer and worker, are outlined in Figure 2.4.

At the top of the wage hierarchy were the firemen, a perfect example of the correlation of skill and a pivotal position within the division of labour, codified by custom. Every technical manual admits that 'of the many processes connected with the ceramic industry, that of firing is the most important'. The entire output of the potbank was in the hands of the fireman during the two or three day firing. Many firemen were so important to the production process that their wages were guaranteed 'work or play'. It is

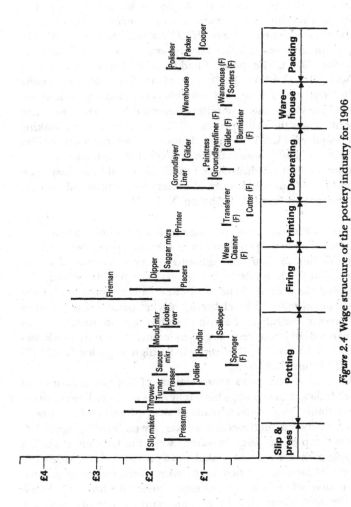

Figure 2.4 Wage structure of the pottery industry for 1906

Source: A. Steel-Maitland and R.E. Squire, *Report to Royal Commission on the Poor Laws and Relief of Distress* (1909), Appendix Vol. XLIV, pp. 371 (251)–373 (253)

not possible to say that any department of the production sequence clearly dominated in wage terms, although pressing and firing do seem to have enjoyed generally higher levels. The existence of wage hierarchies *within* departments is the most distinctive feature (cf Gray 1976: 46-49). For example, in dipping, the wage ranking descends from the dippers through to the placers, saggarmakers, ware cleaners and finally the assistants (CATU Coll L31: makers' proposal 1920).

One startlingly clear aspect of the potters' wage rankings is the way it closely expresses the sexual division of labour in the pottery industry. In 1906 (see Figure 2.4) there are almost two separate male and female wage scales. Note how the highly paid paintresses or female groundlayers only just overlap with the lowly paid male assistants around the 18s. line. As the field notes of Dora Mycock, a union organiser, confirm, women were paid half to two-thirds the wage of male workers, even if women were performing the same task as men (CATU Coll L28: 1908). As Hunt has shown, 'women's wages were determined, in large part, by considerations of what most people believed they ought to earn and this was usually measured as a customary proportion of the male rate' (Hunt 1973: 115, 341). Also, observe how the female wage scale displays the wide range of skill among women workers. Women potters too progressed up skill, career and wage ladders which sharply differentiated the mass of female employees. At the summit were the highly skilled transferrers and paintresses (15-20s. per week). Below them were the semi-skilled workers, such as handlers, sprayers and sorters (10-15s. per week) and at the base came the unskilled cleaners and assistants (2-10s. per week).

The general wage structure of the pottery industry appears to have remained remarkably stable. Notwithstanding the overall rise in money wages during the period 1906 to 1924 (Rowe 1928: 106) the relative position between departments and most occupations was mostly unchanged. As has been found in engineering at this time, the potters' wage hierarchy and differentials experienced no major alteration (Hunt 1973:345-346).

What is noteworthy is the smaller wage range within each occupation in the 1920s compared to 1906; a result of the greater standardisation of tasks and bargaining which the industry experienced. Other detailed changes were in the wage levels of the hollow-ware presser, the turner, the gilder (downwards) and the introduction of the caster at a much lower level than the presser he replaced. A concealed change occurred among the throwers, printers and male ground-layers. These appear to be still high wage earners in 1920s yet their ranks were diminished in numbers. There was also the shift of women workers into a number of skilled male jobs such as printing, placing and even pressing. Each of these detailed changes bear out our earlier conclusions regarding the shifts in the division of labour and the potters' skill hierarchy.

There were many attempts to analyse the general level of wages in the pottery industry at this time by external investigators: all appeared to disagree (*P. Gazette* 1.9.1906, Board of Trade 1908: 216). The wide range of payment among the potters and also the distribution of occupational wage levels across the industry makes talk of pottery as a high or low wage industry meaningless. Instead, let us compare the potters with other sectors of national industry at a number of levels.

The lowest-paid pottery workers (male and female assistants, labourers and women casual workers) were by any industry's standards very poorly paid. In the early 1920s potters' labourers would have needed rises of 38.8% in order to match the wage rates of building labourers. The minimum rates of the women boot and shoe workers were 131.5% greater than female pottery decorators' apprentices, 95.45% greater than warehouse women and 86.3% higher than electrical fitters, dippers and cleaners (CATU Coll 1924 Wage Inquiry, App. 3). Using the average wage levels, the 1906 wage census shows that nationally the average male earned 28s. 6d. to 29s. 6d. while the potters' average was 31s. 3d. The average potter was apparently quite close to the average engineering and building worker yet much better placed than clothing, textiles or rail workers. The average weekly wage for women potters of 11s .5d. did not compare well with the national average of between 13 and 14s. However, the male sanitary pressers, throwers and firemen were among some of the highest-paid workers in the country (Hutchins 1915: 213-231, *L. Gazette* Feb. 1925, Clegg, Fox and Thompson 1964: 479-483, Routh 1965: 86, 90, 92, 94, 96).

The wage system of the pottery industry raises a number of points in relation to an analysis of work and trade unionism. Pottery's general division of labour and skill hierarchy seems to have been reflected in and reinforced by the wage structure. In addition, the wage scale gave expression to the wide variation in male and female pay thereby underlining the sexual division of labour. The wage scale also covered a wide range of highly differentiated occupational wage levels. This range and differentiation of wages was not only a key contributor to the variety of status and lifestyles among the potters, it was also of great relevance to the social relations of the industry. In spite of the absence of radical change in the overall wage pattern of the industry, the detailed movements of occupational wage status proved to be an invaluable aid to the growth and change in the union's membership and social composition.

THE SOCIAL RELATIONS OF THE WORKPLACE

The previous sections have outlined the principal features which conditioned the social relations which arose from work, namely: the industrial process and the division of labour, the prevailing work customs and the wage structure. Here the aim is to highlight how these features interwove and affected the form of social relations. At the same time one is particularly concerned to discover what these features meant for worker or managerial behaviour and how these characteristics were perceived, interpreted and acted upon by potters of differing social backgrounds. Moreover, social relations are not conceived here as neutral; rather, they also involve questions of power and authority. This analysis of the social relations of the potter's workplace necessarily inspects the nature of the control of work.

The hallmark of social relations among the pottery workers was a separatism which arose from the nature of pottery manufacture. Each of the sub-industries, given their product quality, location and workforce composition varied markedly in their social status. Compare the sanitary workers' boast of not being 'bound by custom of the general trade' with the lowly public image of the china workers of 'neck-end' (central Longton) (*S. Sentinel*: 17.4.1907). Wedgwoods or Doultons labour was of higher social rank than the 'penny jack shop's' employees. The piece-rate system and sub-employment helped produce a highly stratified workforce. Piece work was competitive, often leading to divisions of interest between workers. Sub-employment led to antipathy inside departments. A dipper's assistant complained about the behaviour of his employer, the head dipper at Wood & Sons, in December 1919 to the union thus: 'don't you think the head Dipper can *pay* more wages out than this, he gets the money right enough by the Oven ... its a shame don't you think but when you look into it don't come to me individually because if we ask for a rise we get the sack' (CATU Coll L450: 13.12.1919).

Not only was there a wide range of jobs with each occupation, paid differently and encrusted with differing habits or custom, but workers had contrasting appearances and work styles (cf Godelier 1980). The skilled workers were especially conscious of the public definition and image of their work. The mould-runner, stoker or cutter for example could never compare in status with the fireman, thrower or presser. Charles Shaw emphasised this gulf in 1903 when he wrote:

> There was a deep and wide division between one class of workmen on a potbank and another. The plate-maker, slip-makers and some odd branches were regarded as a lower caste than hollow-ware pressers, throwers, turners and printers ... [they] differed so widely in sentiment and habit ... you might have taken one to be the employer of the other.
>
> (Shaw 1903: 193-194)

Sylvia Pankhurst depicted the contrasting work environment and styles of dress in her 1907 series of paintings (Pankhurst, R. 1979: 80-87). Contemporary photographs convey the distinctions of social status as expressed in work clothes. Graham's series (Graham nd 1908?) is an excellent example, showing the different appearance of the young, grubby clay carriers from the neat, smart look of the dish-maker and the assertive stance of the mould-maker. Arnold Bennett, the novelist, distinguished the paintresses from other women potters, with their long black dresses and lace pinafores, dubbing them 'the noblesse of the bank'. The labels 'rough' and 'respectable' continue to have great force on the potbanks today (Bennett 1902: 120, cf Walker 1979: 4).

The phenomenon of social stratification and separatism among workers was not unique to pottery manufacture. In 1906 a group of writers advised leaders that 'rigid class distinctions permeate the rank and file of manual workers. These distinctions are familiar to most social workers, but those who speak generally of the "working classes" or "the poor" can have no conception of their influence or their extent' (Cadbury, Matheson and Shann 1906: 47). The degree of social fragmentation among the potters was a case in point.

There were two further important outcomes of the potters' highly stratified social relations. Workers' reactions to their experience of the production process bred a highly developed sense of workgroup consciousness. Within the array of tasks and occupations the individual potter looked to his team or gang, the primary workgroup, in order to gain definition of status. The words and actions of pottery workers in our period continually betray their workgroup or sectional preoccupations. Divisions of interest developed between workgroups due to piece work. Job Wilcox told of the friction between slip-maker and presser. Pressers quarrelled notoriously with slipmen since 'the slip is given to us, and if we do not get good ware [i.e. if the slip is poor] it is invariably thrown at us' (NCPI mins: 7.10.1925). Similar antagonisms existed between saggar-makers and placers, firing and making, making and decorating: in other words all the main departments conflicted with each other over ware defects and lost payment. Workgroup independence was strong, which made factory-wide organisations unstable. The works' committee of W.H. Grindley, for example, was aborted in 1919 after the glost placers failed to bury their differences with other workers and 'refused to have anything to do with the scheme' (CATU Coll L417: 7.5.1919).

The workgroup was not just a product of the pattern of basic tasks. Given the high degrees of permanence of employment in a company many workgroups developed customs and continuities which augmented their social cohesion. A woman potter remembered that in her pressing shop each Friday the members of her team paid 1d each for a 'cake session' held while the departmental manager checked the weekly count. Local health visitors and philanthropists recoiled at the routine presence of 'footings' and 'jollifications', 'in almost every workshop'. Family connections gave many workgroups their strength (see following section): for instance, Edwin Tomkinson and his father were members of a turning team and backed each other when John Sadler tried to force Edwin to turn extra ware outside of his customary job description (CATU Coll L69: 20.1.1914).

Owners were generally tolerant of workgroup identity because it made sense and money. Workgroup sub-employment lifted the burden of detailed management of production off the shoulders of the owner while stable workgroups developed greater collective efficiency. Conversely, some owners became wary of these groups. The workgroup was primarily a defensive formation but when necessary, if its strategic position allowed, it could become a combative force in the bargaining system of a potbank.

The second distinctive aspect of the fragmented social relations which surrounded work in the pottery industry related to gender. The relations between men and women potters were not simply characterised by mutual enmity or empathy. Historians have mainly portrayed gender relations at work in terms of subordinate female and dominant male roles (Stearns, 1974: 111, Alexander 1984, Rose 1986; on the US see Milkman 1987). While the pottery workers in many respects confirm this view, the differing perceptions and actions of individual potters seriously qualifies the dominant/subordinate model.

Apparently a fairly clear divide existed between men and women's work. The accepted custom on most 'banks was that a broad demarcation should exist between male and female work as it had done for most of the previous century. Only during and after the First World War did women increase their numbers in the semi-skilled occupations. As the 1922 British Pottery Manufacturers' Census shows (see Figure 2.2) women workers were still concentrated in the latter part of the production process: in the decorating, warehouse and packing departments which were popularly seen as containing the more intricate, delicate and less prestigious tasks. Where women did work in the firing or potting shops they were usually the unskilled assistants to male skilled potters.

A combination of factors contributed to the generally subordinate position of most women potters. Male potters continued to explain the job demarcation by maintaining that women were physically incapable of the heavy and dangerous work involved in dipping and placing for example. Tradition was continued so that male workers, as the chief wage earners in a household, should retain the higher-paid skilled work (cf Grant 1989). An observer in 1902 discovered how for the male potter 'his wife and family were his help in the work' (*Morning Leader* 11.12.1902). Custom also ensured that women in the same shop or department as men, seldom earned more than a man. Mrs Ellis was forced in 1912 to cease work by her male tile-maker colleagues since her dexterity led her to earn more than them (Interview E. Ellis, *Women in Ind. Cee* 1919: 121).

In the light of the oversupply of local female labour, and women occupying predominantly unskilled jobs, many women were regarded as replaceable. Indeed women earned amongst some men a reputation as impermanent participants in work. In 1911, Miss Sadler HMI was struck by 'the remarkable mobility of women's labour' in the industry. Of 762 women in 68 potbanks she found that 258 had left in the space of nine months (*HMI Factories Report* 1911: 145). Unfortunately for skilled and more permanent women workers the prevailing image of the woman potter was of a young (see Figure 2.5), unskilled, low paid, and quite marginal worker (*1910 Lead Cee*: Q 6527-6531, 6518).

The subordinate position of female potters can be made clearer by some examples of workshop relations. The arguments around the custom of good-from-oven demonstrate the predicament of the disadvantaged female. As the abuse flew when ware was returned to a shop (damaged after firing) women workers were often the recipients of blame. Some women gave as good as they received yet the conclusion of a factory inspector was that: 'the unfortunate person who is generally supposed to be responsible for it [spoilt ware] is the female' because 'she has the least protection, I suppose, of the others in works; the men can defend themselves' (*Truck Act Report* 1906: 714).

Not all women by any means fitted the subordinate image. As some men privately recognised there was such competition for certain semi-skilled women's jobs that 'if a man did not treat his attendant properly she would leave him to go to another man' and 'in many cases husband and wife or child worked together' (*Royal Commission on Labour, Employment of Women* 1893: 63). Not only were women increasingly employed apart from male worker–employers in this period, but during the years 1914-1920 there was a particular 'self-confidence engendered in women by the very considerable proportion of cases where they are efficiently doing men's work', coupled with higher relative wage levels. As will become clear, women could also exert strong influence at work via their role in workgroups and other social networks. Without doubt

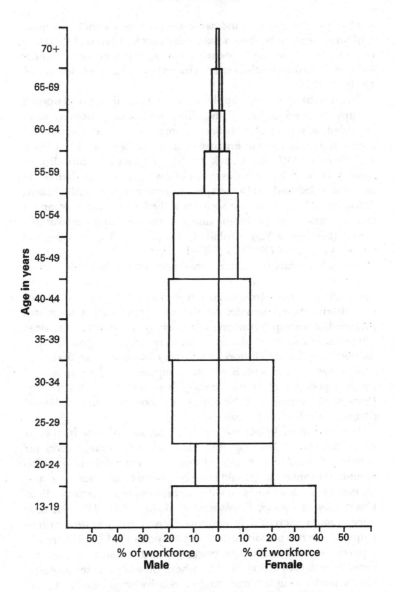

Figure 2.5 Age pyramid of the pottery workforce 1921
Source: Census of Staffordshire, 1921: Table 18, pp. 93–9

the potters' union personified the dominant male influence on the social relations at work. At the same time, in the first three decades of this century, male superiority did not go unchallenged in either potbank bargaining or any of the other forms of union action.

In order to give a full explanation of the social relations inside the pottery industry it is necessary to discover how work was controlled. The work customs, piece-rate and sub-employment systems have told us a great deal about the horizontal control in the industry; how workers sought to control work in relation to other workers. Here the need is to concentrate on the nature of vertical control: how workers as distinct from management attempted to win control of the production process.

Vertical control operates at a number of levels. These levels ranged from the detailed terms of employment right up to decisions about investment or the location of production (Goodrich 1975/1920: xxi). There is a great difference between the control of work and autonomous or discretionary regulation of work. The former involves the complete authority and direction of all the production process whereas autonomous regulation is more limited, implying the regulation by a worker or group of the details of their own tasks. In general there exists a very fluid and imprecise borderline between workshop autonomy and managerial authority (cf Montgomery 1979: 104, 140). The contexts in which workers attempt to establish their regulation of work are vital in determining the strength of their control *vis-à-vis* management.

There existed a strong tradition from the eighteenth century of potters' self-regulation of work. In 1874 the *Workman's Examiner* (19.12.1874) described how flat-pressers 'engage and discharge all their own attendants, and the employer as a rule does not dictate to them'. Many individuals or groups of potters, especially the craftsmen, continued to exercise forms of self-regulation of work in the twentieth century. A pottery manager in 1950 affirmed the strength of autonomous regulation. He wrote:

> The recorded job breakdowns show that much of the responsibility for the production of ware is disseminated throughout the factory. The authority to take action; to set up a machine and to correct faults, is possessed by the

journeyman as a craftsman's right which has not been given
to him by delegation from the management. The right was his
from the start ... there was always this preponderance of
contracted labour which took its own responsibility once it
had been directed to perform a given production task.

(Machin 1973: 179)

This regulation of work was the basis of the skilled potter's pride
in his job. The throwers and turners of Taylor Tunnicliff's objected
to the company introducing a new piece of ware since it was of
inferior quality and beneath their dignity to make (CATU Coll
D45: Taylor Tunnicliff Dispute 1908). Carter Goodrich's seminal
study of control in 1920 relies heavily on the pottery industry for
examples of discretionary regulation of work by operatives
(Goodrich 1975/1920: 37, 98, 109, 131). Perhaps the best indication of a worker's control over his job is his ability to determine
his working hours. There were very few clocks in most potbanks
before the 1920s. As Robert Stirrat explained 'we have no set time
for stopping and starting here' (CATU Coll L492: 26.4.1931).

A by-product of the levels of skill and discretion enjoyed by
many potters was the relative absence of alienation. Alienation
occurs when work is organised so that the worker is forced to
suppress his or her individuality. If the worker cannot relate his
work to a goal, if the work is merely performed through routine,
the production process may be said to exist as something alien for
the operative (cf Gutman 1976: 36, More 1980:22). Admittedly
many unskilled potters did feel powerless and derived little
meaning from their labour, but not so the skilled and even
semi-skilled.

Henry Evans, a ground-layer at Cauldons, like many potters, was
genuinely proud of his 'famous production' (including a set for
Queen Victoria). Potters spoke freely of the gratifying experience
of forming 'ugly looking shapeless lumps of clay into beautiful
vessels' (*P. Gazette* 1.4.1913). J.B. Priestley's description of the
skilled potter in 1934 catches this quality of pottery work
particularly well:

This sound element of craft, in which they can, and do, take a
personal pride, removes all these men from the ordinary
ranks of modern workmen. They are not merely doing a job,
on the contrary these men – and no doubt many of the

women too – become more themselves, enlarge their
personalities.

(Priestley 1934: 204,211)

In terms of industrial relations fulfilment in work did not
preclude conflict arising between masters and workers. Potters
were more ambivalent. Absence of alienation might lessen the
tendency for disputes yet alternatively the fierce craft pride of the
potter could easily have the opposite effect.

Two qualifications of the picture of autonomous regulation of
work by potters must be made. First, regarding the overall control
of the work process, even the most skilled potters or workgroups
had a limited degree of authority. The total arrangement of the
production facilities or major investment decisions were never
within the control of craftsmen. Second, although managerial
control of the detailed elements of production was well known to
be loose, with few foremen or supervisory workers employed on
potbanks in 1900, owners did tighten their control during this
period. By 1925 the numbers of departmental managers and
foremen had increased enough for the union officials to complain
that they saw far too little of the manufacturers in the works and
rather too much of the 'jacket-men' (NCPI mins 1925:29). The
accompaniment to increased numbers of supervisors was the
introduction of clocking-in and other forms of regulation aimed at
developing real managerial control of work. The first qualification
helps explain why even the most powerful craftsmen looked to
union forms of organisation to protect and maintain their
customary rights of control. The second provides us with the
source of much of the potters' individual and collective anger
throughout our period.

FAMILY, HOME AND WORK

Some historians now recognise the intersection of the two worlds
of home and work. It is becoming more common for them 'to
mesh two important specialities, labour history and the history of
the family' because 'these topics embrace two of the more
fundamental areas of human activity' (Pleck 1976: 178, Anderson
1980: 35-36). Applying that perspective to the pottery industry is
especially productive. Although industrialisation in Britain was

accompanied by the decline of the household mode of production, and its replacement by wage labour, the potters show how interdependence of family members could remain strong, especially where there was a high level of female employment (cf Tilly and Scott 1978: 104).

The intersection of home and work in the Potteries can be explored by posing a number of related questions. Is it necessary to discover what was the link between these two areas of working class life? (Bodnar 1982); how was that link perceived and interpreted? (Segalene 1983); and in particular, what relevance did the relationship of home and work have for gender roles? (Hudson and Lee 1989). Ultimately, the answers to these questions will demonstrate how the connection between work and home can illuminate both the form and function of the trade unions.

Two basic features of the potters' lives quickly establish the close association between work and home: the physical proximity of the home to the workplace, and the mixing of work-routine and domestic activity. As contemporary photographs show, the potbank was the predominant physical feature of the Six Towns. The 400 'banks individually and collectively overshadowed their employees' homes. Potters' homes were 'hemmed in by their work'. Inquests, court and press reports indicate that many operatives worked at the very least, in the town or district where they lived. Some firms built company houses. Kirkhams, for example, owned the streets of houses surrounding their London Road works in Stoke (Interview W. Bell). A 1% sample of the union was taken from the records of June 1920. It was found that 89.6% of the members lived within two miles of their workplace. Of these 49.7% lived between one and two miles away and 40% resided less than a mile from where they worked (CATU Coll D40: W. Broad's collector's book 1920). Even the large firms supplied their labour needs from the immediate surrounding areas. Most potters walked to work.

While the residential patterns of the Potteries ensured a special link between home and work, it was the work cycle which bound the domestic and industrial spheres so firmly (cf Young and Willmott 1957: 102, Jackson 1968: 89). Home and work routines were synchronised. Working hours were long and irregular. Oven work was infamous for its lengthy work sessions. David Draycott, a placer, worked 'as long as two days and a night at a stretch' (*P. Gazette.* 1.12.1914). The most frequent breach of the factory regulations was for the length of potters' working days. Apparently, working from 7 a.m. to 7 p.m. was common, especially when meeting deadlines or rush orders. The stoppages and deductions associated with piece work meant extra hours of labour were necessary if lost wages were to be redeemed.

Arguably the strongest social feature of the link between home and work was the family (cf Anderson 1980/1971: 65-80). It was through family and kin relations that the two worlds intersected. Family connections in employment were as old as the industry. It was well known locally that an individual skilled potter, in the previous two centuries, 'might employ his own family', and the observation was made in 1906 how 'that is very often the case to this day' (*Truck Acts Report* 1906: 42, 98). Successive government inquiries revealed to outsiders what potters accepted as commonplace. Collet's study in 1892 found that 'in many cases husband and wife or child work together' in the same factory, and the Royal Commission on the Poor Law found the situation unchanged in the 1900s. The family remained an essential element of the work experience throughout this period and beyond. Individual families 'followed the trade' both between generations and across the family and kin network (Collet to *Royal Commission on Labour* 1893: 61-63, *Royal Commission on Poor Law* 1909: 160-165).

In spite of the unanimity of contemporary commentators and potters, these impressions need testing. Let us take a sample of one neighbourhood in Basford in 1920 (CATU Coll D40: W. Broad's collector's book 1920). Out of the 400 recorded pottery workers and unionists in this area the strength of family employment can be demonstrated. First, 191 or 47.48% of the workers were in families where other members of the family were potters. Second, there were 76 working families: within these family units the mean number of members per family working on the potbank was three. A survey of union contribution rates in 1924 across the Potteries showed that, of the completed replies, 22% of the households had other members working as potters. It would appear from records relating to the Johnsons and Howsons firms that 52.52% of their sanitary workers shared the same surname. Under the entries for 'B', 10 of the 24 workers with surname beginning with B appear related (CATU Coll: Survey of union members 1924). Therefore, one can broadly accept the potter's assertion that 'the men and women working in a [pottery] factory are often husbands and wives, brothers and sisters, fathers and daughters' (*P. Gazette*: 1.12.1893). A stream of examples comes from the pages of William Broad's union collection book covering the period July 1920 to June 1921. Amongst the clearest examples is the Duckett family: Mr and Mrs Duckett both worked at Wengers while their daughters, Ethel and Ada, were pressers at Vickers Limited. Three members of the Munslow family were employed at Twyfords, John the father as a pressman, Edith in the warehouse and Dorothy in the glazing shed. The three Tinsley sisters, Ethel, Annie and Dolly were all employèd at the New Hall Works as gilders. Other families were spread across different firms yet the occupational pattern remains strong. While Christine Cameron was a figuremaker at Wedgwoods her brothers John and Angus both worked in the mill house at Twyfords.

Having revealed that the family or kin relations were common features of the social structure of the potbank it is critical to discover what role the family played at work. One manifestation of the family's role was in transmitting skills and securing job inheritance. Area 23 of Burslem union lodge in 1920 contained thirty-six family membership groups. By tracing the occupations of each member of each family the significance of the family to job succession becomes apparent. In the case of the male workers, 40% of the sons followed the same trade as their fathers. In the females' case, 48% of the daughters worked in the same job as their mothers. If we plot the workers who followed their parents into the same department (i.e. pressing, firing, dipping, see Figure 2.1) the connection is even stronger. Seventy-four per cent of the daughters and 63% of the sons worked in the same department as their parents (CATU Coll: Burslem Lodge membership register 1920).

Job succession was both a source of maintaining a family's collective earning power and a form of craft or worker pride. It was also another example of how potters could attempt to control details of their work. The method of employing labour was not entirely random. Skilled workers, as we have seen, enjoyed the discretion of employing workers of their choosing. Other members of the family or near relatives were a natural choice. Also, potters enhanced their social standing, their commitment to the

74

workshop, by successfully introducing and training relatives. They demonstrated that they could 'speak for' someone. Owners were often happy to make use of these informal recruitment methods. They saved time and they could also become a means of ensuring the loyalty of the sponsor by increasing his or her need to maintain employment. Examples of job inheritance are legion. Instances come readily to hand. In the firing department, D. Corbishley was the fireman at Pratt & Co. of Fenton in December 1909. His father had been fireman there for 53 years and his grandfather had been employed at Pratts for 68 years (*P. Gazette*: 1.12.1909). It was well known that Thomas Edwards, secretary of the Ovenmen's Society followed his father's 'calling'. In 1914 William Hallan worked beside his father as a placer, as he learned the art of firing at Barlow's in Longton (*P. Gazette*: 1.6.1915).

The strength of family employment is important to an analysis of the social structure of the pottery industry. Family and kin relations could strengthen the solidarity of the workgroup and certainly influenced the family consciousness exhibited by the groups. On the other hand owners also made use of the associated family ties. The evidence from the pottery industry generally agrees with Tilly and Scott who have highlighted the extent of family employment in nineteenth-century industry, 'either way they were considered and apparently considered themselves members of a team, earning a family wage' (Tilly and Scott 1978: 113). The example of the potters can also extend the application of Anderson's model derived from the textile industry in Lancashire. He shows how an industry adapted to and respected kin and community ties in recruitment and work allocation (Anderson 1980: 35). Work on the Yorkshire textile industry allied with the pottery case provides a clear criticism of those who assert that by the late nineteenth century worker status was predominantly a function of individual wage labour (Bornat 1977).

Humphries argues that the persistence of the family among the working class can be partly explained by the family's ability to reproduce labour power for employers to use and also because workers defended an institution which enabled them to both organise and come to terms with work (Humphries 1977). A woman potter provided an instance of this dual relevance of the family (Interview E. Grocott). On the one hand she saw how her family, in the 1900s, had been used by her employer. The firm traded on family loyalty during commercial crises and she clearly felt her father, mother and herself were inadequately paid. At the same time she was adamant that it was 'the family' that had found her a job, trained her and provided a physical and emotional resource throughout her days on the 'bank.

The intersection of work and home can be also seen in the direct effect of the pottery industry's economic performance and wage structure on worker housing. One of the best summaries is Harold Owen's study of 1901 (Owen1901: 344-347). He recorded how wage and job status on the potbank was reflected in a potter's home. Yet, as the residential density and tenement surveys of the time indicate, there was an acute housing problem (Astor1922: 295-297). Local building markets and municipal policies apart, the basic problem was that low employment and wage levels meant that many potters were unable to afford housing adequate to their families' needs. It is important to recognise this aspect of the relationship between a potter's work experience and his or her home. At the time, it was the woman potter who received the blame for working 'while the children and homes suffer'.

In fact the reverse was true. Only because women worked did so many potters' families survive economically. Indeed it was the family mode of work which enabled potters to overcome the periodic crises of intermittent employment and poverty. Poor households sent as many members as possible into wage-earning employment. The potters had not reached the stage where, according to some writers, increased productivity and higher male wages permitted a sharper division of labour within the household: married women were not simply 'preferred as child-care and consumer specialists' (Tilly and Scott 1978: 230-231). Traditional work practices, and the need for family income led to almost 20% of the total female population of the Potteries working in the staple industry in 1911. Hilda Martindale found that 'a woman is looked upon as lazy unless she takes her share in contributing to the family income' since the main impulse to work was 'prompted by necessity' (*Physical Deterioration Cee* 1903: 123).

Moreover, since potters' families were large by national standards it became imperative that as many members as possible went out to work in order to contribute to the collective upkeep of the home (*Census of Staffordshire* 1921: Table 10). Children were routine contributors to the domestic purse, making Stoke-on-Trent the second largest area of juvenile (aged 10-14 years) employment in the country after Lancashire in 1907 (*Census of England and Wales* 1917: Diagram XXXIV). A great deal of negative criticism was levelled at the potters by outraged middle-class philanthropists during this period (*Daily News*: 2,8,9.1.1904). Potters themselves were more realistic. A job, and if possible entry to a skilled job ladder, was vital for the family in the short term and the individual youngster (male or female) in the long run. A commentator noted in 1910 that 'the opinion prevails that as parents they have not done their duty unless they have seen to it that *every girl as well as a boy* [emphasis added] is provided with a trade' (*Physical Deterioration C*[ee] 1903: 127).

The potter's family not only united the worlds of home and work but also provided the means of survival for many workers. One needs to look at the family even more closely in order to discover its full relevance to the experience of work and its possible impact on trade unionism. It is necessary to ask what were the gender roles involved and how did the public image of workers' households and working lives compare to reality? In particular what was the status of women in the home, and how did it relate to their position at work? The answers to each of these questions had implications for the women potters' self-image, consciousness and the actions they took.

The roles of men and women in a potter's household were quite different compared to contemporary prevailing middle-class notions. The working-class family has been seen as essentially patriarchal. Bray ventured in 1911 that: 'we are still inclined to regard the family as the one relic of the patriarchal system' for 'we are still apt to see in the home a small world, edged off from the large world outside, self-centred, self-ruled and carrying all the advantages of a benevolent despotism'. Later authors maintain that in the family and domestic sphere 'men stood at its head, their place sustained in the vast majority of working class households by their role as principal breadwinner' (Bray 1911: 92). The potter's family ran counter to both the contemporary and more recent, yet similar, generalisations (Vicinus 1972: 105, Blaxall and Reagan 1976, Eisenstein 1983).

Admittedly many male potters regarded themselves as the breadwinner of the family. A fireman in 1908 based his case to an arbitration committee on the inadequacy of his wage. Five shillings a day was insufficient to 'give adequate support to his wife and family' (*P. Gazette*. 1.10.1908). A tradition of male superiority had been constructed throughout the preceding century. In 1844, William Evans publicly berated women for going out to work since it 'reversed all natural order' (*Potteries Examiner*. 2.10.1844). However, we have seen that there was a strong and continuous presence of female labour across the pottery industry and that women did contribute to the maintenance of home and family. More importantly, there is good evidence to show that women potters were, in their own way, equally important to the direction, organisation and funding of the domestic economy as many male workers.

The male potter may have sustained the public image of being the head of the family, but it was the woman who was so often at the centre of that family. The woman's strategic position was one of domestic manager. In the words of one male potter: 'the lot of a workman's wife, especially if the family happens to become a large one, is one of the most arduous and responsible possible to conceive, for upon her devolves the financing of the too often uncertain income of the family', Union officials reported that the woman was typically the domestic banker. For example, in January 1925 Harold Moore's mother would not let him join the union since it would upset her financial calculations. Another woman ceased to pay her husband's dues (that she was responsible for the payment is itself revealing) since she could no longer contain them within the weekly expenditures (CATU Coll L30: Collectors' Survey 1924). In common with other women workers the female potters combined wage labour with domestic chores. The ability to meet the demands of the workgroup and the family meant that women were not marginal but central figures in the world of factory and household labour. This is not to suggest that women dominated the household, rather to draw attention to their positive yet unnoticed contribution to their families.

The public image of the woman potter was one of dependency. The reality was quite different. Given the economic circumstances of the industry, along with the effects of industrial disease,[1] in many cases the woman became the main and sometimes sole breadwinner for a family. In 1908 Sam Clowes testified that women potters 'are sometimes the sole support of the house' (*1910 Lead Cee*. Q 6511). To take some concrete instances: in 1916 a letter from Messrs Plant & Co. records how a 21-year-old woman requested a wage rise from 7s. 6d. to 12s. because 'she happens to have a grandmother over 80 years of age, and she is the only bread-winner'. In 1910 a woman trade unionist visited two workers. It was noted that 'one was, by reason of her husband's unemployment, bread-winner of her family, whilst the other had a mother and sister dependent upon her labours' (*WTUL Quarterly Report*: 3.7.1910). The Medical Officers of Health reports and the field notes of the factory inspectors are punctuated with such examples (*HMI Factories Report* 1906: 234, 1907: 171, 198).

It was noticeable how the classic roles of male provider and female receiver were reversed in the Potteries, as witnessed by Maud Garnett's testimony to the *Physical Deterioration Committee* in 1903 (*Physical Deterioration C^{ee}* 1903: Q 9351-9354). She was asked:

Question:	Very frequently the man does nothing?
M.G.:	Yes.
Question:	Does he live on his wife's earnings?
M.G.:	Yes, he looks after the children in a certain way.
Question:	Are there many cases in which the man stays at home while the woman goes out to work?
M.G.:	Yes, in Longton [where Maud worked].

Hilda Martindale found that 'men and boys willingly do their part in the domestic work of the house'. The *Committee on Women in Industry*'s findings of 1919 apply precisely to the Potteries: 'the women potters were a stark contrast to the conventional view of women's work, which still recognises for women ideals which are more or less incompatible with the facts of everyday life' (*Women in Ind. C^{ee}* 1919: 37-42).

A danger also lies in assuming that most women workers were part of traditional households made up of parents and children. As the general report of the 1911 *Census* shows (Diagram XXXII), the position of widowed and unmarried women must be taken into account. The demographic features of 'surplus women', especially in urban areas, meant that many women did not marry. Hutchins reminded us of this simple social fact as long ago as 1915 (Hutchins 1915: 78-80, cf Hamnett 1984). The greatest problem for isolated, widowed or single women potters was their low wages. It was estimated in 1906 that 14s. 6d. was the minimum sum necessary for a woman living independently to maintain herself in 'decency and with a meagre degree of comfort'. The average *full-time* earnings of a woman potter at that time was only 11s. per week: nearly 30% of female potters earned less than 10s. (Wage Census 1906: 102).

Clearly some single women were members of extended family units to which they contributed their pay and received bed, board and pocket money in return. However, from a range of local sources it appears that many single women had to work and fend for themselves or were the sole supporters of aged or infirm relatives. Besides the survey work of the Women's Trade Union League and charitable bodies, certain pottery manufacturers in 1908 noticed the problem. A member of the Ridgway firm questioned whether the wages of some women were enough 'to allow a single woman to feed herself properly and to give her all the opportunities which would keep her in health and make her efficient' (*1910 Lead C^{ee}*: Q 13702, 13717). The predicament of unmarried mothers without means of support 'other than their own labour' was unenviable as the recorded cases alone demonstrate (*Royal Commission on Poor Law* 1909:165). Widowed women pottery workers were often in a similar position. The numbers of widowed female potters are conspicuous in the Stoke and Wolstanton Poor Law Union's records (SRO 3506/1/13). One widow for example had five children to support and so she scraped tiles at 1s. for four boards; working at her hardest she could not earn more than 10s. per week.

The relationship of home, family and work is of great value to an explanation of the historical experience of the potters, both individually and collectively. Connections between these three elements of working-class life provide a number of contexts for the development of trade unionism, for the modes of bargaining and conflict and especially for the forms of consciousness among the potters and those will be described fully in subsequent chapters. Yet these contexts were highly ambivalent. A basic feature of the intersection of work and home was the dependency of not only the patriarch but the whole family on their work. With so few alternative forms of employment the potter's family was heavily reliant on the potbank. As in other single industry regions, the succession of generations of potters 'working in the pots' and the close physical presence of the workplace made employment in the staple industry the almost unquestioned basis for working life. The psychological dominance of the industry over the Six Towns combined with the mutual obligations of a potter's family or kin had a critical bearing on how potters responded to what we might construe to be blatantly unreasonable or hostile behaviour by employers or those in authority. In spite of the experience of women potters to the contrary, individual and organised potters seemed to have retained the traditional patriarchal value of both the area and the wider society. Clearly these persistent images and norms presented difficulties for the assertion of independent activity by women potters (*S. Sentinel* 28.12.1903).

Yet there were positive elements for women within the relationship of home and work which have been overlooked. Some of pottery work's informal aspects reveal the potential for workgroup and family solidarity, as well as the active role women could play. It has already been shown how family or kin relationships helped soften the alienating effects of work. This held true for women in particular (cf Grieco 1987). Female potters appear to have enjoyed and valued highly the friendship and sociability of work. A woman jollier remarked: 'I would rather be at work a hundred times than at home, I get lost at home.' Information and trading networks (cf Ross 1983: 4, 14, Hewitt 1985: 302, 309, 315) were useful and accepted parts of potbank life (*HMI Factories Report* 1906: 255, *Physical Deterioration C*^{ee} 1903: App V). Subscription clothing clubs (known as 'maxims'), *ad hoc* medical schemes and workshop parties were all part of the unofficial uses to which the workshop was put (cf Honig 1986). It was therefore in work that many women found a measure of independence and identity. The small-scale unstructured means of pooling information and passing on knowledge were as much the arena for female as male activity. Women found the family, the workgroup and the informal relationships of the potbank were locations where they could play an active part in determining their own lives and helping to sustain others. This relatively untreated feature of the potters', or others', working lives became a vital strength of the emerging potters' industrial union after 1906.

CONCLUSION

The potters' experience of work and their social relations were the result of the coming together of their own, independent orientations to work with the technological and organisational features of the industry. The analysis of work presented here began in the workshop, with the workgroup recognised as the basic social unit of work.

Four features emerged as critical in shaping the immediate form of work within the potbank: the production process, custom and practice, the payment system, and the social relations of work. It was discovered that while the relations within the workgroup were generally cohesive, the relationship between the hierarchically ordered workgroups was competitive and often deeply antagonistic. As was said at the time, the disposition of the different occupations was to 'gang their ain gait'.

The production process was finely sub-divided, lacked continuity of flow and involved a high number of specific occupations. Changes that occurred in the production process were localised and the experience of job redesign and de-skilling was limited to a relatively small number of occupational groups. Contrary to some labour process theorists de-skilling was not the dominant, general experience of the workforce; some workers actually increased their skills (cf Wood 1982). Within the division of labour a wide variety of tasks and skill levels were exhibited and groups were acutely conscious of their abilities and social status. Custom and practice for the potters were a key means of organising and making sense of work. Customary rules, generated by each workgroup, augmented the horizontal differentiation of the workforce while the sub-employment system along with the internal labour market enhanced the vertical separation. The competitive environment of piece work compounded the sectionalism of the potters. Traditional values regarding the role of women workers split the workforce along gender lines.

A conscious attempt has been made to study the mass of the workforce, skilled and unskilled (cf Joyce 1980: xiv). This focus has revealed the natural and continuing heterogeneity of the potters. As has been argued elsewhere, the labour aristocracy may be a useful device for researching certain industries. In the pottery industry such a concept is less appropriate in the period in question. On the contrary, the distinctive feature of the potters was the plurality of hierarchies, divisions and competing groups in each department of the production process and within each sub-industry. Furthermore, the instability of piece rates, the market fluctuations and the changes in skill and status precluded the maintenance of a dominant stratum of workers with the aristocratic credentials required by certain historians (Hobsbawm 1964: 272-315, Gray 1981).

This section began by suggesting that an analysis of work would form a first step towards a study of trade unionism. In this respect a number of features of pottery work deserve highlighting. Although the operation of the production process and wage contract evoked conflict between worker and owner, thereby forming the classic platform for collective organisation, participation in the production process also provided the basis for friction and contests among workers. The sectionalism evident on the potbank alone meant that erecting the common normative framework which gave an industrial union its coherence would be difficult. And yet the strength and permanence of the workgroup on the shopfloor suggests that this might also be the key social unit involved in bargaining and union organisation.

This chapter has also tried to extend the analysis of work outside the workplace. It is clear that the two main areas of a potter's life, the worlds of workshop and home, cannot be separated. The spheres intersected in three main ways: first there was the physical proximity, as home and potbank co-existed, often in each other's shadow; second, was the synchronisation of work rhythms and domestic routines (Whipp 1987a); and third, the strongest link which bound workplace and home was the family.

The investigation of home and work raised a number of related points. The potters' experience highlights how far from reality were the contemporary images of gender roles at work and in the family (cf Davin 1978: 49-56, Segalene 1987). More recently social scientists have seen women as dependent within a patriarchal set of relationships. Yet via family work-ties, women could play an active role in determining the forms of family life. While the man remained the publicly accepted head of the family, women were often the private organisers. On the evidence available, complete male dominance and female subordination is not an accurate picture of the relations within the potter's family (see Lummis 1985: Part III).

Traditional local attitudes towards the role of women, combined with depressed trading, prevented most female potters from joining unions in the nineteenth century. In the period under review women do take a formal part in union activity. One reason was changed economic circumstances. The other was that women were able to use their informal positions and associations derived from the home and the 'bank, to great effect. The potters provide an excellent illustration of Helen Smith's advice that: 'We cannot uncover the realities of women's past if we look at them as adjuncts to or as minor participants in the male power structure' (1976).

The experience of the potters also qualifies the assertion that the early twentieth century saw the retreat of the family from work and its replacement by the individual wage earner. The reconstruction of home and work presented here dilutes the claims of the textile industry to a unique position regarding female and family labour.

Lastly, this analysis has deepened our understanding of social relations in the industry. Income and status divisions on the potbank appear to have been broadly reproduced in residential patterns and housing types. Yet in the workshop, the family workgroup helped to reshape some of the antagonisms which arose from the division of labour. Kin networks contained and accommodated the tensions inherent in sub-contracting as potters often 'employed' their own relatives. As such networks were central to the organisation of work, so they became one of the logical bases for informal action both inside and outside work. The probes into trade unionism and conflict in the industry in the following chapters will therefore be guided by an awareness of this under-researched feature of social life.

One instance of the way family and domestic structures influenced behaviour at work was in the creation of an independent worker mentality over health. Reactions to industrial disease ranged from the defensive to the aggressive. Some potters fought for compensation. Many concentrated on the need to retain their job, while others accepted the customary norms of their families (especially in the case of firemen or placers) towards a necessary evil. Such robustly independent views on similar issues was to prove a recurrent problem for the potters' union; both in terms of its internal relations and its dealings with other outside groups.

Chapter Three

TRADE UNIONISM IN THE POTTERY INDUSTRY

This chapter examines trade unionism among the potters. Subsequent chapters will deal with the wider field of union activity; here the focus is on the union's internal characteristics: its formation, structure and composition. The process of formation, set in context, was a major shaping influence. The origins of many of the paradoxes of union behaviour in the industry may be traced to the NAS's creation. An analysis follows of the union's official structure, as well as an examination of how the union operated over time and on a number of levels. The received wisdom concerning the general relationship of union leadership to the rank and file will be critically reviewed in the light of the potters' experience. Above all, the composition and social organisation of the union will be explored in order that both the forms and meanings of union membership can be revealed: a vital yet neglected aspect of trade unionism. To what extent the union was a product of the workshop or the community, the nature of their interrelations and the reasons for the society's development are the preoccupations of this chapter.

FROM CRAFT TO AMALGAMATED UNION

The formation of the National Amalgamated Society of Male and Female Pottery Workers (NAS) in 1906 and the subsequent realignment of trade unions in the pottery industry was a momentous event. The amalgamation of a number of societies was not an isolated occurrence; this decisive act was the sequel to a train of events and must be set against the rich past experience of trade unionism in the industry. The formation of the NAS helped determine the future of both the trade union and labour movement in the Potteries. The explanations for that formative process, which covered the years 1900-1920, is embedded as much in the nineteenth as in the twentieth century. The interpretation presented here is therefore based on an analysis of the long-term as well as the more immediate contexts.

There was a mixture of union forms, membership, organisation and consciousness in the preceding century. The dominant form of unionism among the potters was the craft union (see Clegg, Fox and Thompson 1964). A range of unions resulted from the differing interests generated by the division of labour and each society served a specific craft or occupational group. Up to twenty different unions are identifiable. Each sub-industry produced its own union formation. The jiggerers in the china trade (320 in total), for example, had their own body separate from the jiggerers in other sub-industries. As craft unions, their membership size was quite small, based as they were on single occupations. On closer inspection two types of union can be seen. The first was composed of the larger, more powerful craft groups and their strength derived from the members' relation to the production process. These unions enjoyed a continuous existence. The second group was based on the smaller, skilled occupations; their potential membership was small and their presence highly unstable (Webb TU Collection, Vol. XLIV: 318-324).

Outside the craft unions the vast majority of semi-skilled potters were almost completely unorganised. The hollow-ware pressers and other male craft unions did try to attract related semi-skilled workers during and around disputes yet they do not appear to have organised the unskilled assistants. Most women potters in the nineteenth century fell into this category, except those organised by the printers' and transferrers' union from the late 1880s onward. The male unions combined, never had more than 400 women members. Major conflicts occurred in the potbank between male craftsmen and unskilled or semi-skilled female potters. The use of women as cheap labour by owners seriously threatened the job definition and status of the craftsmen. At most between 1870-1900, the number of unionised women potters amounted to barely 5% of the total female workforce (Webb TU Collection Vols. CIX, XLIV: 310).

The craft consciousness of the male unions was clearly visible. As their rule books show each union developed around the maintenance and protection of craft privileges and controls. It was around the issues of apprenticeship, wage differentials and the influence of new technology on craft jobs that the disputes of 1879-1880, 1890-92 and 1899-1900 centred. The unions' actions betrayed their craft origins. One can detail repeated instances of bitter conflict between the unions and masters. However, there are examples of the strong sense of 'mutuality' (William Owen's word) which developed between craftsmen and owners (*Potteries Examiner.* 22.11.1879). As one unionist stated: 'let honour be given where it is due. Union is not intended to harass those who right-eously recognise labour's claims, but to build them up in their position' (*Workman's Times.* 28.10.1890). Printers and transferrers, and the hollow-ware pressers regularly had manufacturers as guests of honour at their annual union dinners. Some craftsmen were able to set themselves up in business, which led to their unions framing special rules to accommodate them (*Report on Profit-sharing and Labour Co-partnership* 1920; cf Lummis 1985). The persistence of mutuality and high levels of craft consciousness led some to view the potters' unions in the 1900s as 'a generation out of date'. Yet the craft ideology (Matsumura 1983) of the potters casts significant light on the nature of their eventual amalgamation. Each union's identity and relationship with the pottery owners was an independent one. Amalgamation was seen as threatening to weaken these bases of craft union strength.

The *raison d'être* of the nineteenth-century craft union was the perpetuation of the privileges of small, specialised sections of the workforce. Consequently the unions were narrow and sectional in their aims and actions down to 1900. Despite the collective problems facing the mass of the potters, the craft groups seldom acted in concert. Industry-wide action and collective bargaining was never fully attempted. The major strikes and lock-outs illustrate the divisions within the potters' unions. In 1891 each craft group used the dispute over apprentices to pursue their own sectional objectives. The same was true of the potters' famous arbitration board and hence its intermittent existence. This is not to deny that certain issues (particularly wage cuts) did produce a more widespread collective consciousness, as the events of 1881 and 1891 show (*Workman's Times.* 6.3.1891). Even on these occasions the concentration of the craft societies on their particular interests undermined general solidarity. The stigma of defeat and the mutual recrimination which followed led the flat-pressers' rulebook to admit that, with regard to the 'history of union movements in the pottery trade ... sectional branches have not developed the necessary power' (Webb TU Collection: NOP Rule Book 1891).

Allied to the separatism of the craft unions was the high levels of autonomy within each society. Union size was relatively small (500-1400), administrative structures minimal and a large measure of discretion resided with the lodge or small groups of craftsmen. The secretary of the pressers proudly told the Hatherton arbitration in 1879 that, 'although they had a trade union they did not interfere with individual freedom' (*S. Sentinel* 22.11.1879). The printers saw no reason to develop a central bureaucracy since their members' industrial power on the potbank gave sufficient bargaining strength with the individual master. As late as 1900, the union's agent requested that the members 'settle in the full terms as set forth in the appeal, and where possible the agreement should be ratified by the officials of the society' (*P. Gazette* 12.4.1900). Among 400 potbanks and six townships the local lodge became the focal point of the craftsman's organisation. Loyalty to lodge and neighbourhood was strong. Throughout the nineteenth century, unionism in the pottery industry was dominated by the large number of separate, small male craft unions. Their independent craft consciousness, their sectionalism and well-developed internal autonomy militated against industry-wide combinations down to the 1900s. Moreover, craft consciousness (in spite of the development of alternative attitudes) and its material base remained entrenched throughout our period. Clearly, any amalgamated or industrial union which might emerge among the potters, would be heavily influenced by the long-held status and power of the craftsmen. Indeed the continuing strength of the dippers, pressers, ovenmen, printers and placers would provide a central reference point for any future form of union organisation.

The period 1900-1920 was one of decisive change for trade unionism in the pottery industry. In 1899 almost 20 separate unions were officially recorded; by the end of the era one union, the National Society of Pottery Workers has emerged (see Figure

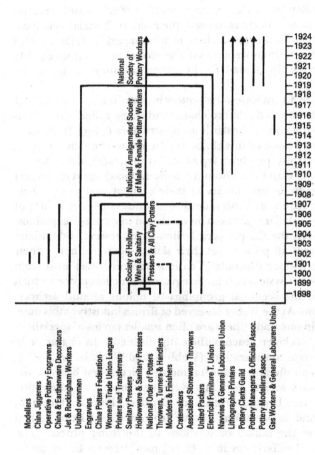

Modellers
China Jiggerers
Operative Pottery Engravers
China & Earthenware Decorators
Jet & Rockingham Workers
United ovenmen
Engravers
China Potters Federation
Women's Trade Union League
Printers and Transferrers
Sanitary Pressers
Holloware & Sanitary Pressers
National Order of Potters
Throwers, Turners & Handlers
Moulders & Finishers
Cratemakers
Associated Stoneware Throwers
United Packers
Electrical Furniture T. Union
Navvies & General Labourers Union
Lithographic Printers
Pottery Clerks Guild
Pottery Managers & Officials Assoc.
Pottery Modellers Assoc.
Gas Workers & General Labourers Union

Society of Hollow Ware & Sanitary
Pressers & All Clay Potters
National Amalgamated Society of Male & Female Pottery Workers
National Society of Pottery Workers

Figure 3.1 Trade unions in the pottery industry 1898–1924

Note: A dotted line indicates a transfer of members but no formal amalgamation

Sources: CATU Coll Annual Delegation mins, *S. Sentinel:* 21.2.1901, *P. Gazette:* 1.5.1910, 1.7.1913, 1.1.1918

3.1). Two main questions arise: why had trade unionism remained so sectional and diffuse, and why should a series of amalgamations occur in this period?

The first question is best answered by using the insights, derived from Chapter Two, into the fragmentation of the potters and the antagonism which characterised their internal social relations. The changes in the production process noted in Chapter Two generated new union groupings. The role of unions from outside the Potteries also added to the range of union forms in the industry.

As Figure 3.1 indicates, the pottery industry is a fine example of what Cole termed the 'mere chaos' and Clegg called 'the unparalleled complexity' of Britain's union structure (Clegg 1979: 164). The primary cause of this chaos in pottery was the rich variety of sub-industries, product types and job descriptions which continued to exist throughout the period. It was logical for potters to first organise the workers in their occupational group, their trade. We have noted the wide diversity not only of skills but of customs, vocabulary, payment methods and trade pre-occupations. For example, the flat pressers, hollow-ware pressers and sanitary pressers were all pressers yet their skills, wages and hence their unions were widely dissimilar. Tensions between trades arose from the piece-work system and the irregular production process which reinforced the sectional groupings of unions around separate occupations. As the Webbs observed of British industry at this time, even within one trade 'there are often smaller circles of specialised classes of workmen, each sufficiently distinctive in character to claim separate consideration' (Webb, S. and Webb, B. 1913: 109).

The major division in this fragmented picture was between the amalgamated society and the ovenmen's union. As their title suggests the 'United Ovenmen, Dippers, Placers, Firemen, Kilnmen and Saggarmakers Labour Protection Association' aimed to organise the skilled occupations in the firing process. The fundamental differences in work regimes between the potting/decorating shops and the ovens had always divided the potters at both the workplace and the union level. Firing faults led to regular inter-workgroup disputes. Though small in number at around 500 members, the oven workers were pivotal by any definition and of immense significance to the course of industrial relations and conflict (*P. Gazette* 1.9.1908). Relations between the leaders of the ovenmen and the clay potters were fraught with difficulties. The open disputes and exchanges of insults enlivened successive episodes of the industry's history. 1908 was an especially bad year with a battle over the arbitration board followed closely by a clash regarding representation on the lead inquiry (S. *Advertizer*: 22.2.1908). Separate industrial action produced a reservoir of ill-feeling. The labour correspondent of the Board of Trade summarised the 1900 dispute of oven and other potters with remarkable understatement when he wrote: 'the requirements of the various sections were not uniform nor were they united in their action' (*Reports on Strikes and Lockouts* 1900: 68-69).

The variegated pattern of unionism in the pottery industry did not remain static. It was augmented by new creations around existing and emergent trades, which sought to protect themselves against changes in technology, management strategy and the action of other unions. The china and earthenware decorators formed a union distinct from the 'printers and transferrers and female decorators union' in 1903 since the older union was not meeting the decorators' needs (*L. Gazette* 1903: 205). The 50 modellers in the industry formed an 'association' in April 1920, 'owing to the modeller not having been treated on all fours [*sic*] with other branches of pottery workers' (*P. Gazette*: 1.4.1920). The modellers clearly felt they could represent their interests most effectively as an independent union. The same was true of the electrical turners who remained a separate society from 1905-1920. The development of new lithographic printing led to the creation of a union which served the lithographers' specific needs.

Two important additions were the societies of the clerks and the supervisory staff. The clerks formed a 'guild' in January 1918, allied to the National Union of Clerks. The late formation of the managers' and foremen's society is particularly interesting and illustrates the character of the division of labour in the pottery industry. Although managers and foremen were appearing more frequently during the period (cf Melling 1980) their position on the potbank was very different from the usual role associated with supervisory staff. There was no neat distinction between worker and foreman. Many foremen or 'heads of departments' were senior craftsmen. The craftsmen owed allegiance to their craft union as the membership ledgers show. Only in 1919 was a separate 'pottery managers and officials association' formed after the manufacturers refused to recognise the NSPW as a bargaining representative of the supervisory grades (CATU Coll NEC mins: 10.1.1920). The position of the manager and the foreman in the workplace was well reflected in the uncertainty which surrounded their union form.

The activity of national unions added to the differentiation of union groups in the pottery industry. The Workers' Union organised among the unskilled labourers. Some of the crate-makers, packers and coopers (many of whom now worked in specialist firms outside the potbank) were recruited by the National Union of Gas Workers and General Labourers. Tom Cusack of the Navvies' Union was especially energetic in bringing unionism to the local tile and brick workers, whose sub-industry had never enjoyed a close connection with the other sections. His efforts came to fruition during the 1910 and 1911 brick, tile and marl workers' strike (*P. Gazette* 1.3.1910). Thereafter, joint action between the NAS and the Navvies' Union appears to have grown and become commonplace. The organisation of the unskilled, essentially auxiliary workers (what today might be called indirect workers) and those in the most distant sub-industry by national unions was quite logical. Given the background of the most powerful groups in the NAS and the difficulties experienced in bringing formal union membership to unskilled direct pottery workers, the NAS decided that the resources of the outside unions could be more appropriately used. Joint action with these external organisations was seen as a practical compromise (CATU Coll L77: Agreement between NSPW and Wengers Ltd 8.2.1919).

The second problem remains: why did this heterogeneous list of unions amalgamate in the 1900-1920 period? The answer lies in the following areas: the short-term experience and events concerning the potters' unions in the period 1890-1906; the pressures which faced all potters' unions during the first two decades of this century and lastly a set of wider influences which affected many other industries at that time.

As Figure 3.1 shows there were really two phases of amalgam-ation: the first around 1906-1908, the second between 1918 and 1920. Let us take the 1900s first. Once the pressers had united officially in one union in 1899 and demonstrated their ability to act cohesively they moved towards becoming a major force in the industry. Their sectional success during the conflict of 1899 and their actions during the difficult trading years around the turn of the century made the pressers a logical base for any further amalgamation. This episode of itself did not make new alliances more likely let alone inevitable, especially given the inhibiting factors outlined above. The combination of certain potters' long cherished designs for unionism with the lessons learnt during the 1892 and 1899 disputes became acutely relevant when the TUC was held in the Potteries in 1905.

The significance of the attempts of various unions to unite in the later nineteenth century should not be underestimated. In 1882, 1892 and 1899 the feeling for wider union forms and the linking of the craft unions was apparent below the surface of industrial conflict. In 1881 an *ad hoc* federation was formed as also happened in 1891: both failed (Webb TU Collection Vol. XLIV: 278).

Many rank and file unionists thought that 'with their petty jealousies' gone and in 'a united society of potting' they could accomplish, it was said, 'more in six months than they had in as many years' (*Workman's Times*: 10.10.1890). The disunity of the craft unions and the feuding between certain leaders during the 1891-1892 and 1899-1900 disputes was an object-lesson for most potters. The 1900 disputes and the failure to win certain demands in a good trade year led Will Thorne to assert that the potters had 'too many unions and too little unity' (*Staffordshire Knot*: 18.4, 10.10.1891). George Hassell, secretary of the pressers, was stung into 'recognising the lack of unity among the workers' which led him to draft an amalgamation scheme which all potters could support, in 1905 (*S. Advertizer*: 2.9.1905).

The short-term determinants of the 1906-1908 phase of amalgamation sprang from the improved performance of the industry at that time and from the role of the TUC and General Federation of Trade Unions. The trade reports for this period show demand and employment was strong with overtime being worked. Exports were up from £195,852 in November 1905 to £230,020 for the same month in 1906 (*L. Gazette* 1906). The success of the two sanitary pressers' disputes of those years was seen to have come from their increasing membership and funds (*P. Gazette*: 1.9.1908). Joining the GFTU in 1903 was an expression of the pressers' society's strength. They thought themselves to be 'in a better position financially than ever before in the history of the society' (*P. Gazette*:

1.3.1903). The meetings and propaganda surrounding the 1905 TUC in Hanley were crucial in boosting the impetus for amalgamation (Barrett-Greene 1905: 7-10). In particular the Women's Trade Union League forced home the need for combination among the male unions as a prerequisite for female union membership. Indeed it was the WTUL who brought the Printers, Ovenmen and Pressers together to consider the 'problem of female labour'. This resulted in first, a joint committee to co-ordinate a recruitment campaign among women and shortly after the formal merging of the Pressers and Printers and Transferrers societies (*WTUL Quarterly Report*: Jan. 1903; Jan. 1905; Jan. 1906: 16-17).

In addition the issues and activity associated with the 1906 election assisted this amalgamation phase. It was noticed that the potters had 'been greatly influenced by the decision on the Taff Vale case' and that the Conservative Coghill blamed his defeat primarily on the issue of the 'trade union question'. The secretary of the North Staffordshire Labour Council, Noah Parkes (agent of the newly amalgamated union) declared at the annual meeting in February 1907 that the past year had shown 'the closest ever support and concerted actions of local unions' (*S. Advertizer*: 20.1.1906, 21.4.1906, 2.2.1907).

In 1908 a number of unions still stood outside the NAS, most notably the ovenmen, packers and electrical furniture societies. However, a second phase of amalgamations occurred in 1917-1921, when these unions finally joined forces with the NAS. In spite of the basic cleavage on the potbank and at the union level from 1906 onwards the NAS clearly intended to win over the oven workers if not their leaders. The strength of the intent is apparent in the remarks of Sam Clowes, at that time president of the NAS. He was reported as saying that:

> they were determined that there should be only one society in the district, and they are prepared to do anything in their power to bring about a united society which was the only workable scheme for the Potteries district (Hear Hear). Whether Mr. Edwards [secretary of the Ovenmen] liked it or not, the day was near when there would only be one society for the whole district.
>
> (*S. Sentinel*: 4.4.1908)

The period 1906-1917 contained a number of events and changes within the pottery industry which facilitated the eventual amalgamations of 1917-1921. The timing of technological change was important. Whereas the pressers and printers had experienced progressive pressure on their job content from the late 1880s, the changes in oven technology only really emerged during and after the 1900s (see Chapter 1). The death of the long-serving oven-men's leader Thomas Edwards in 1911 proved to be an event of great moment. According to his obituary, Edwards had always 'maintained the independence of the Ovenmen's Union, when it was in danger of being absorbed by the Potters' Union'. It was under William Callear, the new secretary, that a closer relationship between the ovenmen and NAS developed (CATU Coll L284: March 1916 settlement). The 1913 industrial disputes saw practical co-operation among these workers and their unions leading to a joint committee of the NAS, ovenmen and the packers being set up in June of that year (*P. Gazette* 1.6.1913).

The 1913 committee's discussions failed to produce a formal merging of the societies. However, the events of the First World War provided a context which made amalgamation almost a necessity. Whereas fairly loose, *ad hoc* joint action between these unions had been sufficient in each of the disputes of 1911-1914, during the war this was no longer the case. Wage negotiations became almost continuous in the face of rapidly rising prices. Temporary bargaining arrangements solidified into something more permanent (CATU Coll L587: 18.1.1916). The increased scale of female employment, especially in oven work made a strong joint stance vital. A permanent joint union committee resulted leading to the establishment of local combined groups of ovenmen and other potters in each of the Six Towns. These groups held detailed negotiations with both manufacturers and government officials over a wide range of issues.

The actions of certain owners during the 1916 pay dispute was fateful. The masters rejected a combined union approach. The result, said the local correspondent of the trade journal, was that 'this reply caused the two societies of operatives to collaborate' (*P. Gazette* 1.9.1919). Rank and file pressure for unity grew again in 1917 when more than one mass meeting saw references to the 'duplication of organisations'. It is interesting to track the feeling for amalgamation in the public meetings of 1916-1919 and the

course of the private negotiations between the societies' exec-
utives. The latter certainly appear to have been propelled by the
former. The establishment of the National Council of the Pottery
Industry in 1917 added greater pressure towards combination
since one of the council's four principal requirements was the
complete organisation of workers throughout the industry. When
the manufacturers' associations combined to form the British
Pottery Manufacturers' Federation in 1918 the need for union
amalgamation was overwhelming as the societies admitted (CATU
Coll NEC mins: 23.10.1918, 30.9.1919). At this point, it was the
relative success of the unions' joint action in the spring dispute
which finally led to their formal joining.

It is also possible to locate the amalgamation process of the
potters' unions of the period in a wider national setting. Cole
thought the era exhibited as strong a 'unity movement' as any of
the previous century. The First World War was a time of greater
common action among unions, even those who had shown few
bases for unity in pre-war years. Permanent federations were
created (Cole 1924: 77-83). The influence of national war-time
bargaining and the pressure on unions to become more representative was well reflected in the potters' case. Pottery
manufacturers, in common with other industrialists, began to
recognise the uses of more representative unions and the
increased prospects for industrial peace if those unions could be
committed to central arbitration and conciliation machinery
(Pollard 1959: 217, Hyman intro to Goodrich 1975 edn: vii). Apart
from being influenced indirectly by the climate of opinion in the
country, the NAS (as will be shown in Chapter 5) had direct
contacts and dialogues with other unions and groups throughout
the period (CATU Coll L161 25.10.1918). The final amalgamation
in 1919 might have been the end of a lengthy process extending
over many decades: in effect it was just the beginning of the real
integration of the potters' unions which took many further years.

UNION STRUCTURE AND ORGANISATION

After the main amalgamation phase of 1899 to 1908 the NAS
evolved a structure far more involved than anything the
nineteenth-century craft unions had produced. In the past, the
craft societies had relied on a relatively simple pattern of

executive, secretary/agent and town-based lodges as befitted their average size of around 500 members (Webb TU Coll Vol. XLIV: item 3). The structure of the NAS was the product of an amalgam of forces. The influences of traditional craft loyalties and of the informal workplace groups were immensely strong. How these craft and informal groups reacted to the events of the period was equally important to the evolution of the new union's form. The physical and social geography of the Six Towns also played a part.

The Annual Delegation corresponded quite closely to the intentions of old craft unions' annual meetings but was more developed. In the nineteenth century the annual meeting was primarily for presenting accounts, reviewing the main policy areas and could easily be attended by the whole union membership. After amalgamation this was no longer possible. A more sophisticated representative body was required in order to embrace the expanded collection of lodges, trade and factory committees. A range of regulations was created for the standard-isation of procedures in order to protect members' interests. Each annual meeting elected a president and vice-president who oversaw the working of the delegation and the national executive for the coming year. It was at the annual delegation that broad policy decisions and commitments were made. All lodges, district committees and executive members could lay down motions; voting was by district or lodge (CATU Coll Annual Delegation: 28.8.1911, NEC mins: 12.1.1918).

The national executive committee (later called a council) and its sub-committees were made up of elected representatives from each district. By 1915 there were seventeen members of the NEC including the president, his deputy, the full-time officials and three trustees of the union. In common with other unions, as Frederick Parkin put it, in 1915, 'the society shall be under the management and protection of the National Council', between annual delegations. The NEC processed and resolved most of the problems received from the trade committees, lodges and officials 'affecting the whole of the members of the society'. The district committees dealt only with their local matters.

District Committees were established in January 1915. The reasons for their creation were two-fold. They were the product of the increase in membership, which led to far greater workloads for the NEC and lodges, allied with an increasing desire for wider representative forms within the union (CATU Coll NEC Report: 30.1.1915). The society's membership was divided into four geographical areas. The lodges within each area elected annually a committee of seven. The district committees' function was to deal with issues which arose within their areas. In particular, the committee acted as a court of appeal for lodge members; co-ordinated the work of the trade committees regarding changes in wage and employment conditions and was responsible for propaganda and organisation in the district. They were not given powers to vote money towards or to decide independently on 'general questions relating to strikes and lock-outs'. Instead they were supposed to process information concerning such activities to the NEC via the full-time union officials (CATU Coll NEC mins: 21.4.1917, 2.1.1918).

The lodge had been the principal administrative unit of the individual craft unions and was retained by those societies when they amalgamated. It was accepted that the lodge 'should be the centre of trade union activity' (CATU Coll Annual Delegation: 1914). Most craft unions had one lodge per town. The NAS made direct use of some and merged others to give three in Burslem, three in Hanley, two in Tunstall, two in Longton, one in Fenton and one in Stoke. Lodges' duties included the collection of dues, the dispensing of benefits, the maintenance of membership registers. Lodge officers were entrusted with raising members' questions and problems with national officials and the higher committees (*P. Gazette.* 1.9.1897, cf Francis and Smith 1980: 4).

Working alongside the lodges were the trade and factory committees. The lodges were geographically based and dealt with administrative matters while the trade and factory committees were responsible for representing the detailed interests of the workers in individual occupations, trades or in a sub-industry. The importance of the trade committees was demonstrated during the formation of the district committees. It was carried unanimously that the new bodies should be modelled 'on the same lines as the China, Sanitary, Jet and Rockingham and Stoneware Trade Committees, as the exigencies of the trade demand' (CATU Coll Annual Delegation: 1915). The factory and workshop committees did not fit easily into the official structure of the union. These were the temporary, self-sustained inventions of small groups of workers in one potbank or workshop. Their immediate concerns were factory based and their basis and actions were often unofficial.

The picture presented thus far of the union's structure has been, of necessity, institutional and directed at the official shape and the nominal structure of the union. In order to understand how the union operated in practice and why it developed in a particular way, a more dynamic approach is necessary. The sections of the union functioned in different contexts and underwent a number of changes. The distinction is between the image presented by the protocols of union conferences and the practical, everyday behaviour of officials and members. As H.A. Turner pointed out: 'in every institution, the structure's actual working, in terms of the relationship between its constituents and members, is as important as the formal rules that guide it (Turner 1962: 270). In common with other unions, the potters also faced the central problem of how to convert the spontaneous actions of a heterogeneous mass of workers into permanent organisation (Flanders and Clegg 1970: 38-47).

After amalgamating in 1906 the potters' union became progressively more centralised. The combined forces making for greater standardisation and conformity were formidable. Leaders saw that as the union increased in size, co-ordination of the various segments became vital if a unified approach was to emerge. If the union were to fulfil its basic obligations regarding funding and benefits, centralisation was an agreed prerequisite. The commitments involved in the national insurance and unemployment acts, the political fund, the moneys spent on litigation in cases of industrial disease and the many short-term funding operations, all produced a far greater administrative workload than under the craft union. The financial basis of the union and the co-ordination of the accumulated rules, contributions and benefits was a major problem. Moreover, for trade unions, money was a traditionally sensitive issue and the potters' were no exception. The demand for monetary accountability was strong. Weekly, monthly and annual balances and accounts were kept by both lodge and central office. Even so, in common with others (cf Cole 1939: 195, Clegg 1954: 88), the NAS's accounts were continually found to be 'unsound' given their precarious actuarial basis, as the deficits of 1908-1909, 1912, 1914 and 1921 showed (CATU Coll NEC mins: 14.5.1917, 22.7.1922).

The Webbs felt that centralisation was necessary for effectiveness: in their words 'the growth of national trade unions involves, for strategic and what may be called military reasons, the reduction of local autonomy to a minimum, and the complete centralisation of all financial and of all executive government' (Webb, S. and Webb, B. 1913: 138). However, workers themselves also pressed for centralisation. In the NAS some of the craft-based lodges and trade committees were inappropriate to the needs of many of the semi-skilled and unskilled who joined the union after 1906. The creation of the district committees and the widening of the NEC to a larger council in 1915 were the clear attempts to create a geographically based representation. It was hoped that this arrangement would eliminate some of the inequalities of power and influence inherited from the craft institutions. As the secretary, Joseph Lovatt admitted, 'this important change in the system of government' was 'in accordance with a general desire to act on more democratic lines ... making it more representative of the whole of the members' (CATU Coll NEC mins: 30.1.1915).

Moreover, the union became aware of the changes in structure being carried out by other unions: a survey of the major national unions organisation was made by the NAS in 1917 (CATU Coll L161, 15 point questionnaire). Furthermore, pressure was generated by the increase in collective organisation by the manufacturers and the trend toward industry-wide bargaining forms from 1910 onwards. Union leaders argued for a more concentrated structure and mode of decision making to match the trends in industrial negotiations and agreements (cf Fox 1958: 253, Clegg, Fox and Thompson 1964: 246, Price 1980: 116-124).

An examination of the continuous operation of the central office, lodges, collectors, trade or factory committees and activities of both union members and officials makes their significance and interrelations clear. It can show the circumstances in which they operated and may help determine how the potters managed to convert 'movement into organisation'. As will become clear, the union contained forces making for centralisation and non-conformity; elements of upward as well as downward control co-existed.

The central office is a good example of how the union's institutions reflected both the changes and continuities the membership required. Under the craft unions, the upstairs rooms of pubs sufficed. Early on, Joseph Lovatt's front room served the purpose for the NAS (Horace Barks Library, Parkin nd: XIX). In 1908 a set of offices was built in Hill Street, Hanley, to cope with the union's increased activity and processing of information. However, the offices were not purely an administrative unit; they continued to be regarded by potters as a social and advice centre. Union rules stipulated that the general secretary had to live there so that he would be personally available to help members who called.

Nowhere was the social basis of union organisation more visible than in the lodges. The lodges provided a link in organisation between the craft union and the amalgamated society. Loyalty to the lodge was intense and always had been due to their localised constituency and support. During disputes the lodge helped mobilise action and opinion. For example, in May 1923 Longton lodge directed the 1,000 members involved in the Cartwright and Edwards dispute. Though bound by the union's official administrative rules and requirements the lodge exercised a good deal of discretion and independence. In January 1909, one lodge held a concert, given by its own choir, 'devoted to helping a number of working potters who, through no fault of their own but largely', it was said, 'owing to the introduction of new processes of manufacture' were unemployed (*P. Gazette* 1.1.1908). Lodges were often based at workmen's clubs which is indicative of how close they remained to their social base. Rambles, day-trips and 'entertainments' punctuated the lodges' year. The Albany Glee Club was an important feature of lodge life in the Fenton and Longton lodges (*S. Advertizer* 8.2.1908, *P. Gazette* 1.6.1921).

A lodge's status within the union was related to its size, past activity and the ability of its officials. Burslem and Hanley were always the strongest. In 1899 their membership was almost double Tunstall's and fifteen times that of Longton and Stoke. They were regarded as 'the strongholds' of the potters' union. Lodge secretaries built up large banks of knowledge and expertise on local issues (CATU Coll Finance C^{ee} lodge returns 1909). Their influence on the day-to-day running of the union led to a continual tension between the larger lodges especially and the NEC over autonomy of action.

The collectors and canvassers system has remained unrecorded and yet it proved to be one of the reasons why the union successfully translated 'movement into organisation'. The collectors were a response to the large informal union membership as the president admitted at the 1915 annual delegation (CATU Coll Sub-c^{ce} mins: 28.10.1915). A lodge's jurisdiction was divided into areas with a collector responsible for each. Longton lodge, for example, had 23 areas, covering 203 streets with a collector for every group of ten streets. His or her job was to visit each member or family at home, weekly, in order to collect subscriptions, pay out certain benefits and initially deal with any member's problems (CATU Coll Longton membership ledger).

The collectors were of immense significance to successful maintenance of the fabric of union membership. They were the means of organising workers when manufacturers refused to allow unionists on their potbanks. The collectors were able to process a diversity of problems for the individual member or their families. A collector lived in his 'area' and could respond quickly to calls for help. J. Elliott intervened in 1924 on behalf of a group of girls in Normancot after, to use his words, 'the master told the girls over a settlement that he would send for the union himself, as he could get better terms for them, which was a lie and he deliberately robbed them'. The collector proved to be a remarkably efficient means of exchanging views and information between members and officials, as the union's response to the groundswell against non-union labour in the early 1920s showed. Also, the collecting system was a key means of creating an industrial union. The collectors were based on areas and not trades or occupations. They were crucial to the union's ability to accommodate the wide range of occupations and sectional interests which emanated from the workplace (cf Drake, 1920: 219, Fox 1958: 241, Roberts 1971: 65, Walker 1979: 204).

The trade and factory committees were not simply administrative blocks within the union but a direct product of potters and their workplace relations. They are not easily defined and confound the niceties of organisational science. The factory bodies, which often sent representatives to the trade committees, were formed by all or part of the workers on a potbank. Their coverage of the industry was patchy, reflecting the differing traditions, circumstances and distribution of power among the potters. No full-time official could assimilate the diversity of ware type, size and price in even one trade: he or she had to rely on the relevant committee. Certain committees such as the sanitary or mouldmakers, became immensely powerful, because of their members' wages or status on the potbank and the performance of their sub-industry (*P. Gazette* 1.11.1911, CATU Coll NEC mins: 30.5.1918, 13.9.1920). The array of committees and the considerable autonomy and influence of some was partly responsible for the increased pressure for greater centralisation after 1911. However, whilst the leadership and executive attempted to unify the actions of the trade and factory committees, the forces which created these committees were pulling in the opposite direction (CATU Coll NEC mins 21.11.1918). The widely differing contexts in which they operated meant that as a united, centralised organisation the growing union was being continually tested and put under strain.

There was a wealth of union activity outside the formal lodges and committees. These activities were as relevant to the maintenance of union organisation as its more publicised, official layers. At a very simple level, badges became popular among the 'jet and rock' workers in the 1900s for drawing attention to non-unionists (Interview W. Bennett). The device was adopted by the executive as union policy in 1911 (CATU Coll Annual Delegation: 1911). 'Show card days' and 'window-card weeks' were used to drive the message into the neighbourhood concerning local membership drives or disputes. Home-made handbills were a standard means of workers in one factory or workshop spreading information about their actions, especially during disputes. Much of this type of informal activity has gone unchronicled. The impact of these actions was demonstrated by the manufacturer who took the trouble to prosecute those workers involved in distributing handbills concerning his wages in 1917 (*P. Gazette* 1.3.1917).

The union might hold mass meetings or 'annual demonstrations' at the Victoria Hall, Hanley, but these were underpinned by the dozens of smaller meetings or demonstrations which were regularly held within the neighbourhoods of the Six Towns. The strength and persistence of these 'organic' features of union activity were eventually recognised by the union executive: district committees were then made responsible for helping to co-ordinate and finance them (*WTUL Quarterly Review* Jan. 1897, cf Liddington and Norris 1978: 41,106-109).

An explanation of the working organisation of a union must

obviously pay attention to its leadership. The NAS's officials were at the heart of the society's formal, and to some extent even its informal activities. They were often the meeting point for the opposing pressures for centralised or local control and played a mediating role between the sections of the union. The leaders brought their own characteristics and backgrounds to their jobs. Their actions, however, were constrained by the limitations the union imposed upon them and as individuals they were moulded by the problems and events which faced them. The point of convergence for the institutional union histories and the proponents of the 'incorporation thesis' is the relevance they ascribe to leadership (Burgess 1975: 309).

The leaders of the NAS were given a controlled degree of power by the constitution after being elected by a ballot of all members. The general and financial secretaries along with the organisers had permanent posts. They were directly answerable to the NEC and the annual conference, and could be dismissed by ballot of the members. Within these constraints, the duties of the officials, combined with the relationships they developed throughout the union, meant that they accumulated considerable power. The secretaries and organisers attended all NEC meetings and many district, trade and lodge gatherings. Their job required that they were conversant with a wide yet detailed knowledge of not only union practices but the current work process, prices, sizes, counts and wage rates across the industry. Any secretary who couldn't give the price and count on, for example, a '6 inch cast breakfast' at Woods was an impostor. A request from Tom Wikin regarding an 'oceanic' mould shape price shift over two years, for dinner and toilet ware on 5 January 1909 to Joseph Lovatt, assumed the secretary's competence to answer (CATU Coll: L422 5.1.1909). The officials had to be experts.

Yet despite their expertise the influence of the leaders varied according to which section of the union they were dealing with. The general secretary nursed the inexperienced lithographers of Myott's through two months of negotiations over apprentice ratios in 1912; bringing them to his office to coach them on tactics and telling them to let him do the talking since, as he told them, 'a still tongue makes a wise head' (CATU Coll L484: 16.12.1912). Whereas the trade committees, at most, were prepared to use full-time officials only as advisers: the craftsmen's specific knowledge of their case could seldom be matched. Often the official found himself caught between manufacturer and worker in these cases. Indeed the officials could not ignore the response of any members to their actions. In the early 1920s, 12.63% of a collector's membership search left the union because of dissatisfaction at the way officials had treated them (CATU Coll: 1924 membership survey).

The potters' leaders brought two sets of characteristics to their job: the individual and the collective. From 1900, a new generation of union officials emerged. The foundation of the NAS coincided with the death of Thomas Pickin, long-serving secretary of the hollow-ware pressers and the retirement of Joseph Hassall, their agent. Joseph Lovatt and Jabez Booth were completely new appointments as general secretary and organiser respectively of the NAS in 1906. Sam Clowes became president in 1907, his first union position, and only became a full-time organiser in 1909. Arthur Hollins, described as 'the alert, young Assistant Secretary', took office in 1910. Only Noah Parkes had previously been a union official, a secretary of the Printers and Transferrers Society (*P. Gazette* 1.1.1908, 1.8.1910, 1.9.1911). Therefore, all the full-time officials came to their jobs anew and were able largely to construct their roles from scratch. Their lack of in-grown attitudes and habits was noted and is one of the reasons why the union was able to make the mixture of trades and groupings cohere within one organisation. The friendship of Clowes with Callear of the ovenmen is a case in point (*P. Gazette* 1.12.1908).

The other notable feature of the new leaders was their occupational and residence patterns. They were mainly craftsmen 'makers' or pressers and, except for the organiser responsible for Longton, virtually all of them came from Hanley or Burslem, the central area of the Potteries where the bulk of the membership was concentrated. Both these features were to influence union policy and action. On the available evidence, the stability of the officials is remarkable. Even the annually elected officers show a marked degree of permanence with only twelve people occupying the forty-two possible positions between 1907 and 1928. Leadership crises do not appear to have figured in the union's development.

The individual personalities and backgrounds of the leaders help explain the evolution of the union at such a critical stage and also qualify the collective picture of a narrowly based and unchanging group. Arthur Hollins was austere and 'very academic'. As financial secretary he appears to have been the necessary counter-balance to the more extrovert general secretaries. In contrast Joseph Lovatt and Sam Clowes were sanitary, not hollow-ware pressers, who were proved in the fire of the sanitary disputes of the 1900s. Lovatt's character as general secretary was shaped by his experience of addressing mass demonstrations in the 1907 sanitary dispute and observing the evil of large-scale unemployment around 1908. He honed his renowned negotiating sharpness during the arbitration of 1908-1911 leading a manufacturer to remark on his 'considerable skill in cross-examination' (CATU Coll S. Clowes Scrapbook: 25.3.1917).

Sam Clowes and Jabez Booth had different skills (cf Walker 1979: 203). Clowes, organiser from 1909 to 1918 and general secretary from 1918 to 1928 stands out as a man of singular traits. His special hallmark was the ability to communicate with all sections and levels of the membership. He won widespread acclaim amongst skilled and unskilled alike for the public stances he took against masters. Organising work in Longton and the out-potteries won him many future allies. Apparently he had the gift of being able to explain the technicalities of the industry 'with the simplicity of a child'. As an organiser he learnt platform techniques and style (Interviews D. Robinson, R. Gibbon). In 1907 he was speaking on waste ground in Fenton. As he drew to a close at 9.30 p.m. he saw that the lights were on in a nearby 'bank. He quickly used the light in the window as a motif around which he constructed a final blistering attack on owners who abused labour. A neat turn of phrase and a telling use of imagery distinguished his speeches. Clowes attacked manufacturers who refused to make up workers to journeymen and employed 'apprentices as grey as myself' (he had striking white hair). On the problems of lead poisoning he spoke of how 'once a man was certified as suffering from plumbism he might as well be branded on the forehead' (S. Sentinel: 6.4.1907, 26.3.1928). His long-held advocacy of industrial unionism which included women and young potters, learnt from his time in organising the china trade, made him especially popular with a very broad range of workers (S. Advertizer: 25.1.1908).

Jabez Booth, organiser from 1906 to 1918, built his reputation by organising the unorganisable in the 'jigsaw puzzle' of the jet and rockingham trade. While Hollins, Clowes and Lovatt excelled in the formal negotiating forum, Booth was a prime example of the local, small-scale bargainer and union agent. Angered by the managerial onslaught on his hollow-ware presser's craft, employed by one of the toughest firms in the Potteries (Grindley's was once described as 'not having a trade unionist on the place'), Booth was engaged in the guerrilla war of small potbank conflict and bargaining for nearly twenty years. His tactical skills and knowledge bore fruit in the wider negotiating machinery which developed after the First World War (*P. Gazette*: 1.1.1906, 1.12.1908, 1.3.1918).

A view current in the historiography would predict that the full-time officials' life-style became distinguished from that of the average worker's. Union leaders were, it is said, 'reluctant advocates of rank and file grievances after a period in office'. The isolation of the union official made him vulnerable to the prevailing ideology of employers. According to Burgess, 'instances of "incorporation" are legion' (Burgess 1975: 309). In the case of the potters, the argument does not hold.

There was no great jump in income for the officials, although their job was much more secure (CATU Coll Annual Delegation: 1911). It has already been shown how the jobs of secretary and organiser were founded on accessibility and intimate knowledge of the industry's continuing operation. Even after bargaining became more formalised, the officials still dealt with factory and trade groups. There were dangers within the job of leadership. Clearly the union officer's expertise and range of contacts set him or her apart from the potter at the bench. As a negotiator the official necessarily had to deliver his part of an agreement. It was only human that Clowes or Lovatt, caught sometimes between masters' and workers' aspirations, fought for their own judgement (cf Clegg 1979: 231). Perhaps Sam Clowes' case shows why he and other officials could not separate themselves from the work experience of their industry. As Clowes put it towards the end of his career, 'I myself worked at the bench 34 years and I feel the effects of it every morning with about half an hour's hard coughing' (CATU Coll 1924 Wages Inquiry: 18).

The evidence for the 'incorporation' argument among the potters is very shaky. Superficially, it would be possible to derive a picture from the comments of masters and the local middle class, of the potters' leaders as sober, respectful and respectable, at ease in the world of manufacturers and judges. For example, in 1916, an owner described Clowes as a 'sturdy, straightforward leader ... generally carrying himself in such a way as to earn the confidence of employers and employed' (*P. Gazette* 1.11.1916). Yet, looking more closely, it becomes clear that the potters' leaders were being constantly reassessed by local figures of authority. Throughout the period the same Sam Clowes was attacked by manufacturers for being too 'rugged in his way of expressing things' and found guilty 'of indiscretion in speech' (*P. Gazette* 1.3, 1.5.1918). Jabez Booth was marked down for showing 'advanced democratic leanings' and 'speaking injudiciously' (*P. Gazette* 1.6.1918). To argue that these trade union leaders were sucked into collaboration with manufacturers' values is to ignore the evidence (cf Steed 1980: 148ff).

One further preoccupation of writers on trade unionism has been the question of democracy. Vic Allen's observations are particularly apt. He pointed out that a trade union was 'not based on theoretical concepts prior to it, that is on some concept of democracy, but on the end it serves' (Allen 1954: 62). In the potters' case there seems to have been an implicit balance between the aspirations for self-government and problem of how the union was to be an effective organisation. The checks and balances of the rulebook seem to have operated. The annual delegation functioned as planned with a healthy turnover of delegates each year, scrutineers employed and members free to see the books at any time (CATU Coll Annual Delegation mins: 30.9.1920).

The range of the representative committees and lodges appears to have provided a means of expressing the interests of the different occupational groups. Clearly certain groups had more industrial and therefore union power than others: in that sense the union was very much a reflection of the workplace. Yet in many ways it was the flexibility of the union, as shown in its operation, that prevented any one group from enjoying complete power or suppressing internal opposition. The craft groups were extremely influential yet they, the executive and the union leaders' authority were circumscribed by numerous traditions and strengths of local organisation which the union contained. The resulting tension between the aspiration for self-government and the need for collective effectiveness was a theme which ran through the activity of the potters throughout this era and beyond.

MEMBERSHIP

It is a strange thing but a major aspect of trade union history which receives relatively little attention is the membership. Apart from numerical extent, the social dimensions of membership may provide insights into not only how a union operates but also the meaning individual workers ascribed to trade unionism. The following section will explain therefore both the extent and growth of the union as well as exploring the composition of the rank and file. The intention is to develop a clearer idea of what it meant to belong to a union and also to draw out the relationship between the member and the formal structure and organisation.

The potters in the late nineteenth century were often categorised as poor supporters of unionism (Shaw 1903: 183, Warburton 1931: 12ff). There is a distinction between formal, recorded membership and informal unrecorded union support. Many potters supported the craft unions and the early NAS by word and action although they could not afford to become fully paid-up members. For instance, in Longton in 1901, Noah Parkes found that, due to poverty, many china workers could only informally associate with the union. He explained that 'since the last great strike they had obtained a good many members from that district, but they were not financial members' (i.e. full fee-payer). Potters moved in and out of financial membership as circumstances dictated (*S. Sentinel*: 4.3.1901). There were continual references during the period to unionists and non-unionists working and then acting together in disputes (*P. Gazette*: 1.3.1908, 1.1.1909). As has been shown elsewhere, interpreting low union membership as being a product simply of worker apathy is dangerous and superficial (Gutman 1976:297, Spaven 1978: 216).

The total union membership figures may be examined with these qualifications in mind. Figure 3.2 outlines the progression of membership in the NAS and among unions nationally during the period. Bain and Price show how the industrial power of a union 'depends more upon union density than upon the absolute number of union members' (Bain and Price 1980: 160-163). Figure 3.3 therefore indicates the levels of union density, locally and nationally for the same period. Broadly speaking, absolute union membership for the potters appears to have followed the

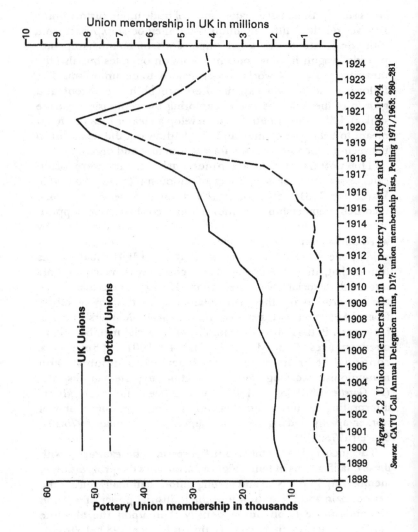

Figure 3.2 Union membership in the pottery industry and UK 1898–1924

Source: CATU Coll Annual Delegation mins, D17: union membership lists, Pelling 1971/1963: 280–281

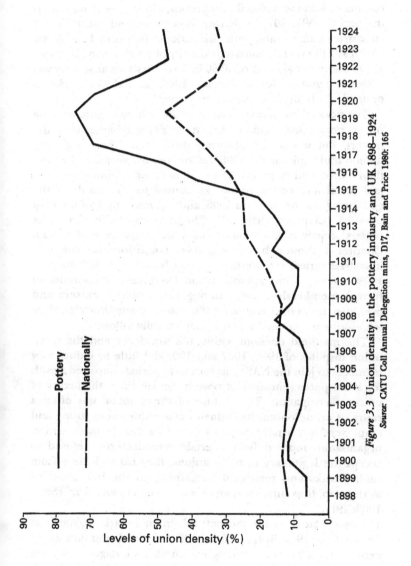

Figure 3.3 Union density in the pottery industry and UK 1898–1924

Source: CATU Coll Annual Delegation mins, D17, Bain and Price 1980: 165

national trend. However, if union density in the pottery industry is compared with the national proportions, differences stand out. In the period 1898-1907 the density in pottery stood at 6-12% and compared unfavourably with the national figure of 12-14%. By 1918-1921 the pottery industry's density of 68-75% had risen well above the national mark of 40-50%. Two questions arise: why was pottery's density so low in the early 1900s, and why did it rise so dramatically in the later part of the period?

The potters' low density relative to the national figure must be put in perspective. National union density was higher than the potters' but it was not uniformly distributed. There were two million trade unionists in 1906, yet four out of five unions had less than a thousand members. The coal, building, engineering, iron and metal and cotton unions accounted for two-thirds of the country's trade unionists in 1906, and still made up half the total by 1913 (Clapham 1938: 321, Phelps-Brown 1959: 216). The potters' relatively low union density still requires explanation. Chapter 1 showed how the market conditions for the sub-industries varied, with certain sections badly depressed down to 1908. Low wages, unemployment and defensive postures inhibited formal membership, even among the sanitary pressers and ovenmen. It was the irregularity of the wage system which led Shaw to describe the potters' union as 'haphazardly followed'.

The manifold divisions within the workforce and the inter-union disputes of 1900, 1907 and 1909 did little to induce new members to join the NAS in its formative period. Impaired health for some potters meant that poverty denied them the luxury of union participation. The culture of the potbank was often a restraint on unionism. Individualist craft values were strong and employers' paternalist regimes (see Chapter 4) made union organisation more difficult. Certain manufacturers refused to accept the legitimacy of trade unions: they banned them from their 'banks and restricted bargaining to the individual or workgroup, thus shrouding unionism 'in secrecy and fear' (Shaw 1903: 191).

The explanation for the potters' union's marked growth in density from 1911, in spite of the difficulties and restraints which existed, must be taken through a number of stages. First, the potential for unionism did exist. As one potter remarked: 'the industry was so localised ... they ought to have the strongest union of any trade in the world' (*S. Advertizer.* 16.1.1909). Second, models of union growth are available. Davis shows that positive changes in union membership correlate more closely with sharp changes in prices than general prosperity (Davis 1941). As wages lag behind prices, so workers must organise if they are to avoid a drop in their standard of living. In the past, a period of rising prices was nearly always a period of increased production and decreasing unemployment. He also points out that there must be major grievances involved for the workers concerned. Davis's model only helps to explain part of the potters' experience in the period 1911-1920. There is a need to focus also on the role of employers and key actors (cf Price and Bain 1976). Economic prosperity may have set the preconditions for union growth but it was the activities of certain individuals and groups which proved to be the all-important triggers of expansion.

During the period 1911-1920, rising wages and increased trade led to regular wage income and rises in real earnings for many in the pottery industry. Some of the poverty-related barriers to union membership were dismantled. Unemployment dropped to its lowest for a decade. In common with other unions the potters recorded an increase of around 20% in membership between 1910 and 1912. The labour market tightened, especially during the war, and so the perennial problem for the union of surplus labour virtually disappeared (*L. Gazette* 1912: 267, *P. Gazette.* 1.12.1915, 1.6.1916). In conditions of full employment and high demand for products and labour (except in sanitary and tiles), the union was able to make demonstrative stands on certain issues. These issues attracted a wide range of members. In May 1915, a 10% increase was put forward by the union for *all* workers. Minimum wage levels for women and equal pay for equal work for men and women became union policy. Strong feeling among the membership developed against non-unionists receiving the same wage increases as unionists thereby increasing the pressure to join the NAS (*P. Gazette.* 1.5.1915, 1.3.1916).

The context of the period 1911-20 was one of rising demand with owners needing to maintain production to ensure profits. When 3,000 potters left to answer Kitchener's call, manufacturers were unable to continue production without worker and union co-operation. It was observed in 1915, that 'labour never stood in a more autocratic position in the Potteries than it does at the present time' (*P. Gazette* 1.8.1915). Masters gave unionists recognition at the formal and, to a great extent, the informal level as well. Isolated workgroups were free to join the union officially without the fear of open victimisation. As a master admitted in 1917, 'some explanation for the large accretion to the membership of the unions is due to the recognition which manufacturers themselves are now giving to these organisations of their workpeople' (*P.Gazette* 1.5.1917, cf Bain 1970: 122-135).

By this recognition the union became the prime means of gaining the successive 'war bonuses': these four sets of bonuses were of great importance being described as 'the largest single increase in the history of the trade' (*L. Gazette* 1917: 27, 45, 211). One seasoned official was under no illusions regarding the phenomenal rise in membership. Looking back from July 1918 he observed how 'many workers have joined through the economic pressure of the increased cost of living and have only become members for the purpose of obtaining an increase in the war bonus' (NCPI mins: 25.6.1918).

The events of the period ensured that these factors making for union growth overcame the traditional sectionalism of the potters. The impact of technological change on certain craft and skilled workers was critical. As the period progressed, craft unionists and especially their leaders became acutely aware of the threat to their status on the 'bank and their bargaining power. Changes occurred across the production process; organisations to combat them could no longer remain sectional. As early as 1909, Thomas Coxon, a presser, saw how 'they were still in a very backward position from a trades unionist point of view, since a revolution was taking place in methods of production in the Potteries, and it was time that they should organise so efficiently that they would be able to take a proper share of the results of their production' (*S. Advertizer* 16.1.1909). At the same time, Sam Clowes was aware that 'the employers were wide awake enough to play one section of workers against the other' and therefore 'they [the NAS] wanted to organise all sections of workers. They recognised that the time had arrived when one class of workers should not be organised and the other left untouched' (CATU Coll NEC mins: 24.1.1919).

During the war, the large-scale substitution of women for absent skilled male workers made the need for industry-wide organisation even more necessary. Popular feeling among workers regarding

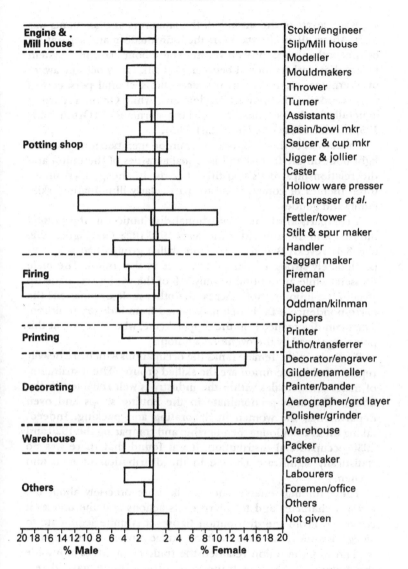

Figure 3.4 Occupational composition of Burslem Lodge of the NSPW
1920
Source: Reconstructed from Burslem Lodge Membership Registers, CATU Coll

the wage levels of the unskilled, the labourers and assistants was high. Above all, in the war years the individualism and separatism of the potbank was broken down. The labour 'pooling' system meant that workers moved between potbanks: they became aware of alternative methods and practices; the sectional perspectives were eroded. The potters underwent, what Orton recorded generally for the period as, a 'social transformation' (Orton 1921: 125, cf Price 1980: 176, Hunt 1981: 295).

An analysis of the composition of union membership may shed light both on the formal and informal activities of the union and the relationships of its constituent parts. In the potters' union three themes of composition are particularly illuminating: skill, family and gender.

A comparison of the occupational distribution in the pottery industry and the union, for the years 1920-1922 (see Figures 2.2. and 3.4) reveals that the craft and skilled groups had a disproportionately strong numerical presence in the union. The male pressers, while amounting to only 2% of the workforce made up 12% of the union sample. Across the other male occupations the correspondence is fairly well maintained from industry to union. The main divergence is in the dippers' case, who were still at this point organised by the ovenmen's union.

Similarly, in the female ranks the occupations which are heavily represented in the union are the skilled groups. The distribution of males and females within the industry is well reflected in the union. The men predominate in the potting shops and oven departments, the women in decorating and packing. Indeed, taking the Hanley lodge membership and comparing the 1920 and 1930 occupational distribution, it was found that there was no statistically significant change in the distribution of men and women.[1]

These findings enable one to talk more precisely about the union's character and to interpret its actions and the images it conveyed. From the distribution figures it is quite legitimate to categorise the NAS as a craft or skilled union. Those figures explain why the union retained the trade committees alongside the lodges. It was the trade committees which gave direct expression to the craft and skilled groups' interests within a wider, growing union. The occupational profile also provides the reason why the Balfour Committee and local writers still refer to the potters' *craft* union in the late 1920s, in spite of the NAS's declaration of industrial unionism (*Balfour C* 1926: 296). Skill continued to provide the framework for the union therefore from the nineteenth well into the twentieth century.

Yet, the profile also emphasises that by 1920, whilst the skilled groups still dominated the union, the dispersion of members' occupations was across the whole industry, across all departments and across all skill levels. Comparing the newly amalgamated craft unions of 1906 and the NAS in 1920 or 1930 it becomes clear that the union shifted from being a closed to an open union (cf Hunt 1981: 295, 311).

The figures also point to a further feature of the connection between workplace and union. The relationship of the workgroup to the organisation of work and the social relations of the potbank has already been shown (see Chapter 2). It is interesting that the union lodges categorise the membership by their workgroup function. If placed beside other evidence, this categorisation is indicative of the workgroup as a means for not only job but also union entry. The workgroup was also the main point of reference for most workers once they were inside the union and for any action which they took there. This workgroup consciousness is illustrated by the letter of H.J. Salt who wrote to Sam Clowes on 20 January 1920:

> I want to know if you can do anything for our Department
> that is the polishers. I think we are about the only department
> without a wage scheme. As we are now its really no benefit to
> me being a member I am only one in out of four men and
> one woman but I think they would join if we became
> represented as a department.
>
> (CATU Coll L445: H. Salt 20.1.1920)

Similarly the family was not only directly relevant to the social organisation of work, but one of the strongest threads in the social fabric of the union. The linkage of home and work via the family was reproduced in the NAS. The potter's family appears clearly in the membership ledgers. Using Burslem, the largest lodge, and its register for 1916-1920, a sample equivalent to 1% of the NAS was taken. It transpired that 30% of the women and 45% of the men members were in the union as part of a male or female family group. In other words each male or female register recorded large

117

numbers of fathers, sons and brothers or mothers, daughters and sisters from the same family. It was then possible to merge the male and female registers and reconstitute whole families of potters who were members of the union. For instance, Area 23 of Burslem, consisting of 20 streets and 341 members, contained 36 families or groups, amounting to almost 30% of the area's membership.[2] A clear example comes from the Leese family of 27 Wain Street in 1920. On page 21 of the Burslem male register appears Richard Leese (aged 52) the father and his three sons, Richard (26), Ernest (19) and Fred; all were flat pressers. On page 15 of the female register one finds Richard's two daughters Annie (24) and Edith (29), both employed as spongers. In other words, all the Leese family who were potters worked in the potting shops or the 'clay end' of the potbank.

The relevance of the family for the behaviour of trade unionists and the relationship of individual members to the unions was repeatedly shown. Collectors highlighted the role of the family as a mediating force between the rank and file and the union bureaucracy. George Eardley, a collector, reached this conclusion:

> After the little experience I have had in the way of canvassing, it appears to me a difficult proposition to get these people to join the society, unless the atmosphere of trade unionism prevails *in the house or workshop* (emphasis added).
>
> (CATU Coll: G. Eardley December 1924)

The words of pottery workers leave one in no doubt of the effects of family life on individual or group union membership. A union official recorded the following indicative remarks in 1924: 'father refused to pay as he thinks society ought to pay sick benefit, also son refuses because his father does'; or 'one home in Brook St. I have visited there are 5 pottery workers and only 1 in the Society. Their father says he does not believe in unions' (CATU Coll: 1924 union survey replies). Many workers clearly joined or left the union as a family, which is in line with the collective family bases survival strategies identified above (CATU Coll Longton Lodge register: 58).

While studies of trade unions have recognised the relationship between the workplace and the union, the contribution of the home and family to that relationship is unexplored. Bornat's work remains one of the few British studies to analyse the inter-relationship of the work situation, domestic economy and trade unionism. For industries with a high percentage of female labour such as pottery, one would agree that 'the close link of home and work maintained through dependence on and exploitation of family ties provided the context for participation in trade unions' (Bornat 1977: 65). This contradicts the suggestion that the role of the family in work was diminishing and its functions being taken over by trade unions by 1900 (Joyce 1980: 61-62, 229). In the potters' case the family continued to be a principal feature of work organisation well into the 1920s: for many potters it provided the bridge between workshop and union.

One of the distinguishing characteristics of the NAS's composition and growth was the high proportion of female members. By 1918, 58% of women potters were formal union members compared to 21% for the clothing industry, 27% for printing and paper, and 63.5% for textiles. The explanation for the sharp rise in official female membership lies partly in the set of factors already outlined for the whole union. Women benefited especially from the higher wages, constant employment and the new job opportunities which the war period presented (*Women in Ind. C^{ee}* 1919: 11). Given a stationary level of around 1,000 for the preceding period, the large increase during 1914-1918, from 2,000 to 23,000, is at first sight puzzling.

Orthodox reasons for the subordination of women in home, workplace and union are readily available for the 1900-1914 period (*Royal Commission on Labour 5th Report* 1893: 96, Hamilton 1941: 28, 57, 162, McCarthy 1977: 162). Yet these explanations fail to account for why such apparently deep-rooted obstacles to female trade unionism could be demolished overnight. An awareness of the ideological and institutional constraints is insufficient. A study of the unofficial, informal modes of behaviour reveals the ability of women workers to act as trade unionists or, if that were not possible, to act alongside unionists and to display high levels of union consciousness. These forms of female activity existed before and during the period 1900-1914. When economic and institutional restraints lifted after 1914 these small-scale, often unreported types of female action were given formal recognition and became organised on a larger scale.

Following the largely pessimistic tradition of the history of women and trade unions, it is possible to uncover evidence of the subordination of women at work and in unions (Lewenhak 1977). It has already been shown how women potters, by virtue of customary values, age and skill were overshadowed by male workers in terms of public status and authority. Some women in particular faced the problems of irregular employment; being used as cheap labour by manufacturers, which led to male unionists' enmity; and the restraint on female union activity produced by the traditional contemporary norms of behaviour. As Isabella Ford put it: 'trade unionism means rebellion, and the orthodox teaching for women is submission' (*Nineteenth Century* Aug. 1898: 256). Initially, the NAS appears to have been an example of the subordinate role of women in trade unions. Women paid dues and received benefits at half to one-third the rate of men. No female delegates to the annual conference appeared before 1916. Union attitudes apparently continued to embody male dominance: thus the one-week notice for women compared to the two-week or month's notice for men was part of union policy (CATU Coll Annual Delegation 1915: 60-61).

However, to be guided by the pessimists' view would mean missing a whole world of female union activity (cf Kennedy 1979, John 1986, Cooper 1987). Women potters did take part in formal and especially informal types of union action. The WTUL, following their campaigns in the 1890s, undertook regular organising work among the women potters from 1900-1915. The anti lead-poisoning campaign, led by Mary MacArthur and Gertrude Tuckwell, and their urging of women to claim their statutory compensation rights, won high praise from male unionists. During the changed economic circumstances of the war the unpublicised preparatory work of the WTUL bore fruit (cf Braybon and Summerfield 1987). The NAS's official recruitment of women at that time bears all the brush strokes of Marland Brodie, one of the women's earliest organisers (*WTUL Quarterly Review* Oct. 1906, *Annual Review* 1909: 20). Similarly the work of Sarah Bennett and unnamed women activists who assisted Clowes in the china, and Booth in the jet and rockingham sub-industries should not go unnoticed.

As Barbara Drake noted there were several women on the district committees after 1915 and men and women potters mixed freely in the lodges. Women's presence was particularly strong in the collectors' ranks, where they performed at an equal rate to men. In Fenton lodge, there were seven women and only five men collectors (CATU Coll Longton and Fenton Registers). The work of female organisers Dora Mycock and Agnes Lawton, though less publicised than Lovatt's or Clowes', covered all sections of the women's workforce (*S. Sentinel* 14.2.1901, *S. Advertizer* 23.7.1898, 23.11.1907). Lawton even won recognition from the notorious Grindley & Co. Both women were regularly winning, signing and holding companies to agreements regarding female potters on the shopfloor: both were front-line negotiators in the 1916-1924 industrial negotiations (CATU Coll L639: Grindley to Lawton 29.8.1911, L145: Furnival to Mycock 22.1.1920).

At the lowest, informal levels of union activity in the workshop women were active in defending their own interests either independently or jointly with male workers (cf Kessler-Harris 1975, 1982, Milkman 1980). The available evidence indicates a continuous strain of small-scale action by female potters long before the 1914 rise in union membership. The 1907 sanitary dispute has gone down in Potteries folklore, yet the strike of women tile workers at Henry Richards in Tunstall at the same time has received less attention (*S. Sentinel* 30.3.1907). In November 1911, seven women aerographers were given a few hours' notice of wage reductions by Grindleys. The entire female workforce of 160 struck successfully in support of the aerographers (*P. Gazette* 1.11.1911). The union's files contain regular accounts of women workers' activities ranging from the large sectional disputes down to workshop flare-ups lasting barely an hour.

Men and women acted together just as they worked with each other. Emily Hall worked as a transferrer with Mr Birch, a printer in 1912. While ill, the manager tried to replace her and on her return gave her notice of dismissal. Joint action by the printers and transferrers in the workshop was taken to recover her job (CATU Coll L673: 3.12.1912). Much female action was subsumed within the workgroup and went unreported. During the war period women were in high demand for often pivotal positions in the work process, earned high, regular wages and their activity was more widely reported. Their wartime behaviour was seen as novel. In reality they were continuing at an official union level what they had practised at the routine, unofficial level for years.

Lastly, within the total membership of the union there existed a wealth of rank and file activity which undermines the assertion that union leaders easily became the 'managers' of their union (Hyman 1972: 74-77). The assumption behind such views is of a strict, static, unchanging relationship between leadership and rank and file. As has been shown, in the potters' union there was a continual interplay between officials, the differing levels of organisation and all areas of the union membership. The heterogeneous mass which the union became after amalgamation and the growth to a 40,000 membership made the tight, bureaucratic direction, alleged by certain writers on unionism, impossible. The authority and power of leaders and certain sections were considerable but they were nowhere near absolute. To attribute such capabilities to union leaders or groups is to deny the worker or workgroup independence of thought. In the 1920s members left the union precisely because they rejected the advice of union officials. Whole families in the china section tore up their cards after the 1924 china agreement (CATU Coll L489: 26.4.1916).

The period abounds with examples of autonomous rank and file activity which union leaders had to react to rather than create, organise and direct. A group of women towers at Booths was exasperated by the lack of official union activity and told Arthur Hollins, 'the men do not seem willing to fight for us. So the best plan was to fight for ourselves' (CATU Coll L547: Booths Towers nd). The mosaic of pottery manufacture produced such tension constantly. The china saggarmakers in 1916 rejected the union earthenware saggar demand since china saggars were far heavier than in earthenware. Equally indicative of the limits to the union secretary's power was his admission to a firm on 22 December 1913 that: 'regarding the refusal of your litho transferrers to go with the Shrewsbury pattern. It is quite correct that they are acting entirely on their own and against advice given to them by myself on Friday' (CATU Coll L470: 22.12.1913).

CONCLUSION

The creation of the NAS has revealed a great deal about the institutional (Coates and Topham 1988) and more importantly the social dimensions of trade unionism. The combination of the nineteenth and early twentieth-century experience of the potters' craft unions conditioned the formation of the NAS in 1906 and constrained the amalgamated union's growth and relations with other unions. In spite of formal amalgamation, trade unionism remained sectional and diffuse. The amalgamation process extended over almost the whole period. The nominal structure of the NAS was the outcome of the combined influences of craft loyalties; the range of occupational groups; the Potteries' geographical features; and the responses of the varied workforce to the events of the period. The craft groups ensured the continuance of their trade committees yet pressures for broader representation resulted in the formation of the district committees and the restructuring of the NEC after 1915. In operation the union structure was highly flexible as the attempt was made to convert the spontaneous energy of the pottery workers into permanent collective organisation. The official structure at first appears rigid and mechanistic: its operation was far more organic and became the key to the NAS's survival and growth (cf Flanders and Clegg 1970: 38-47, Merritt 1986).

The distinction between formal and informal action has enabled a more subtle explanation to be offered of the meaning of union membership. At the informal level, workshop collective action (cf Child, Loveridge and Warner 1973) was continuous: only at the formal level was there marked discontinuity as changed economic conditions after 1914 enabled workers to translate informal practices into formal, paid-up union activity. The union therefore came to mirror the workplace very strongly (cf Matsumura 1983: 35, Price 1980). Yet only by accommodating the diversity of skills, by embodying the linkage of work and the family, and by adapting the ability of women to play an active part in the workshop, was the NAS able to progress decisively from being a closed craft society to becoming an open, industrial union. The roles played by women and the family in such a process are as important as they are unnoticed (Bodnar 1982).

The incorporation thesis (Burgess 1975: 309) and the contention that unions were in effect managed and manipulated by their leadership is unsupported by the potters' experience. The union's constituents produced a shifting set of forces making for both centralisation and dispersion. Modes of control emanated from the top and the base of the union's structure. The relationship between officials, the intermediate levels of the union and the rank and file was one of conflict alternating with co-operation. Compare the praise Clowes earned for his organisation of the unskilled in Longton with the fist fights which broke out at a meeting over his stand on wage levels in 1921.

The natural rhythm of the NAS's history was created by the countervailing forces within the union, both generated from across the varied membership and played out between the differing organisational levels (cf Penn 1985: 37-55, Batstone 1988). Union strategy was not superimposed on an inert membership: it was as much the outcome of internal conflict as it was the result of struggle with the external pressures which surrounded the union. The contradictions between the logic of collective strength and the basic desire for worker autonomy were apparent in the actions of the potter trade unionists throughout the period (cf Palmer 1979:199, Perrot 1987). These countervailing forces and contradictions were given full expression in the pottery workers' and their union's relations with other classes and groups, as the following two chapters will show.

Chapter Four

POTTERS, MASTERS AND UNION

This chapter investigates the role of management in the work process, one of the most critical yet under-researched elements of the patterns of labour. The portrait of employer–worker relations which emerges from the pottery industry questions a number of the assumptions made by social scientists about the development of managerial control and industrial bargaining. The evidence provided by the potters and workers in other industries points not so much to employer domination as the limitations on managerial authority and control. Above all, the employment relation appears remarkably difficult to encompass or predict, even in a single industry, given the extent of the contributing forces and the fluidity of their interaction.

The result is that the simple axioms regarding paternalism in traditional British industries are shown to be of limited use. Similarly, the preoccupation with national bargaining can now be seen as a distortion. In sectors such as pottery there have been multiple bargaining mechanisms and arenas eminently suited to the stratified workforces, socially diverse owners and complex union structures which helped create them. Blending the concepts of historians, sociologists and management specialists allows not only a fuller reconstruction of the way work has been regulated, but also the chance to revise some of the established images of conflict in industries such as pottery.

THE POTTERY FIRM

What were the core characteristics of the pottery firm? In the early twentieth century the most important features were its size, social composition and form of ownership. Each aspect was of direct relevance to the industrial relations of the potbank and the industry.

In terms of firm size the pottery industry exhibited a wide range. At one extreme was a group of exceptionally large firms. By 1920, Cauldons had fourteen factories employing 3,000 workers. The largest firms (Wedgwoods, Johnsons, Mintons, Doultons, Grindleys, Maddocks, Meakins, Grimwades, Copeland and Cauldons) were recognised as a 'leading sector'. These were international firms, which dominated certain markets and developed the 'best practice' techniques of the industry (*Times Eng. Supplement*: 21.4.1913). Numerically they amounted to under 10% of all pottery firms and employed under a quarter of the total workforce. Yet within these large outfits plant size was small since production was based on craft skill and hence there was no necessary virtue in large unit size (Manners 1980: 234). The period in question is generally seen as an era of 'growing concentrations of production' which stemmed from 'the logic of capitalism'. By that logic a firm strives to lower its unit costs and to do so has to create larger units of production (Clapham 1938: 212, Pollard 1962: 10, 62). In this sense the pottery firm was an exception.

Although the leading sector firms had a disproportionate influence, they were only part of an industry made up of almost 500 firms (*Census of Staffordshire* 1901: 69, 1911: 49, 548, 1921: 54, 491). In 1911 the average potbank employed 84 workers. At the opposite extreme to Wedgwoods or Johnsons were the back-street operations of men such as James Shaw. In 1924 he was in business on his own, 'modelled all his own creations, made his own moulds, and undertook the pottery throughout, whilst he relied upon his two daughters to undertake the decoration' (*P. Gazette*: 1.8.1924). As today, the 'penny-jack shop' provided an easy, if risky, entry to the industry. This explains why the total number of firms within the industry remains so high throughout the period, the periodic trade depressions and bankruptcies notwithstanding (Fogarty 1945: 328).

As in the nineteenth century, many firms were found between these two extremes. The medium-sized unit employed from 100 to 500 workers. These included many of the standard brand names of the industry such as Howsons (450 workers), Edmund Leigh (500) or James Kent (300). Moreover, while Mintons, Doultons, might win international awards for their techniques and products, as in the Brussels fair in 1910, the small and especially medium-sized firms were the backbone of the industry (*P. Gazette.* 1.10.1910). The latter supplied particular product markets and each market had its own trade leaders and competitive structures (*US Report 1915*: 389). No simple distinction existed therefore in the industry between large and small firms (cf Gattrell 1977), the one employing high-quality technology and labour, the other cheap techniques and low-paid workers. Given the craft components of production, all firms had to use skilled potters. Moreover, a number of small to medium-sized firms were leaders within their own markets. Therefore craft potters and craft union groups were not only found among the larger companies but across the range of firms in the industry.

With smaller production units common, the popular notion of employer and worker cannot be easily applied to the potbank. The clear separation of owner, management and labour had not been completed by any means. Many pottery firms were run by newly self-employed potters. For example, in 1898, the brothers William and Robert Stubbs raised enough capital by a sale of furniture to start up as china manufacturers in Longton. In 1906, William was drawing only £3 in salary which compared unfavourably with the wages of most firemen or modellers (*S. Advertizer.* 3.11.1906). Owners such as the Stubbs were of necessity as personally involved in production as their employees. In the same year a visitor to Thomas Cone's works found him 'actively engaged in the warehouse'. These types of masters saw themselves as self-made men. They were not absentee owners but, as H.J. Colclough, the china manufacturer, put it, 'they were self-made men who had to look personally after their business' (*P. Gazette.* 1.10.1908).

Both in the past (Cadbury, Matheson and Shann 1906: 205-206) and more recently (Ingham 1970: 15,141), authors have maintained that small firms enjoyed less turbulent industrial relations. As Joyce argues for textiles 'in a shared social environment, where craft status and the social relations of craft production were still substantial realities, feelings of class opposition were noticeably absent' (Joyce 1980: 167). Admittedly, pottery owners 'felt it an advantage to get into direct touch, wherever possible with the personnel of the establishment' according to Mr Ray, the proprietor of the Grosvenor works in Longton in 1922 (*P. Gazette.*

1.12.1922). Yet personal contact does not preclude conflict developing between master and worker. The economist Shadwell, on a visit to Longton in 1906, found that 'there are some ninety pottery works; everyone of them was originally started by a workman, and some so lately that they are still carried on by their workman founders'. However, he went on to say that 'no men are

Table 4.1 Analysis of pottery manufacturers' obituaries and profiles 1900–1924

Number of manufacturers in sample	100
Born in Potteries	38
Born outside Potteries	5
Father, grandfather in trade	43
Family firm	56
J.P.	24
Councillor	40
Officer of political organisation	10
Member/officer of philanthropic body	23
Officer of sporting or social body	7
Nonconformist	20
Anglican	11
Catholic	2
Lives outside Six Towns	20
Self-made	24

Source: Pottery Gazette 1900–1924

harder taskmasters than such employers ... they have a hard struggle to succeed, and as they do not spare themselves they are not minded to spare those whom they employ'. He concluded: 'it is a delusion to suppose that workmen who "rise" have a fellow-feeling for those they leave behind' (Shadwell 1906: 308).

Equating size of firm with the degree of conflict in master/employee relations does not work. It was not that the small units were less likely to experience conflict but that the relationships between worker and employer were personal and often limited to the individuals or working group involved (*1910 Lead Cee*: Q 11905). Industrial relations operated necessarily on a very small scale and bargaining was highly sub-divided, features of the potbank to which the potters' union had to adapt.

An outstanding attribute of the pottery firm was its family base. Just as the pottery workers organised their working lives with strong reference to family and kin, so did the pottery owners. In common with Britain's other staple industries, the family business remained the typical form of enterprise down to 1900 and beyond (Allen 1954: 12, Pollard 1965: 266, Musson 1978: 252).

In the Potteries it was regarded as self-evident that pottery companies were run by an owner and his family. By using a sample of 100 manufacturers' obituaries and portraits from the trade journal it was possible to test how extensive the family firm was in the period 1900-1930. Table 4.1 indicates that 56% of the sample were members of a family firm. The continuity of pottery making within families (though not necessarily in the same firm) is shown by the figure of 43% of the sample having followed their father or grandfather into pottery manufacture.

Examples are ready to hand. The Wedgwood family enterprise is well-known but two of the other largest firms were also run by families. Johnsons had three brothers at its head, while Meakins included grandfather, father, son and uncle in their business (*P. Gazette* 1.3.1907). The large firms were not unique in this respect as the career of Ezra Bourne shows. He worked under his father from 1868 until 1882, whereupon he joined his uncle in business. In 1890 his uncle died and so Bourne's brother-in-law John Leigh went into partnership with him. A small firm like Allerton of Longton had relied on three generations of family management by 1906 (*P. Gazette* 1.3.1906).

The extent and persistence of the family firm in the pottery industry is explained first and foremost by its ability to supply sufficient managerial competence (cf Payne 1974: 27). Since craft organisation and sub-contract were relied on so heavily management could be relatively unsophisticated. Bakewell Bros. coped adequately with John looking after 'the commercial side' and Wilfred appointed 'manager of the works'. Moreover, four generations had been involved in many pottery companies by 1900 and had developed reasonably efficient methods of training and integrating their sons into the business. Albert Spencer began work in his father's firm when he was 13 in 1872, 'learned the trade' and spent most of his working life as manager until his two brothers succeeded him in 1913 (*HMI Factories Report* 1908: 143, *P. Gazette*. 1.4.1916, 1.1.1926). It was also logical to confine management to the immediate family, if possible, in order to minimise the loss of recipes and technical knowledge and to ensure the transmission of in-house trade secrets which made the ware distinctive (*P. Gazette*. 1.11.1915, 1.2.1917). As will become clear, strong family-based management and ownership succession resulted in distinctive modes of control and labour relations.

It has been claimed that between 1880 and 1914 the adoption of company organisation was one of the most prominent and widespread of all industrial changes. The pottery industry qualifies this view in an important way. From a listing of pottery manufacturers of 1921, 120 out of the total of 278 or 43.17% were limited companies (*P. Gazette Diary* 1921: 71-75). The reasons for adopting the limited form elsewhere were usually connected with obtaining increased scale, facilitating the introduction of specialist managers and separating ownership and management (Payne 1974: 17-20). These reasons applied to only some of the larger firms in pottery: to most, economies of scale in production and sophisticated management were not strictly relevant. The main reason why an increasing number of pottery firms took up private, as opposed to public, form was in order to obtain security through limited liability. In fact this represented a consolidation of traditional company form. Thomas Twyfords 'went limited' in 1896, yet in 1906 the shares in the company were still held entirely by the family and its factories were funded mainly by their own profits and reserves (*P. Gazette*. 1.4.1906).

Indeed pottery owners were anxious to assure the public that though they were limited companies they were private and retained the same ownership and therefore the same reputations. As one manufacturer anxiously pointed out in 1910: 'many of the leading businesses are now, it is true, conducted under the aegis of companies, but they are not public companies, they almost all remain in the hands of the families which built them up' (*P. Gazette.* 1.4.1906). The basic tenor of the public statements of the Heath family or Sydney Malkin on the assumption of company form was their rejection of change (*S. Advertizer.* 4.5.1907). None the less, to some workers the mere appearance of the label 'limited' was deeply disturbing, smacking of outside interference. As early as 1906 a Mr Edwards told the engravers' union that 'the old private employers had been supplanted by limited companies, for whose shareholders profits had to be made' (*S. Advertizer.* 29.9.1906).

In effect the pottery firm, in terms of size, composition and ownership remained remarkably unchanged from its nineteenth-century form. A wide range of unit size continued to exist. The average pottery firm in the early twentieth century was still the small to medium-sized 'bank, run by a self-made entrepreneur; owned and run by himself and his family in a partnership or private company. Yet the manner in which firms of different size, status and power reacted to the events of the period diverged considerably and helped to account for the variety of forms industrial relations took in the industry.

MANAGEMENT

The following section is concerned with how ownership was translated into managerial control in the pottery industry. A number of conclusions have been drawn regarding the development of management technique during the first three decades of this century. Pollard demonstrated that little attempt was made to generalise or rationalise the experience of industrial management into a science during the Industrial Revolution. He also found it difficult to isolate the managerial role from the entrepreneur's (Pollard 1965: 250). Yet by 1919 Marshall claimed that the 'wholesale transference of authority and responsibility from the owners of each business to salaried managers and officials' had occurred (Marshall 1919: 321-328). Landes and others see the period as notable in the sense of the increasing awareness of scientific management (Bendix 1956: 435, Landes 1969: 322). Critiques of this view have stressed that Taylorism made relatively little practical impact: British manufacturers were still operating with nineteenth-century *laissez-faire* principles, although trying to develop standards of professionalism (Merkle 1980: 209). Pottery firms show just how limited was the development of the managerial role in British industry. At the same time the industry offers a clear warning against categorising such management action as simple or self-evident.

Large parts of management action can be related to the desire and attempts to control resources whether in the form of technology, motive power, materials or labour. Bendix realised that 'subordination and discipline are indispensable in economic enterprises' (Bendix 1956: ix). Braverman and others maintain that discipline or control was the essential human task of the process of capitalist development (Braverman 1974). Since labour was the least predictable element of production it became necessary for management to construct regimes of discipline specifically for labour. However, given that the forces of production were closely linked this meant that control had to be exercised over technology, power, materials and labour *together*.

The forms which production and therefore managerial control took in the past have varied widely. No simple unfolding of increased managerial control occurred. The progression has been uneven: the forces of production, especially labour, have proved to be difficult to control and the relationship between these forces has not remained constant. Different variants of managerial control have emerged depending on the circumstances. A broad distinction exists between 'formal control' and 'real control'. Formal control involves only the legal title of ownership and the claim to control production. Under real control management enjoys detailed direction and regulation of the forces of production. Real control may also appear in different degrees of sophistication: simple control by the use of foremen and piece work; technical control using machines and systems of work organisation, and finally bureaucratic control involving the construction of highly developed internal administrative hierarchies and rules (Stedman Jones 1975: 54).

A reconstruction and explanation of the modes of control which developed in the pottery industry between 1900 and 1930 involves three main considerations: first, identifying the main contextual influences on managerial action and how they changed; second, evaluating the levels of control in the industry against the typology outlined above; and third, recognising that managerial control was not created in isolation. Control of production was attempted by both workers and management. In the period in question these opposing bids for control converged around a number of issues. These included the content and nature of work itself, the official and unofficial 'welfare' benefits associated with work, and the thorny question of trade unions.

The characteristics of pottery manufacture which had the most immediate influence on managerial control were capital availability, profit levels and relative costs. Pottery owners found great difficulty in attracting investment. Instead they relied on reinvested profits which led them to be labour rather than capital intensive. Control of labour, given its importance, became a prime concern. In the smaller works control was imperative since those firms could only survive by carrying as little capital as possible tied up in stock, and turning their capital over many times a year. In 1924, it was estimated that the average firm had to produce and sell £900 worth of goods per week before profit was earned. This meant 3,000-dozen pieces of ware per week had to be made and moved in order to realise a profit. In the smaller firm the figure was as high as 9,000-dozen (CATU Coll 1924 Wage Inquiry: 3-5, Warburton 1931: 197-198).

The intensive local competition (outlined in Chapter 1) of the period, lowered prices and profits thereby increasing the need to direct production and control labour. The necessity for controlling labour also grew as manufacturers became increasingly aware of relative costs. By 1914 cost analyses of pottery manufacture showed that the traditional division of a third each to wages, material and standing charges was no longer valid. Materials by then accounted for 33.53% of total costs; fuel and power 13.11%; overheads 5.74% and labour 47.63% (CATU Coll 1924 Wage Inquiry: 3-5, Board of Trade 1946: 3).

Given the small average unit size personal control was common. Joseph Gray, proprietor of the Brittannia Works, Hanley, supervised the production process from buying materials right through to selling his ware to factors. Many potbanks were 'characterised by an absence of anything like an office' in 1921 (*P. Gazette* 1.4.1921). The census of the same year did not separate the category of employer from manager indicating the lack of bureaucratic structures of control in the industry (*Census of England & Wales* 1925: 215). Pottery owners in 1920 thought that their industry was 'one in which there is the closest possible touch between the employer and worker'. Whilst one should be aware of the positive image which manufacturers might wish to present by such statements it does seem that even the largest companies did not have elaborate supervisory hierarchies or rules of procedure. In 1913 Thomas Watkin, one of the directors of Grimwades, wrote how he personally worked out (with the mould-maker Mr Patterson) the shapes and prices for a new range of wares and flower pots (CATU Coll L460: 30.10.1913). Apart from small unit size, personal control was logical since the family firm could comfortably supply the necessary personnel. In 1907 Robert Lewis Johnson, head of the multi-plant company of the same name, used his sons to manage the Tunstall and Cobridge factories. On a smaller scale Reuben Floyd, in 1914, divided supervision of his potbank between his three sons (*P. Gazette* 1.9.1908, 1.6.1914).

In spite of the debate around scientific management only the larger and more innovatory companies possessed a sound costing system. W.G. Fox told the English Ceramic Society in 1916 that 'there is abundant evidence that cost taking was a minus quantity with many firms' (*P. Gazette* 1.3.1916). In 1940 it was estimated that only one-third of pottery manufacturers kept costs accounts that informed them of labour and material costs for each sub-process of production (Board of Trade 1946: 17-21). While outsiders castigated the pottery firms for 'want of system', management relied on more implicit forms of control.

Piece work was used since the piece price was a crude mechanism for ensuring worker output: a worker could only earn a given wage by producing a set amount. Potters developed counter-strategies to piece work and so internal sub-contracting was a complementary but still simple type of labour control. Contracting had the advantages of saving managerial time, removing the need to control all workers directly and also dispersed the risks of production from owner to sub-contractor. As was shown in Chapter 2, given the pivotal role of craftsmen in the production process it was sensible for employers to rely on craft organisation. Overall managerial control was retained by ensuring that craft control was limited to very specific parts of production and therefore fragmented (cf Schloss 1907: 197). As will become clear, the use of sub-contract and piece work was highly risky for management since their bases and terms were being continually questioned and challenged by the workers who operated them.

There were changes in the contexts in which pottery management operated during this period. Foreign competition for certain sub-industries increased, prices fell in the period 1900-1910 and during the 1920s, and internal competition in the industry intensified. The greater need for increased productivity and cost control led some manufacturers to rationalise certain methods and attempt to increase their real control of production. As new technology was introduced, women workers were put on the new jobs as directly paid employees of companies. Sub-contracting was diluted. In order to retain the benefits of the new technology management had to become more systematic.

How far this process had gone by the 1920s is suggested by the remark of B. Wethered and H. Clay that 'the old personal touch between the various sections of the industry – between master potters and operative potters, to a considerable extent had been lost owing to the organisation of modern business in limited liability companies and in large firms' (CATU Coll 1924 Wage Inquiry: D). Whilst it is difficult to quantify the increase in managerial supervision and control, the opinions of the potters were broadly in agreement. In the larger or technically more advanced companies, ceramic consultants were used and the role of managers and supervisors developed and became more specialised. In 1921 a manufacturer noted that 'the responsibility of the manager's position was being more and more recognised' (*P. Gazette* 1.2.1921).

Admittedly these changes did not occur uniformly across the industry but the demonstration effect on workers of new managerial practices was clear. Trade unionists complained in 1924 that now they saw 'too little of the master and rather too much of the jacket-men' (CATU Coll, Hollins 1924). Yet there was no sharp break in the development of management technique. Instead traditional forms of control co-existed alongside the new. The result was a range of managerial control methods which matched the differences in unit size, knowledge of ceramics, market location and labour supply.

However, the forms which managerial control assumed were not only the result of managerial choice. Control of production and labour especially, was the product of the interaction of management and workers. The precise nature of control emerged day by day from specific issues and contests. There were three broad areas where managerial control was concentrated during the period. The first concerned the issues which arose directly from work; the second centred on paternalism; and the third on the question of trade unions.

The major issues which the work process yielded were wages, technology, the stratification and movement of the workforce and health. Wage payment provided a constant test of control. Control of the size and movement of wages was imperative in the labour intensive pottery industry. Manufacturers were acutely aware of the high cost of the potter's skilled labour. As one master recognised in 1908, 'the disadvantage of hand-making saggars is the large amount of skill needed', whereas 'little or no training is needed for a man to become clever at casting (saggars), and consequently the wages of the saggar maker can be considerably reduced' (*P. Gazette.* 1.8.1908). In the depressed trading of the 1900s and 1920s, wage costs were an important area of change for manufacturers wishing to maintain profit margins and who were unable to reorganise production.

Management accordingly used every possible device to control wages. They fought to maintain the myriad allowances or deductions and consistently opposed minimum wage proposals. Companies would often ignore arbitration awards and take unilateral action in order to retain their control over wage costs and profit margins. In a 1920 survey of 53 earthenware firms, 34% of the operatives had not received the 5% wage advance for their trade of 1900, and 26% had never seen the 5% rise of 1911 (CATU Coll L58: 18.5.1920). Wages, argued manufacturers, were to be fixed primarily by the market. In the 1908-1910 disputes, 'lifeless trade' and the strength of competition were cited by manufacturers as adequate reasons for lowering wages. Numerous forms of wage-cutting were used such as not allowing apprentices to become journeymen, increasing ware sizes while leaving the piece price unchanged, or packing ovens more tightly (*P. Gazette.*

1.6.1908, 1.9.1910). It was precisely because wage control was so central to managerial cost strategy that wages remained the central area of dispute and conflict.

Technology was not merely a means to more efficient production. As Chapter 2 showed, new technology had direct impact on the detailed organisation of work, its intensity, the levels of skill, pay and status involved. The contests over new technology were not only about costs but control. During 1908 Twyfords attempted to introduce casting to a section of their sanitary works. The issues raised during this episode as workers contested the nature of casting are instructive. Casting involved new technical knowledge and therefore the pressers would have to pay, via reduced wages, 'the cost of their acquiring knowledge of a business which at present they do not understand'. Craftsmen's authority was to be reduced and 'the whole of the men to be under the control of Parkes (a new foreman) who shall have power to suspend any man'. Compared to the previous forms of craft control over working times and recruitment, there were now to be 'set hours of work' and 'that only young men shall be selected and that we entirely control the selection of such men' (CATU Coll L689: 11.2.1908).

Manufacturers also sought to control production by reinforcing the existing divisions within their workforce, and using their firms' internal labour markets (cf Reich, Gordon and Edwards 1973: 359-365). Primary workers such as the highly skilled designers, modellers, firemen and department heads were treated quite differently from the less skilled. They were often put on 'the staff' and made permanent salaried employees as opposed to piece-rate workers employed on a weekly or monthly basis (*Inquiry into Pottery Regulations* 1911: 36). Various attachment devices were used to tie these workers to the firm. Twyfords, as early as 1896, issued shares to their 'chief staff'. Skilled workers were often prevented from moving freely between firms given their knowledge of the companies' recipes and methods. The Central Pottery in Burslem had employed Samuel Williams since he was a 17-year-old apprentice. As the proprietor wrote to the secretary of his manufacturers' association in 1913, 'there is plenty of work for him but he wants to go journeyman somewhere else and we don't think it is the right thing to allow him to do so as he is now useful to us. We shall certainly not give our consent for him to leave' (CATU Coll L761:

1.8.1913). By contrast unskilled workers received few of the 'staff' benefits and were often subject to instant dismissal.

The workforce would also be divided on gender lines. As C.T. Maling & Sons stated in 1912, 'it has not been customary for us to accept, or give, our girls a week's notice' (CATU Coll L486: 16.9.1912). Women were clearly used as cheap labour. Manufacturers were often able to disassemble craft jobs and increase control of work by substituting unskilled women jolliers and casters for traditional pressers and throwers. Some women were treated as casual workers with very few contractual privileges (cf Macdonald 1904: 47, Cadbury, Matheson & Shann 1906: 119, Amsden1980: '11,29). Doultons in 1908 were prosecuted for making deductions from certain of their girls' wages without any written notification or contract (*P. Gazette* 1.2.1908).

The prevalence of industrial disease and the attempts by workers and trade unionists to find remedies had important ramifications for profit levels and the control of work. The private and public definition of illness and its causes became an area of fierce contest. Manufacturers strived to redirect the explanations for the potters' ill health from the working conditions of the potbank towards personal, individual responsibility (cf Figlio 1978: 196-197). The relationship between health and profit for some owners was shown in the technical manual which stated that 'a strong (and heavier) saggar as a rule lasts longer than a very light one and it is better to tax the muscles of the kilnmen than the purse of the proprietor'.

William Callear was asked at the 1911 inquiry why manufacturers had not introduced the protective health regulations for their industry. It was put to him that it was a 'question of time and money'; he replied 'that is all your honour. It has never been anything else but such questions' (*Inquiry into Pottery Regulations* 1911: Qs 636, 938, 966). Manufacturers frequently used the argument of foreign competition for not changing their methods. As one owner put it, 'so long as foreign and continental potters are allowed to use lead, our potters must do the same, or be left behind' (*HMI Factories Report* 1920: 57). At the same time the 'blame' for lead poisoning was passed from owner to worker. In 1925 Ashly Myott could still publicly assert that 'I believe a great deal of lead poisoning comes about through uncleanliness on the part of the worker' (CATU Coll Werner: 16).

Underlying the arguments over health was the question of control. If it could be shown that pottery-making led to ill-health, the implications for management's ability to control costs and their authority to direct their workers were immense. Reorganising production, admitting liability, paying compensation and allowing the state to regulate production were seen by manufacturers as major erosions of their authority. Pottery owners continually opposed the protective legislation for silicosis which workers demanded. One manufacturer told the Samuel Commission in 1906, that if medical inspection was implemented 'it would simply paralyse our work' (*Samuel Comm. Report* 1907: Q 6929). Even when manufacturers were forced to accept a measure of government legislation they did their utmost to ensure that its detailed implementation affected their control of production as little as possible.

The second main variant of managerial control strategies involved the use of less direct and more subtle devices. Pottery owners attempted to construct a dominant image of the social relations of the potbank and thereby establish norms of behaviour for their workers to follow. Some industrial sociologists have recognised that conflict was not universal in industry and that management has often worked hard to elicit the co-operation and consent of workers to the pursuit of profit (Fox 1958: 315). Writers have been quick to use the term 'paternalist' for this kind of management activity which was to lead to social stability. The term has been used rather loosely. It has often led to a model of social relations viewed from above; the workers' part in the relationship has been underestimated. Paternalism has been confused with general ideals rather than what happened and the label has been applied irrespective of the specific historical context. In so doing writers have minimised the importance of paternalism as an ideology of work and as a critical force in the relations between master and worker (cf Thompson 1978: 133, Roberts 1979: 2, Joyce 1980: 111, 138, 164, 179-180,).

In the Potteries the existence of paternal forms of management was often noticed. In 1908 one observer remarked of the industry, 'like master like men is an established maxim here'. In 1920 a Captain Sydenham from the Ministry of Labour thought that 'employers in the pottery industry were still in direct personal contact with their workmen to an extent that was unknown in many other industries'. However, the exact relevance of paternalism to the pottery industry requires a reconstruction of both management action, and above all the response of pottery workers.

Certain employers did seek to build up personal relations with workers. The depth of that relationship could be quite shallow, no more than the occasional exchange of a greeting. Employers certainly made use of the appearance of those relationships. Such relationships with owners could also be vehicles for exploitation. Masters' provision of worker housing was double-edged. On the one hand this fits in well with Roberts' (1979: 2-4, 173) notion of obligation within paternalism, yet, besides binding workers to a company, housing provision could also be used as a sanction. J. Bowden, after a dispute at his potbank was forced to leave his company house on 15 January 1920 (CATU Coll L126: 15.1.1920). Employers also made individual arrangements with workers during stoppages and lay-offs to pay part of their wages in advance. But during the 1921 coal strike it was noted how owners made use of this device 'to look after skilled craftsmen' not their whole workforce (*P. Gazette* 1.6.1921). Clearly, these personal relations alone could not guarantee worker co-operation.

More grand were the public rituals which manufacturers used to construct their ideology of 'common interest' with the employer as the provider of work. Bendix saw manufacturer ideologies as vital in his model of British paternalism. He argued that masters constructed ideologies which interpreted management authority in a positive way and neutralised conflict (Bendix 1956: 13). In the pottery industry the manufacturer's images of work were exhibited in two main ways: the general social events of the potbank and, in particular, the long service presentations. The object of these exercises was to minimise the contradictions within the wage bar- gain and instead highlight the moral duty of worker to employer.

As Mr Fielding told his workforce while giving presentations to nineteen employees for twenty-one years' service: 'These were people who thought not simply of the £.s.d. question but who showed an appreciation of loyal service and had aims which were apparently above simple money making' (*P. Gazette* 1.10.1911). Some owners tried to establish the appearance of a natural succession of family workers. The managing director of Bullers in 1919 spoke to his workers of how many instances there were of three generations working together on his works. He remarked that 'when people had been with them through all their boyhood and manhood, girlhood and womanhood, that they had the desire to bring their children and their children's children there' (*P. Gazette*. 1.10.1919). Presentations were routinely made for twenty-five to fifty years' service with the same company. The family atmosphere of the potbank was fostered with certain workers' weddings, promotions and retirements marked by employer gifts and collections among the workers (*P. Gazette*. 1.1.1911, 1.8.1916, 1.1.1920).

The social events organised by owners symbolised what they saw as the acceptable codes of worker behaviour. Many firms were formally recorded as organising a range of social activities for their workforces. These included celebrations of employers or members of their family marrying; marking the majority of an owner's son or the wedding anniversaries of the master; and a mixture of works outings, concerts and whist drives. The ideological component of these activities was striking. The foreword to the programme of T.C. Wild's & Co.'s party at Longton Town Hall in 1919 read:

A bond of comradeship and sympathy happily exists among us, which is most gratifying to those whose duty it is to guide the policy and manage the affairs of our various businesses ... So long as we all work together harmoniously, and with the same spirit of mutual respect and goodwill we may look with great confidence to the future.

(*P. Gazette*. 1.1.1919)

Similarly, at a Gibson's social evening in 1906 it was declared that 'the firm recognised that they were supported in their efforts by reasonable workpeople' (*S. Advertizer*. 13.1.1906). The workers of A. Harley-Jones were told during their day-trip to Chester that 'the way in which they could best repay their employer for his generosity was to do their duty at the works' (*P. Gazette*. 1.8.1920). The images involved in these events were important. Some of the largest manufacturers invited workers to the grounds of their home as an annual treat, where the owners 'presided' over the 'guests'. These occasions often reinforced the larger firm's internal labour market as separate events were held for managers and officials, distinct from those for the production workers (*P. Gazette*. 1.10.1910).

The pottery owners' paternalism did not remain unchanged during our period. Joyce asserts that paternalism broke down by 1900 (1980:186, 338). In the Potteries, paternalist policies still operated in the 1920s. The change occurred in the content and emphasis of such approaches. In the late nineteenth and early twentieth centuries paternalism was based on largely individual, informal employer benevolence and worker's duties. By 1920 the use of paternalism as a tool of managerial control had become more 'rational' and formally defined. Instead of being based on the responsibility of the rich to the poor, as union bargaining increased in scope, the guiding notion became one of rational efficiency (Shadwell 1906: 173). As in other industries, the shift in approach was labelled 'welfarism' (Merkle 1980: 229).

As one pottery owner argued in 1920, there was now a need 'to devote a very real attention not to the mechanics of industry, but to its humanics' (*P. Gazette*. 1.5.1920). The potters' campaigns over industrial illness and the need to reorganise production during the war led to a recognition by manufacturers that efficiency and welfare were closely related. Many of the larger works built 'Rest and Health' recreation clubs and 'welfare institutes' run formally by rules and committees (CATU Coll NCPI mins: 2.10.1922). Yet welfarism was also used by manufacturers to prevent government intervention in their industry. The retention of managerial control over welfare schemes runs throughout the pottery manufacturers' responses to government inquiries. John Ridgway therefore opposed the National Insurance Bill in July 1911 on the grounds that his own sick club scheme was better suited to his company (*1910 Lead Cee*: Q 14995).

Whilst it is possible to construct a picture of strong attempts by pottery manufacturers to develop paternalist or welfare-based strategies as a means of securing worker co-operation and a stable workforce, the crucial test is the actions of the pottery operatives. Some workers did respond to paternal acts with deference (cf Meacham 1977: 21). It is noticeable how employer gifts were repaid. In 1906 the employees of William Morley entertained his son Gordon on the occasion of his majority in the potbank warehouse, where workers made speeches regarding the esteem they held Mr Gordon in and the goodwill which existed between them. Though owners clearly produced their own representations of such events, the actions of workers towards their employers are well recorded. In 1910, the workers at Bain & Co. celebrated the homecoming from a world tour of Elijah Bain, the son. The female operatives presented Mrs Bain with a gold brooch and the oldest male employee made the gift of a gold-topped walking stick to William Bain (*P. Gazette* 1.9.1910). The inscriptions on such presents are indicative. The lettering on a gift to the Jarvis family from their workers recorded that it was to mark 'the cordial relationship which existed between them' (*P. Gazette* 1.5.1909). Workers even supported their masters in rejecting the government health regulations and asking for their own sick clubs to be returned.

Owners expended great energy to legitimate their authority in the workplace and to ensure an identification of interests between master and worker. Yet these are not sufficient reasons for their inevitable success. As we have seen, manufacturers used less subtle means of control such as wage-cutting and the increasing use of foremen which could not be masked by whist drives and presentations. Many casual and unskilled workers were omitted from these events.

Above all, the ideologies and imagery offered by management was just that: workers could still make an independent choice and interpretation of these activities (cf Gray 1976: 1-6). Whilst it was clearly in the interest of workers to participate in paternal relationships, the sources of conflict arising from work remained plentiful. The experience of the struggles for family survival in the 1900s could not be easily wiped out by an owner's tea-party. One example shows how fragile paternalist relations could be. In September 1919 the New Hall Porcelain Company took its workers to Blackpool for the day. During speeches that evening much was made of the longevity of service of women employees (one was 80 and still working). Two months later, in December, the entire workforce came out on strike over the stoppages made by the company out of the women workers' wages. The women won the strike (*P. Gazette* 1.10.1919, 1.1.1920).

The third main area where managerial control was tested and modified was in the relations between companies and unions. The concern here is with the manufacturers at the individual firm level. Pottery management did not simply accept or reject the rights of unions to represent workers. On the contrary there were ways in which management accepted certain union activities as complementary to their own policies. Yet proprietors' attitudes towards unionism varied according to the areas of union activity involved and the changing contexts in which they occurred. As Walker put it, union 'recognition is, however, a habit of mind and a continuous relationship as much as a once and for all publicly conferred capitulation' (Boraston, Clegg and Rimmer 1975: 180, Walker 1979: 292, 313, Price 1980: 193).

There were very specific ways in which pottery management rejected union activity on their potbanks. The obstruction often derived from managers or supervisors whose ability to control their workers was made especially difficult by union agents. Owners were often quite prepared to deal with union leaders. In January 1911, a union organiser visited Furnivals over a disputed payment to Charles Poole. The manager, S. Rowley, 'refused to deal with the Trade Union although he said he had respect for the leaders personally' (CATU Coll L617: 16.1.1911). Similarly, Johnsons met the union leadership but would not allow organisers on their works. Management apparently did not reject the union as a general spokesman for the pottery workers but objected to direct union intervention in the questions which directly affected control of production. In 1916 H.J. Plant recognised the NAS yet wrote to Sam Clowes indignant that a union canvasser had set foot on his works. As Mr Plant put it, 'personally, I consider it to be a case of impudent interference in our private business' (CATU Coll L560: 30.5.1913, L554: 7.1.1916).

Against these rejections of union legitimacy it is possible to set the varieties of acceptance. Three main sources were used in order to draw up a measure of the extent of union recognition. The union's correspondence files indicated who officially dealt with the NAS; the union price count records were derived from access to firms; the union's records of official notices received from firms indicated companies which dealt formally with the union. Clearly these sources do not capture the fullest extent of the firms involved but they do provide an estimate. In broad terms it appears that around 30% of the firms in the pottery industry had recognised the potters' union, by establishing bargaining procedures by 1920. The three sets of records also indicate that the medium to large, well-established firms (with notable exceptions such as Cauldons) had individually accepted, even in a limited way, the presence of the potters' union.[1]

From around 1910 onwards, in the context of expanding trade, individual companies increasingly recognised the use of trade unions. By the 1920s some of the larger companies were frequently exchanging information with the NAS. Meakins and the Campbell Co. were routinely sending the union's central office schedules of price changes and copies of settlements in their workshops (CATU Coll L221: 26.4.1923). Certain firms believed they could use the union officials to help control their workforce. The manager of the Midland Pottery Co. wrote to Lovatt in June 1913 over the irregular attendance of his workers asking him 'to take your members in hand'. As the union grew in size during the period, it became one of the best sources of specialist labour as Peake Co. found in 1911, when they were short of jiggerers (CATU Coll L683: 18.11.1911, L428: 19.6.1913).

Edmund Leigh, one of the more prominent manufacturers, felt that weak trade unionism was dangerous for the industry (*P. Gazette.* 1.7.1906). Only a united, recognised trade union could carry out what it agreed with manufacturers and therefore provide a stable basis for industrial relations. It is noticeable that employers rejected unions from outside the Potteries almost entirely. Moreover, the recognition of the union often came to depend on quite personal friendships between manufacturers and officials as the correspondence of Frank Williamson and Sam Clowes showed (CATU Coll L426: 8.11.1913). One distinction remained between the smaller firms and the rest. The smallest potbanks could not afford to operate under union regulations and did their best to avoid formal bargaining commitments. Finally in times of trade depression and over major issues of change as in the 1900s and 1920s, all manufacturers were capable of demolishing existing relations and tearing up union agreements (*P. Gazette.* 1.10.1910, 1.9.1923).

INDUSTRIAL RELATIONS

The industrial relations of pottery manufacture have been greatly misunderstood. An orthodoxy has developed which characterises the industry as almost conflict-free, stable and unchanging. The object of the following sections is to revise fundamentally the existing interpretation.

An examination follows of the terminology and concepts

relevant to a study of industrial relations. By using these insights it will be possible to reconstruct how bargaining occurred on multiple levels, appropriate to the complex division of labour, the fragmented union structure and the range of managerial strategy. What becomes clear is that between 1900 and 1930 the pottery industry underwent arguably the most important changes in both union and employer organisation and bargaining in its history. In contrast to the prevailing accounts the industry contained widespread conflict.

Clegg and others have defined industrial relations as the study of the rules governing employment. Collective bargaining then becomes the bargaining over such rules between trade unions and employers, as well as the making, interpretation and administration of employment rules. Some writers see the history of trade unionism as the history of the development of collective bargaining (Rowe 1928: 121, Charles 1963, Clegg 1979: 1-3). Historians have been critical of this institutional approach which ignores workers' ability to think and act independently, omits social pressures and reduces the study of industrial relations to formal bargaining structures and procedures (Cronin 1979: 28, Hyman 1972: 66, Rubery 1978). For some authors the starting point for examining industrial relations is the exchange relationship, whereby property owners buy labour and the property-less class sells it. The basic disparity between the buyer and seller makes conflict inevitable. Yet an understanding of industrial relations requires a study of both the structures and the actions of those involved. The dynamic of industrial relations derives its force from the struggle for power and authority.

The pottery industry confirms the well-known picture of the disorder and complexity of British industrial relations (Clegg 1979: 15, cf McCabe 1932). A Ministry of Labour inquiry of 1917 was perplexed at the extreme range of bargaining forms. It was said of the 1908 dispute that 'among the whole body of manufacturers it would be difficult to find half a dozen who had received a precisely similar set of notices' (*P. Gazette.* 1.6.1917). The sectionalism of the pottery companies, workforce and unions was reproduced in the variegated pattern of their industrial relations.

The Donovan Commission of 1974 reported on what most workers had always known: in industrial relations two modes are in operation, the informal and the formal. The informal relations are

146

those between workers or unionists and employers in the workshop or plant, as opposed to the formal level where unions and employers bargain in a regional, industrial or national setting. The informal level involves customary, often unwritten understandings, the formal relies on written agreements (Boraston et al. 1975: 165, Batstone et al. 1978: 14). This perspective provides a key insight into how potters experienced and organised their particular form of bargaining. However, the distinctive feature of the pottery industry's industrial relations and indeed the main explanation for the pattern of conflict during the period was the *multiple* levels at which bargaining operated.

Five levels of bargaining were distinguishable in pottery, each with its own set of participants. The levels ranged from the individual or workshop level to the plant, the occupational group, the sub-industry or the industry-wide.

Phelps-Brown concluded for the 1900s that 'four out of five employees made their own bargains' and that 'the immediate relations between employer and employed at the place of work remained remarkably unregulated' (Phelps-Brown 1959: 279). It was entirely consistent with the social relations of the potbank that bargaining was predominantly between the individual or workgroup and the employer. A sample of the union's dispute files shows almost 80% of the bargaining problems related to individual companies. In a second sample of disputes, 35.42% of the disputes involved individual potters and 47.92% workgroups.[2] As these figures suggest, localised and informal bargaining was widespread and almost certainly the most common means of experiencing industrial relations for a potter.

Three main reasons underlay the prevalence of this small-scale bargaining. Management clearly found it easier to deal with relatively isolated individuals or workshops rather than tackle questions affecting a whole potbank. In October 1908 Cauldons issued notice to every one of its employees telling them that 'every one employed on these works will be under one month's notice from this date ... during the month each person will be seen with a view to possible rearrangement of their work and wages' (*P. Gazette.* 1.11.1908). The technical differences between occupations in the potbank meant that common problems and issues did not readily present themselves. In addition, the piece-rate system reinforced the individual basis of bargaining since it relied on the pricing of single items produced by one worker or small group. Owners had developed this form of bargaining into an art form out of the annual hiring system of the nineteenth century (Warburton 1931: 149). Manufacturers used individual notices for each employee as a means of preventing bargaining points becoming of wider relevance. In 1908, it was estimated that 16,000 workers had given in notices to their employers and one year after the 1911 arbitration board 3,000 notices were still being negotiated. Even when industry-wide bargaining became more established later in the period the months after an agreement were taken up with hosts of individual bargains on the potbanks as each worker translated the award into figures related to his ware pattern, size and workshop custom (*P. Gazette* 1.11.1911).

The workgroup form of bargaining sprang naturally from the primary social groups which made up the division of labour in the potbank. In the 1920s the seven mould-makers at Twyfords formed a separate bargaining group for both their employer and the union (CATU Coll L572: 14.1.1920). Each small collection of workers wrestled with the issues and problems specific to their workshop, which were not easily transferable or understood by other groups. Certain women's occupational groups also developed similar bargaining techniques, especially among the skilled lithographers, transferrers and paintresses. Group modes of bargaining were the natural extensions of the strength of workgroup control. The new occupations created during the 1900s, such as casters, developed bargaining forms and techniques similar to the traditional, existing forms (CATU Coll L601: 24.8.1911).

The prevalence of small-scale, individual or workshop bargaining meant that this level occupied the majority of the union's activity throughout the period. This local form of negotiating was the most direct contact point with union action for most potters. In April 1923, the jiggerers and jolliers of Minton's, according to the manager, when asked to sign a settlement 'refused to sign the same, unless it has previously been submitted to the Union' (CATU Coll L220: 25.4.1923). Moreover, it was from these localised workgroup questions that many of the larger industry-wide disputes arose. The sanitary pressers' dispute of 1907 grew originally from the introduction of one article on a single potbank. Even in the 1920s, when supposedly more formal systems of negotiation were in operation, the head office of the union was still directing that 'all individual notices on both sides to be dealt with at the factories concerned' (CATU Coll NEC mins: 17.2.1923, 24.10.1925). The small-scale forms of bargaining were so entrenched that when the union and manufacturers tried to establish a single, fixed, annual settlement date many workgroups were unable and unwilling to keep to such a uniform procedure.

British trade unionism has exhibited a strong factory consciousness (Flanders and Clegg 1967: 24, Tolliday 1986). Yet in the pottery industry, while union and worker action occurred mainly within the factory, it seldom concerned the whole workforce of a potbank. The division of labour separated the workers and relatively few issues arose which were common to all the workshops on the potbank. Differences in skill, status and work experience militated against factory-based action. Of the 72 recorded issues which arose between Grindleys and the union in 1912-1913, or the 20 subjects arising at Johnsons in the same period, none relate to disputes involving all the workforce of a plant (CATU Coll: Grindley File, Johnson File). Only when an issue was seen by all workers to be a common threat did a potbank workforce mobilise, as happened at the New Hall works in 1920 over arbitrary wage deductions from a group of women workers (*P. Gazette* 1.1.1920). Clearly the reason for the failure of the National Council of the Pottery Industry sponsored works committees after 1918 lay in their attempt to erect an inherently illogical institution with no real social base.

By contrast the occupational group within a local geographical area provided a remarkably strong basis for bargaining. This level of bargaining was based on the common interests of a single occupation or 'calling' drawn from a number of potbanks in a particular district. It was far easier to establish common prices and practices for a single occupation in an area than to attempt to combine the divergent interests of widely different occupations in a potbank. It was entirely natural for flat pressers to pool their resources with other flat pressers locally, given their common vocabulary and the broad similarity of the technical problems they faced. Although the union dispute files show that under 10% of bargaining activity took place at this level, the figure must be qualified. The actions of the occupational groups may have been quantitatively small but in qualitative terms their impact was far

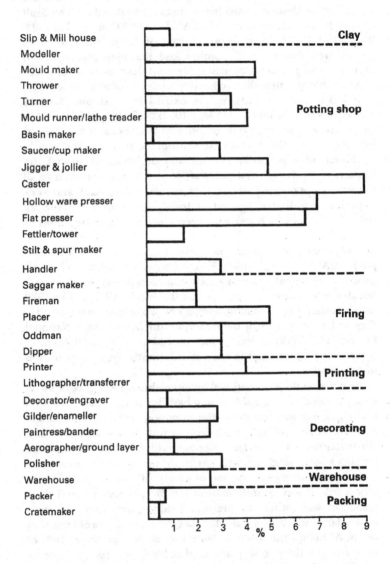

Figure 4.1 Level of union dispute activity 1906–1924

Source: CATU Coll, Union Dispute Files 1906–1924, covering 288 recorded disputes

greater. As the analysis of union structure showed (Chapter 3), the skilled occupational groups did not need to ask for official union intervention in their bargaining. For example, the sanitary pressers' committee for Hanley was exceptionally strong and by 1914 had established bargaining and monitoring procedures with the principal sanitary firms. The saggarmakers of Burslem and Tunstall acted in a similar way (CATU Coll L433: 16.9.1915, L116: 27.1.1920).

The 'trade' or 'district' price for an article or pattern became benchmarks for occupational or craft bargaining. The strongest area bargaining units were the craft or skilled groups. On 28 July 1910 Bishop & Stonier were routinely corresponding with the union central office that 'we herewith accept the offer made by you on the 19th inst., at the Handlers' prices sub committee'. It was often the craft area-based groups who responded to the problems of an isolated workgroup as happened in 1907 when Cauldons sanitary dispute was generalised to cover the whole sanitary sub-industry (*P. Gazette* 1.3.1907). As an analysis of union dispute files shows (see Figure 4.1) the craft and skilled occupations appear to have dominated the union's bargaining activity. This was perfectly consistent with the strength of the skilled workgroups on the potbank, allied with their connections with their fellow skilled potters.

Moreover, it was the craft groups at the potbank and area level which were responsible for the main episodes of bargaining during the period: episodes which historians have mistaken for industry-wide bargaining. When manufacturers and union met therefore in 1921 to discuss the general level of wages in the industry it was 'the consideration of departmental (or trade) notices', which was of paramount importance. After the 1920 general settlement it was noted how negotiations were really 'an all year business, with departmental meetings called for saggar makers, glost placers, odd men, dippers, biscuit bedders, hollow ware placers, kilnmen and handlers' (*P. Gazette* 1.12.1921). The national agreements of the later part of the period were essentially amalgamations of layer upon layer of departmental or trade group bargaining. Nor should it be assumed that sectional bargaining was divisive. Many of the craft and trade groups' demands served as blueprints for smaller or less skilled groups (cf Price 1980: 46). In 1911 the tactics of the turners in Longton became a model for other groups in the china sub-industry (*P. Gazette* 1.11.1911).

Some manufacturers and groups of trade unionists tried to establish bargaining units based on the seven sub-industries. These were less permanent and far weaker than the occupational group level since employer and union involvement varied markedly in relation to their relative strength within a sub-industry and according to trade conditions. In 1907 seven sub-industry manufacturers' committees existed yet in that year alone attitudes towards sub-industry bargaining diverged widely. The china manufacturers, as a result of foreign and domestic competition, were 'dropping down to prices never heard of before' due to 'want of cohesion among the manufacturers' (*P. Gazette* 1.1., 1.5.1907). In contrast, the jet and rockingham and sanitary masters were well organised (CATU Coll L240: 25.3.1915).

Yet attitudes to sub-industry bargaining varied between manufacturers. While the jet and rockingham masters readily negotiated, the sanitary owners refused. The sanitary masters were determined to fight the men at any cost and had formed an employers federation, on the lines of the engineering employers. Alternatively, pottery workers found it equally difficult to establish and maintain sub-industry-wide organisation. Sanitary organisation and bargaining was especially active in 1908-1912, when casting provided a central issue, but collapsed during the war when the market fell (CATU Coll L174: 28.5.1909, L106: 25.3.1918). Stoneware never bargained at this level and even in 1926 still lacked a standard wage scale (CATU Coll NEC mins: 22.9.1917, 26.3.1926). The largest sub-industry, earthenware, produced a form of bargaining which was meant to apply to all its member companies during and after the First World War. The diversity of products and firms within earthenware always limited the applicability of any agreements which might be reached. The sub-industry level of bargaining was impermanent and varied greatly in its strength and coverage where it did exist. At best these forums dealt with certain occupational groups and never covered all the workers in the sub-industry. The factory and the sub-industry were both inappropriate locations for dealing with the problems raised by the multiplicity of trades they contained.

It has been generally assumed that industry-wide collective bargaining was established in British industry around 1900 and has since been the norm (Allen 1964, Burgess 1975: 291). In the pottery industry, bargaining on this scale did not exist before 1916 and even after that date the terms must be used very carefully. The differing settling times used by sections of the industry made industry-wide bargaining impossible until the Great War. The dispute phases of 1900, 1906-1908 and 1911 never involved the entire industry, although the *Labour Gazette* and the language of some press reports implied the opposite. The 1900 episode principally involved the printers and transferrers, as well as the pressers but only in the earthenware sub-industry. In 1911 the negotiations of that year involved 'sectional (trade) committees'. As a potter observed 'as regarded the case of the clay workers other than flat pressers, it was pointed out by the manufacturers that the notices given by the men were by no means general' (*Times I.F.T.S.*: 13.4.1911). Only by 1916 did a single union bargaining association (of the NAS and the ovenmen) exist (see Chapter 3). In that year it was noted how:

a precedent was fixed by the workers, inasmuch as instead of apprising the manufacturers of their demands individually, or in individual groups or classes, as has long been the custom, a general formal notice was served upon the secretary of the Manufacturers Association by the secretary of the Pottery Workers' Union.

(*P. Gazette.* 1.4.1916)

Yet even the epoch-making qualities of this event cannot sustain the argument that industry-wide bargaining was permanently established. Manufacturer and union action remained highly sectional (cf Batstone et al. 1978: 51, 61). Annual negotiations between the organisations of employers and employed only signified the beginning of a widespread, fragmented process. The tensions between individual, workshop and wider collective forms of bargaining continued. The workgroup and area-based occupational group remained strong and active after the erection of industrial bargaining forums. Both management and workers were anxious to retain the local forms as the potters' union recognised. In 1920 the NSPW informed the manufacturers' federation that 'the above increases shall apply to slip and mill-house hands and kiln firemen, but the Union recognises the right of Employers to pay these workers at the rate per hour arranged between the

153

individual employer and employee' (CATU Coll L552: March 1920). Similarly the 'Handbook of Agreements for the China Trade' used in the 1920s states that for decorators, although an industry-wide pricing committee will be established, 'no prices shall be fixed for any decoration without consultation by the management with these decorators who are wholly or partly to do the work' (CATU Coll Handbook of Agreements 1926: 21). It was the customary base and strength of the lower levels of bargaining which ensured they remained in operation in the 1920s when the attempted industrial forms broke down.

Labour historians have placed great significance on the apparent shift from the informal to the wider formal modes of bargaining in British industry during this period. Price asserts that the 'transition from an unformalised to a formalised system of industrial relations was the critical event in modern labour history whose significance can hardly be underestimated' (Price 1980: 55, 95). Rowe considered the change as predetermined. As he put it: 'the establishment of collective bargaining on a national basis must be viewed as a more or less inevitable process of evolution' (Rowe 1928: 132, 143). The pottery industry shows how the dynamic of industrial relations is rather different (cf Allen 1964: 69, Clegg 1979: 3).

There is evidence to suggest that industrial relations did become increasingly formalised during this period in the pottery industry. Arnold Wethered, in 1924, thought the National Council of the Pottery Industry, established in 1917, was 'quite the leading example of what a Whitley Council can be' (CATU Coll 1924 Wage Inquiry: D). Leading pottery owners certainly wanted stable industrial relations, if possible, through public formal agreements. By binding the union to written procedures the strength of informal, customary action might be minimised and workers brought under greater managerial control. The owners' attempts to establish an arbitration and conciliation board for the industry were impelled by this basic desire to create rules which would limit independent worker action. In 1908 a manufacturer observed how 'trades unionism is now more than ever before a great fact to be reckoned with in industrial affairs': his main hope was that 'it forms a great safeguard against rash or ill-considered action by the operatives' (P. Gazette. 1.4.1908).

The potters' leaders, at certain times, favoured the creation of

154

more formal industrial relations. They saw real benefits were obtainable for pottery workers, but they did not enter formal negotiations blind to manufacturer strategies. The union officials' prime aim was to establish a degree of order in wages and conditions. They wished to make employers accountable and control manufacturers' freedom of manoeuvre. For the potters this was an immense achievement when set against the previous century's experience of chaotic piece rates, companies under-cutting each other on price and the dense undergrowth of impermanent informal bargains. Given that in 1892, 1900 and 1907 a number of manufacturers had tried to cripple and destroy the potters' unions, holding masters to public, formally recognised agreements were considered a great triumph. In 1911, therefore, the union could pressurise Furnivals into changing their treatment of their pressers by using the company's and their association's agreement with the union (*P. Gazette* 1.7.1911). Formal recognition of the union by manufacturers was also used as a means of recruiting members of the NAS.

While pottery manufacturers wanted more formalised industrial relations in order to increase their control over organised labour, this did not result in the emasculation of the union. The outcome of the changes in industrial relations in the pottery industry were more problematic: they did not have the effect on the potters' union of 'rendering them comparatively harmless' as some have argued in relation to other industries (Burgess 1975: vii). Manufacturers, including the largest, continued to act unofficially when they felt their interests threatened by formal agreements. Above all the institutional, formal procedures were never permanent or complete in their coverage. The richness of workshop custom and independent, informal bargaining were not easily brought under control by union or manufacturers and constantly threatened the official forms of bargaining. From November 1912 through to January 1913 at Twyfords, a leading member of their manufacturers' association, a running dispute was fought over two trade customs: the right to second firing and the right of workers to check the counts. Thomas Twyford was quite clear that, as he put it, 'I will have my business conducted in my own way' and he refused to negotiate or be involved in the generally agreed conciliation committee of two masters and two union representatives (CATU

155

Coll L736-740: Nov. 1912-Jan. 1913). The struggle for control of production in the potbank continued to be fought over wages, prices and allowances in their local settings. Even during the war when formal, industry-wide bargaining was at its strongest, independent action by workers and separate bargaining was common (*P. Gazette* 1.5.1916).

An examination of the activities of the conciliation and arbitration board, the manufacturers' associations and the National Council of the Pottery Industry confirms that the development of a formalised system of industrial relations was not only partial but highly unstable. The disparate motivations and actions of both workers and masters, at all levels, never allowed these three institutions to direct their constituents effectively. The arbitration and conciliation board, though nominally in existence since 1868, was periodically disbanded (*Workman's Times* 12.12.1890, 14.8.1891). Between 1891 and 1908 no board operated since the unions were 'sick of the name of arbitration'. Owners might boast that it was 'the first and most successful of the Labour Arbitration Boards in the country' yet it only officially sat between 1908-1911 (*P. Gazette* 1.6.1907, 1.1.1908, 1.4.1911). The unions did not submit to the rules constructed by manufacturers as the contest over the board's reconstitution in 1907-1908 showed.

It was hardly surprising that formal bargaining procedures were so fragile when the manufacturers' associations were so weak (cf Turner 1962: 373, Charles 1963: 39-41). From 1890 to 1910 *ad hoc* groups of masters combined during disputes to confront workers yet they consistently failed to act collectively on any larger scale. As one of their leaders admitted in 1906, 'the pottery trade, from the time of Wedgwood to now, has invariably been in want of union. There are the different sections ... and each has fought its own hand' (*Truck Act Reports* 1906: Q 679, *Royal Commission on Trade Disputes* 1906: 281).

Government intervention, the war and the growth of the union's strength led to a period of stronger collaboration between manufacturers. Legislation regarding workers' compensation and industrial illness potentially affected all companies and resulted in temporary collective action by the more established firms to resist the outcomes of the Lord James inquiry of 1900-1902, the Workman's Compensation Bill in 1906 and the lead investigations of 1908-1910 (*P. Gazette* 1.7.1906, 1.10.1910, 1.11.1911). By 1914, as masters conceded, these episodes combined with 'labour troubles' and 'the Insurance Bill' had 'impressed upon manufacturers, as perhaps nothing else could have done, the urgent necessity for combination'. The immediate problems of raw material and labour supply during the war produced a 'special war committee of manufacturers associations' in 1914 which became the British Pottery Manufacturers' Association in 1918 (*Times I.F.T.S.*: 1.12.1918). But the composition and actions of the new organisations reveal their ineffectiveness. The association's membership list shows that over half the employers were not included. The smaller masters were notably absent. The rules were so loose that when trading was disrupted and prices fell in the 1920s, enforcement of their regulations was a problem and therefore the cohesiveness of industrial bargaining broke down (*Workmens Comp. C^{ee}* 1920: Q 18669).

The intentions of the National Council, formed in 1917, were ambitious. The new body was to bring about uniform organisation and pricing in the industry, roll back foreign competition and even help create a new transport system: these were the understandable aspirations born of the reconstruction era (Bowley 1921: 21, *P. Gazette.* 1.2.1918). The council's standing orders, however, underline the limitations of its scope. A two-thirds majority was necessary for motions to be carried. The statistical, research, organisation and wages committees were designed as information gatherers and discussion devices. The council could not compel manufacturers or workers to accept its decisions nor had it the powers to enforce agreements. The council was an entirely voluntary body (CATU Coll NCPI mins: 11.1.1918, 11.4.1918, 19.9.1919). The attempt to encompass so complex an industry failed. In 1920 on the basic question of wages and profits it was found that 'no summary of information could be obtained which would be of any practical use'. The 1920 and 1924 disputes did involve a committee from the Council, yet in 1920 a government investigator found that with regard to the works committees scheme, 'the vast majority of operatives know little or nothing of the recommendations of the joint industrial council' (CATU Coll NCPI mins: 17.10.1918, 17.3.1920). In the 1920s union members questioned the council's relevance. The annual delegation of 1922 was asked if the union's payments to the council were justified by the results. In 1923 one delegate put it to the union that the council 'looked like doing little or nothing in the actual interests of the workers' (CATU Coll Annual Delegation mins: 111, 136). Many manufacturers did not want the council to deal with industrial relations; they preferred the body to operate as a means of lobbying government. The fall in attendance by manufacturers from 1921 further undermined the council's efficiency (CATU Coll NCPI mins: 2.5.1922, 2.1.1925).

The National Council failed to alter fundamentally the industrial relations of pottery manufacture (cf Wrigley 1986). At the very most it gave temporary reinforcement to the formal industry-wide bargaining between 1917 and 1924. As one of the architects, Henry Clay, confessed: 'the previously existing machinery for dealing with wage questions was left to function undisturbed' while the executive strength to carry out the ambitious objectives was missing (Clay 1929: 162, 165, Charles 1963: 196).

Professor Williams believes that there has been a 'remarkable record of industrial peace in the pottery industry' in this country. He cites the uniformity of bargaining forms as a major reason for the lack of conflict (!) (Williams 1958: 298). Yeaman also claims that 'there has been no strike or dispute since 1899' (Yeaman 1968: 150). Both conclusions are particularly curious. In fact the potters participated in major industrial battles and the contest for the control of production was a continuing theme involving a wide range of issues.

At its narrowest industrial conflict is equated with the strike. The strike has been defined as 'a temporary stoppage of work by a group of employees in order to express a grievance or enforce a demand' (Hyman 1972: 17). Conflict arises from many sources and may be expressed in differing forms. Scullion and Edwards distinguish between the behavioural, institutional and structural variants. The behavioural form is where conflict is actively recognised and expressed by participants; the institutional arises when conflict is expressed by customary procedures and practices; structural conflict refers to the forces making for conflict which may be implicit within a given situation, though they may remain dormant for long periods (Edwards and Scullion 1982: 12). Recent studies of conflict highlight the variety of its expression and point to the strike as a relatively exceptional form. The typical strike has been found to be the spontaneous, small scale and short stoppage

(Batstone et al. 1978:51). Even though this form is so common in industry, it has gone largely unnoticed by official statistics and by commentators on the Potteries and other industries (cf Cole 1924: 124).

The pottery industry of the early twentieth century in fact exhibited conflict in all its forms. The depth of individual or workgroup bargaining was indicative of the conflict generated in the workshops of the potbank. The 'day-books' of union activists record the high incidence of small-scale, short-term disputes involving between one and half a dozen workers and lasting no more than a day. The majority of these tiny events never required union recognition nor action. It was the density of this routine form of conflict that led the union in 1911 to request that members reported the outcome of their disputes to the lodges in order that the union might record their incidence (CATU Coll Annual Delegation 1911:9). In 1909 a local observer reflected on the strength of localised disputes. In his words: 'for three or four years now, the sanitary trade has been upset by dispute after dispute, and much of it might have been avoided had more reliance been placed in the leaders (of the union)' (*P. Gazette*. 1.10.1909).

The large-scale co-ordinated strike was in fact the exception. Put beside Stearns's strike model much of the potters' strike activity was, to use his terms, 'unsophisticated' (Stearns 1974:4). Yet in practice there was a wide gulf between the forms of potters' strike action. At one extreme was the spontaneous, unofficial sometimes violent strike action, for example, in 1907, during a dispute at Doultons, sanitary workers fought a group of blacklegs, forcing them to shelter in Hanley police station (*P. Gazette*. 1.5.1907). At the other extreme was the calculated, planned offensive over a major issue. As in 1881, 1890, 1906-8 and 1920, for example, these strikes were played out with deliberate union ritual and theatre. They involved the entire apparatus of bands, daily marches, mass meetings in the main squares of the Six Towns, backed up by the organisation of temporary stewards, collectors and the trade committees (*Workman's Times*. 14.11.1890, CATU Coll Clowes' Scrapbook 4.4.1907, *P. Gazette*. 1.12.1920).

During this period in the pottery industry, some of the most notable episodes of conflict occurred. It was said of the 1908 disputes that 'never in the history of the trade probably, has a more serious crisis arisen' (*P. Gazette.* 1.4.1908). Although the surviving union records are incomplete, the main phases of dispute activity seem to have occurred in 1910-1915 and 1919-1920. 1908-1909, 1916-1917 and 1923-1924 were years of active but less intense conflict. The early 1900s and 1920s were relatively quiet. The disputes which involved large sections or all the workers in a sub-industry occurred first in 1900 when a dispute involving printers, transferrers and ovenmen in earthenware arose over a wage increase claim. The conflict of 1906-1908 in the sanitary sub-industry was really a series of rolling strikes concerning the introduction of casting. The 1906-1907 phase was sparked off by a workers' offensive as prices rose: in 1908 masters counter-attacked with wage cuts as prices fell (*S. Advertizer.* 22.2.1908). The disputes of 1911 were over wage levels in the earthenware, sanitary and tile sections and the rules surrounding the arbitration board (*The Times.* 13.4.1911). The strikes of 1913 involved jet and rockingham, tiles and the cane and white makers while 1914 witnessed disputes over wage structures in earthenware and china (*P. Gazette.* 1.5.1914). The 1919-1920 disputes were over the reduction of wages by manufacturers. During 1923-1924 workers attempted to recoup the wage losses which had followed the extensive price cutting of the early 1920s (CATU Coll 1924 Wage Inquiry).

The explanation for this pattern of conflict rests on a composite set of interlocking causes. The dominant role attributed to the trade cycle by Hunt (1981: 321) or Burgess (1975: 82-84) is not borne out by the experience of the potters: their dispute activity sprang from four main origins – wages and the cost of living, the organisation of work, and less obvious deep structural causes. Wages remained at the forefront of potters' demands yet their arguments changed. In the late nineteenth century they argued that workers should profit from buoyant demand, in a market economy, just as they had suffered from depressed trade. By the 1900s, and in common with other industrial groups, the potters maintained that not only should their wages reflect 'commercial prosperity but that a social criterion should govern wages' (*S. Advertizer.* 22.2.1908). The 1924 dispute therefore rested on the assertion that 'we want to put a minimum rate below which no one shall go'. Even the issue of work organisation led to its own constellation of disputes. The ovenmen resisted an intensification of work whereas the hollow-ware pressers faced the threat of

unemployment and the possible end of their craft due to casting
(*P. Gazette* 1.6.1908).

Although in broad terms conflict in the pottery industry was
related to industrial performance, it cannot of itself explain that
conflict. The major dispute phases of 1900, 1906-1907, 1911, 1913,
1919-1920 and 1923-1924 occurred in periods of increasing
output, exports and employment. Yet why potters chose to act at
these points also relates to their perceptions of previous disputes
(Whipp 1987b). Never visible in strike statistics, none the less the
role of memory is crucial in explaining the full motivation behind
strike action. An industrial correspondent noted how pottery
workers in 1907 bore grudges from the 1900 disputes. As he put it:

> eight or nine years ago a section of the employers unwisely
> adopted the attitude that the workmen's unions were a
> negligible quantity, and could be ignored. The spirit begot a
> feeling of bitterness and antagonism on the part of the men
> which has led to many of our difficulties.
>
> (*P. Gazette* 1.1.1908)

CONCLUSION

Anyone trying to summarise managerial behaviour in sectors such
as pottery manufacture composed of almost 500 separate firms is
wise to be cautious. However, there are a number of themes which
arise and require emphasis. First and foremost the pottery industry
supplies considerable evidence of the limitations of British
management in the early twentieth century.

As in other labour-intensive industries with markets under
renewed challenge from more recently industrialised countries,
control of labour was vital. Yet management control of work was
never established overnight nor once and for all. The social
relations of the potbank were seldom in a state of equilibrium.
Rather, control was constantly being attempted by management
and workers alike. Indeed, the pottery industry shows how difficult
it can be to identify in practice the owner, manager and employee
in such industries. In spite of the clear imperatives involved no
implacable establishment of managerial domination is discernible
(Burawoy 1985). The employment relation is much more
demanding in reality (cf Poole 1980). As the potters show, wage

payment, technology and working practices might be the more visible occasions for contest yet all facets of work were the subject of competing interpretations. It is an indication of the general weakness of managerial control that management in the Potteries had to put such extensive effort into constructing the responsibility for industrial disease or creating ideologies of common interest and attachment around their firms. What stands out is the fragility of the employment relationship and the uncertainty of its outcome.

This profile of pottery management combined with the fragmented production process and sectional workforce resulted in a highly pragmatic form of bargaining which complemented the 'chaos' of industrial relations across the 500 firms. That pragmatism found its strongest expression at the local level – in the potbank workgroups or the area trade bodies. In contrast to certain orthodoxies, the formal, industry-wide, national forms were far less important and the most difficult to sustain. Recent work by industrial relations specialists on the 1980s (Batstone 1988, Sisson 1989) suggests that such patterns are still vital in understanding contemporary bargaining forms and managerial practice as the limitations of 1970s national industrial relations machinery are exposed.

Managerial action around the employment contract in no way simplified the meaning of work in the pottery industry; instead it added to the complexity of the patterns of labour. In order to appreciate the full extent of that action it is necessary to examine the role of employer and employed in the wider context of the Six Towns.

Chapter Five

COMMUNITY, MOVEMENT
AND STATE

THE POTTERS AND THE COMMUNITY

No study of the potters in relation to their community, the labour movement or the state exists. The subject constitutes a substantial research topic in itself; space is available here for the first stages of such an inquiry. What follows is not a full-scale cultural or political history of the Potteries: instead we will attempt to map out some of the basic features of the potters' community, their relevance to class and the growth of the area's labour movement in the 1890-1930 period. The relevance of community to labour history is readily apparent. Hobsbawm directed historians to look at the internal divisions of classes as well as their relationship to other groups. As he put it, 'class defines not a group of people in isolation, but a system of relationships, both vertical and horizontal' (Hobsbawm 1974). Gray noted the danger of writing the history of the working class in isolation, with assumptions about the structures and ideologies of other classes (Gray 1976). Others have opened up new lines of explanation for the development of trade unions and the labour movement by examining the communities workers inhabited and created besides studying the interaction of local occupational groups and their relationship with other bodies or political parties. These analyses have tried to penetrate 'the life beyond work' (Dawley 1976, Palmer 1979, Williams 1980, Bodnar 1982).

The concept of community requires careful specification before it can be used in a historical setting. Jackson emphasises the shared experience of those who make up a community based on a common economic position: the experience is reinforced by kin relations and joint attachments to work (Jackson 1968). Though these features may be found within a community they are, by themselves, insufficient to capture its full dimensions. Others have stressed the role played by forms of association (Frankenberg 1966: 201). A community is then a geographical area, in which mutually dependent groups act together to satisfy their needs through common sets of organisations. Calhoun offers a sharper conception by including both individuals and groups and basing it on social relationships. Community suggests, he argues, not only face-to-face contact, familiarity and commonality of purpose but a pattern of self-regulation. Moral obligation becomes the essence of community. A person is not necessarily conscious of the abstract object 'the community'. Yet he or she is absorbed via numerous relationships into the community and is aware of helping to determine the experience of others and of being affected by other people. Community as a pattern of social organisation and as a defined way of life depends on a high degree of stability. Rules or standards define appropriate action within the community (Calhoun 1980: 105). Calhoun also asserts, as does Foster (Foster 1974, MacFarlane 1977), that the growth of working-class collective action depended on the social integration of working-class communities. Divisions within the ranks of workers and the differences in work patterns and local traditions could inhibit that growth.

As an analytical device the community, seen as a set of social relations, can illuminate a study of the potters' experience and their way of life. This concept of community leads to a questioning of the ties and contacts among the potters outside the workplace, and to ask how strong was the sense of common purpose; what kinds of traditional moral obligations existed; and how far did the potters' collective action depend on the integration of the community? The forces making for divisions within the community and the impact of other groups and classes on the potters require investigation. One needs to know what factors mediated between the potters' experience of work and their expression of union, class and political consciousness.

The close physical relationship of industries and their surrounding communities was a common feature of Britain's industrial and urban development. In the Potteries the link was especially strong as the region's name suggests. The Six Towns were physically dominated by the staple industry. A visitor in 1892 thought the towns were 'to all intents and purposes one place', given the industry which united them. The interpenetration of home and work within the lives of the potters has been demonstrated already, along with the overlap of trade unionism and the domestic sphere. Outsiders have noticed how being a potter became 'a whole way of life' (*Daily Chronicle* 14.11.1892, *P. Gazette* 1.5.22, Board of Trade 1946: 12). However, it has also been shown how the stratification of the workforce by skill, authority and income at work was reproduced outside the factory (Matsumura 1983). A closer look at the Potteries reveals that the potters were highly localised in their social relations outside the potbank. This localism in many ways echoed the small scale of the potters' workplace and union groupings.

Attachment to the town or neighbourhood where a potter lived and usually worked, was strong. The lack of easily transferable skills between some sub-industries and the marked longevity of employment with a single firm made changing residence between the towns unlikely. Local districts had developed physically and socially during the nineteenth century whereby, as Harold Owen noted, 'the names of Longton, Fenton, Stoke, Hanley, Burslem and Tunstall had an individual and sufficient significance'. Potters today still regard fellow potters from different towns as 'foreigners'. Elsie Grocott worked in Stoke yet lived in Newcastle and like other workers earned her nickname 'Castle Black' from where her home was (Interviews with E. Grocott and J. Owen, 1976). People locally were introduced as 'Miss Bennett, of Burslem' or 'William Tunnicliffe of Longton'. The toast at a celebration was often to 'the town and the trade' where those assembled lived and worked (*S. Advertizer* 23.5.1908). The growth of new suburbs at the end of the nineteenth century notwithstanding, the lives of the potters remained highly 'district-centred' (cf Daunton 1977: 143). Between 1902 and 1910 there was fierce controversy over proposals to federate the Six Towns into one county borough as each town zealously guarded its own identity and independence.

Potters, their families and their kin, developed patterns of social relations which helped bind these areas together. From the available evidence, local status, mutual respect and assistance were strong parts of neighbourhood codes. Co-workers and neighbours regularly saw to it that families afflicted by ill-health, accidents or poverty were given aid, whilst preserving the independence of the assisted. In 1907, a 33-year-old woman and her eight-year-old daughter only received 5s. 3d. per week compensation from the firm where she contracted lead poisoning. Her neighbours temporarily ensured that she had at least the basic necessities of life (*HMI Factories Report* 1907: 170). In 1910, a woman asked how she coped with illness and unemployment replied: 'We had to manage. The neighbours were very good and helped the children. My husband was not at work, and he looked after me' (*1910 Lead Cee*: Q 11789). Unofficial midwives and 'wise women' were local sources of medical advice and help. The nursing arrangements for infants were also neighbourhood based, usually reserved as occupations for the older women who did not work on the potbank. Although such support strengthened the social ties of an area, mutual assistance had observable limits. Assumptions were never made about access to homes or involvement in domestic decisions. Respectability was founded on independence and self-determination. This was what puzzled the middle-class settlement workers from outside the potteries. In Fenton when they tried to open crèches for the potters in the 1900s, nobody attended. As the settlement head found out, 'it was said by the working people that it was taking the bread out of the mouths of the elderly people' (*Physical Deterioration Committee* 1903: Q 9024).

It was these local codes of behaviour and social relations which helped to shape the potters' union structure and its activities. The linkage of the potter's home and family with his or her union and the role of the neighbourhood street collector have already been noted. During disputes local rules of dependence and equity found expression. For example, striking potters at Doultons collected money in a cigar box outside the factory gates and then divided the collection between the strikers' families. In the 1907 disputes union collectors gave out financial assistance to union and non-union strikers in their areas because of the poverty among certain occupations. Workers on strike established their own local distress committees, often in association with the local working-men's clubs. In 1907, one club organised relief to 179 families during the sanitary strike. Demonstrations and meetings respected traditional locations and rituals (CATU Coll S. Clowes Scrapbook: 30.3.1907). Local allegiances were part of the union's social texture. Factory or neighbourhood 'Glee parties' and choirs provided entertainment. Charity collections for the Haywood hospital or the Red Cross were organised on the potbank or in the surrounding district (*P. Gazette*. 1.6.1916). For those who flouted local codes of behaviour the reaction of their neighbours could be swift and violent. In 1907 John Woburton defied a strike call at his sanitary works. His home was besieged by his fellow pressers and neighbours with Henry Adams leading the shouts of 'you nob stick' (CATU Coll S. Clowes Scrapbook: 30.3.1907). It was the detailed knowledge of these local relationships and customs which provided the bases of Booth's, Parkes', Clowes' and Tunnicliffe's union authority each of whom lived and worked in the area they organised (*P. Gazette*. 1.12.1923, *S. Sentinel*. 26.3.1928, cf Walker 1979: 26).

The community and its attendant social relationships could clearly affect the nature of class consciousness among the potters. Thompson implicitly located the generation of class consciousness in the community. He sees class as highly subjective, in that 'class is defined by men as they live their own history, and, in the end, this is its only definition'. Whilst there may be objective determinants of class consciousness, class arises, he argues, as people perceive their productive relations within the wider 'ensemble of social relations', informed as they are by inherited expectations (Thompson 1968: 9-12). Class and class consciousness involved not only a person's relation to the means of production but the perception of class derived from his experience of his position, or his group's position in relation to other people and groups (Palmer 1979: xvi). Class consciousness was mediated by particular cultural contexts. A reconstruction of the class consciousness of the potters therefore necessitates combining what is already known of the potters' experience and interpretation of the work on the potbank, in the family and in the neighbourhood, with the potters' relations with employers, local leaders and groups outside the workplace.

However, the degree of class consciousness could be affected by a number of pressures which social scientists have identified. The apparent viability and stability of the economic system influenced the propensity for class opposition. Social fragmentation among workers is regarded as critical to the strength of collective action and consciousness. In his study of shipbuilding, Reid argues that 'while all workers shared a common subordination to their employers, it was a subordination integrally linked to sectional divisions' which weakened their sense of class identity (Meacham 1977, McDougall 1978, Reid 1980). The structure and activity of elite groups and their relations with others could modify class awareness. Moreover, workers may act collectively yet they may not necessarily see themselves in opposition or antagonism to other classes. The collective activities of the potters, in their union and in other groupings, will be examined as well as their ideology. The aim is to discover whether the potters were merely an introverted, interest group or whether they were highly aware of their status leading them to try and change the inequalities existing between them and other classes.

The pottery owner's attempt to establish his authority and the pottery worker's acceptance or rejection of management control were not confined to the social relations of the potbank but were continued in public. In the textile industry down to 1900 employers enjoyed an extensive command of politics, municipal affairs and local institutions (Joyce 1980: 4). The South Wales mine owners found little need to demonstrate their authority in that way since the strength of their industrial power was abundantly clear (Williams 1980: 108, cf Stedman Jones 1977: 162-170). The role of the pottery owners is much less obvious. First, their cohesive strength was not uniformly strong. To some workers it appeared that 'all the masters' families were related'. For example, Edmund Leigh in 1906 married the sister of Arthur Wilkinson, master potter of Burslem, and in 1910, the Wild and Poole pottery families were united in marriage. The evidence for inter-marriage between the pottery owners' families suggests it was more characteristic of only the larger firms (*P. Gazette* 1.7.1906, 1.6.1907, 1.11.1910, CATU Coll 1924 Wage Inquiry: 71). In the absence of the manuscript census we know relatively little of the smaller-sized companies. The manufacturers' associations were never uniformly supported yet a central group of families did become more active and influential than others. A comparison of the membership and leadership of the trade committees with the chamber of commerce indicates that the Wedgwoods, Johnsons, Baileys, Ridgways, Leighs and Grimwades were the dominant figures. Many of these larger, old-established owners used the solicitor, Llewellyn and Mr Bullock the accountant to provide a unifying link among them during trade disputes and debates over local issues (*P. Gazette* 1.6.1919, *S. Advertizer* 22.5.1909).

The impact of the pottery owners was perceived differently within the Potteries. To some the larger pottery manufacturers had an absentee image. During an inquiry in 1904 a resident was asked 'Is it not true that the owners of factories live somewhere outside in the country?' She replied: 'Yes, and many of the big ones do not even drive in' (*Physical Deterioration C^{ee}* 1903: Q 9161 and 9206).

The Aynsleys lived at Blythe Bridge; the Johnsons were members of the North Staffordshire hounds; Eliot Meakin owned Creswell Hall and lived near Francis Benham at Stafford. Local town leaders such as alderman Green complained in 1907, that 'Stoke suffered from the fact that many of its leading men live out of the town. They were never to be seen in Stoke at night time' (*P. Gazette* 1.4.1907). A radical such as Gertrude Tuckwell agreed in 1911 that 'the richer class has fled before the cloud, and made its home among the green fields and wooded districts' (*P. Gazette* 1.11.1911). Outsiders concluded that the Potteries had no 'west end' and was to a great extent devoid of a residential leisured class.

The potbank owners may not have displayed a clear collective social cohesion and many did not live in the Potteries. However their status and image was to a large extent derived from particular representations of public activity and display (cf Cannadine 1982: 107-130). Some of the potbank frontages and entrances were clear attempts to demonstrate the position and wealth of the owner. John Aynsley's factory in Sutherland road was a good example with its arched entrance, Venetian windows and pediment along with numerous cornices and quoins. Potbanks such as Johnsons, Doultons or Mintons were among the most famous buildings in the Potteries (Smith 1965: 81-94).

In terms of action many manufacturers continued their paternalism outside their factories, usually in the town or district where the factory was located. The assumption behind contemporary reports of pottery owners' lives was that being a master naturally involved becoming a benefactor. Traditionally and throughout the period manufacturers played their parts as paternalists to the full. Meakins were recognised to be 'large benefactors' and of Cartwright Edwards it was said, in 1909, that there was 'not a benevolent or philanthropic organisation he has not assisted' (*P.*

Gazette 1.4.1909). The spread of types of largesse was considerable. Gibsons in 1906 gave £1,000 to provide meals and clothing for the local elementary school. John Aynsley was the main backer of the cottage hospital at his home town, Longton, while the Twyford family underwrote the Hanley museum. Thomas Taylor gave an 'annual treat' to the 200 poorest children in Hanley (*P. Gazette* 1.2.1906). During the depressed trade of 1909 certain masters felt it was their duty to help relieve the local distress among the workers (*S. Advertizer* 9.1.1909). The war also provided them with opportunities to exhibit their generosity: in 1917 some china manufacturers proudly announced they had contributed a 'motor ambulance' for the troops. Female members of the masters' families were also active. In 1918 the Misses Audrey and Phoebe Wedgwood called together a local meeting to consider the shortage of workers' housing (*P. Gazette* 1.5.1918). On Christmas day 1909, it was reported how Mrs Cecil Wedgwood and Mrs Johnson gave the children in Stoke Workhouse a gift of a tree and afternoon tea (*S. Advertizer* 2.1.1909).

The local press always welcomed such behaviour warmly. Their verdict on the kindness of the Wedgwood ladies was that 'another generation of the Wedgwood family shows a disposition to maintain the high standard of life'. To many people these activities were born of unalloyed generosity and boosted the prestige of the pottery masters considerably. A report on the Johnson firm pointed out that 'the community was greatly indebted to such men as the Johnson brothers, whose foresight, enterprise, and business ability found regular employment for nearly 3,000 workpeople'. W.H. Grindley was spoken of almost apologetically in 1926 since he was 'not a local leader', as he clearly was expected to be given the importance of his firm; he redeemed himself by being a 'great benefactor' (*S. Advertizer* 26.1.1907, *P. Gazette* 1.3.1926).

The influence of these kinds of actions and attitudes on the social relations of the Potteries is shown by the souvenir programme of the Hanley TUC of 1905. The Meakin Concerts, funded by George Meakin and his contribution of one-third of Queen Victoria's jubilee fund in 1887 were proudly announced and the contemporary charitable works of the masters reported as worthy of praise. The photographs of Noah Parkes and Thomas Pickin the pottery union leaders, appear in the programme along with the full page portrait of the Duchess of Sutherland (CATU

Coll TUC 1905: 38, 51 and 68). The image presented was one of apparent acceptance of the leading roles of the pottery owners and their associates in the public life of the Potteries.

Employers and their families also took up positions in local institutions, and organisations. The manufacturers concerned were clearly seen as leaders and figures of authority. The sample of 100 masters (Table 4.1) shows that 24% were magistrates, 40% were councillors, 10% held office in political bodies, 23% were involved in philanthropic organisations and 7% were found to have held office in a sporting or social body. Their participation was spread throughout the Six Towns. Traditions of employers' involvement in local public life were strong. George Meakin's appointment as JP in 1906 was warmly greeted since he was 'following his father's tradition with the public and charitable movements'. Ten of the twenty-six new magistrates in 1914 were pottery manufacturers (*P. Gazette*: 1.4.1906, 1.2.1914, 1.6.1920). Nor were employers merely remote figureheads. Ezra Bourne, in common with other masters, not only funded chapel building but took 'an active part' in preaching. He was 'an earnest Wesleyan' and had 'held every office a layman could hold in connexion with the Wesleyan Chapel at Burslem'. In 1913, Daniel Linyard, the jet and rockingham manufacturer, was steward of the Alsager Primitive Methodist circuit. In the sample of manufacturers, non-conformists outnumbered Anglicans by 2:1. The Potteries were a 'stronghold of non-conformity' for both masters and workers (*P. Gazette*: 1.10.1906, 1.7.1908, 1.2.1909, 1.5.1913, 1.6.1919).

While workers did not simply follow their employers to chapel or join the same institutions the image of the employer was clearly portrayed in terms which might inhibit class antagonism. The manufacturers' position as provider of employment on the potbank was enhanced by his role in other spheres of local life. His authority took on a wider dimension. An image of trust and probity was constructed from his actions in friendly and building societies, sports clubs, organisations for the blind or on hospital boards (*S. Advertizer*: 14.12.1907. *P. Gazette*: 1.1.1910, 1.2.1913, 1.2.1915, 1.9.1918). Clearly the pottery owners felt these positions were significant as they figure so prominently in the public reports of their careers and life styles. Even the local labour press admitted that 'our leaders in political, social and religious movements are manufacturers' (*Staffordshire Knot*: 21.2.1891). Employers were able to

171

use their image as leaders both in the workplace and in the community when contentious issues arose. During the lead poisoning legislation campaign in 1906 one outsider was so impressed by the dominant and authoritative influence exercised by the masters that he reported that, in psychological terms, they had 'established a reign of terror in the district' (*P. Gazette* 1.9.1906). This image of authority certainly led manufacturers to ascribe to themselves the role of leaders and spokesmen for the community who defined public notions of wisdom and rationality. Hence William Burton assumed in 1900 that he spoke for all potters when he outlined his 'wise settlement' of the 'lead question' (Letter to Home Office, 8.6.1900, PRO: HO45/1018/B12393P).

Pottery manufacturers' activity outside the potbank included participation in politics. Evidence of owners' political allegiance is, however, fragmentary, although the actions of the leading figures are fairly well recorded. A high proportion of manufacturers were councillors. Harry Shirley was on Hanley council from 1893-1910 and was mayor twice. Party allegiance was not readily apparent since the prevailing ethos for many councillors was that council work was really 'financial management' (*P. Gazette* 1.3.1910, Bealey 1965). Elijah Bain, the china-maker, was therefore elected to Fenton council in 1908 not on any political platform. His appeal was apolitical and based on his being 'closely associated with the administration of the town since 1885' (*P. Gazette* 1.5.1908). Owners traded heavily on their image as leaders in local institutions as a basis for their almost natural suitability for council office. Indeed, some manufacturers blatantly united their council and business positions. Aaron Edwards, 'the popular Mayor of Longton' used the coincidence of his mayoralty and his fiftieth year in business in 1908 to take his 530 workers on a celebration to Blackpool. The assumption of leadership in the affairs of the local authorities by 'the trade' was demonstrated clearly when A.P. Llewellyn, secretary of the manufacturers' association, was appointed without question in 1908 as presiding officer of the federation poll (*S. Advertizer* 4.1.1908). Moreover, it was the apolitical atmosphere of council elections and business created by the masters and dominant groups which made it so difficult for workers' representatives to gain access by using party political arguments.

For the principal owners parliamentary politics was important.

During the elections of the period manufacturers were recognised to have taken 'a prominent part' in electioneering. There was no uniformity of allegiance. In 1922 it was observed that the 'manufacturers differ in their politics as much as in their methods' of production (*P. Gazette.* 1.8.1922). Thomas Twyford contested North West Staffordshire for the Tories in 1907 and was president of the area Conservative association. Francis Benham was a pillar of the county party and John Hall was chairman of Burslem conservatives. Prominent Tory backers included the Aynsleys, Robert Copeland, Arnold Greatbank, S. Mear, H.J. Colclough, E.J. Ridgway, H. Boulton and Enoch Massey (*S. Advertizer.* 6.1.1906, 27.11.1909, *P. Gazette.* 1.11.1911, 1.3.1919). The balance of the owners' support went towards the Liberals and was based largely on the strength of manufacturer non-conformity and its traditional ties with Liberalism (Pelling 1967: 273, Anderton 1974: 111). The political alliance of certain owners with working potters' representatives had ensured a traditional Liberal domination of the constituencies of the Six Towns. The Liberals numbered amongst themselves some of the largest manufacturers in the Potteries (*S. Advertizer.* 13.1.1906, 20.7.1907). They included Robert Twyford, Harold Plant, Leonard Grimwade, Edmund Leigh (president of the North West Staffordshire Liberal Association), Walter Meakin, (candidate for West Staffordshire) and Sydney Malkin (candidate for Burslem and Tunstall) (Anderton 1974: 108, 113ff).

Although constituents voted according to a wide array of influences and issues it was observed how manufacturers of all political persuasions attempted to use their roles as local leaders in political questions. Some were quite open about the mutual duties of employer and community representative. The Conservative candidate, Sir James Heath, told an election meeting during his campaign in 1906 that his firm paid out £3,000 a week in wages and so 'Kidsgrove did owe him something' (*S. Advertizer.* 13.1.1906). In a more subtle way candidates often made use of the industry as a reference point for their arguments. They turned national issues such as tariff reform or national insurance into pottery industry questions. These questions were presented in very inclusive and unitary terms. Candidates spoke broadly of the trade, always avoiding the differing relationship of master and operative to work. Edmund Leigh in 1906 worked whole speeches around the

notion of 'efficiency' in the trade and how this truth was recognised in 'the just claims of workmen' (*P. Gazette* 1.7.1906). In
opposing the campaign against lead poisoning, manufacturers
emphasised the cost to the industry of the remedies suggested by
workers and trade unionists (*WTUL Quarterly Report* April 1911:
11). Manufacturers such as Leigh were trying to transfer their
efforts to define the 'correct' approach for the industry and
community on a given issue, to the political sphere (cf Palmer
1979: 98). The following explanation given for the Conservative
defeats in 1906 is based on the assumption that working potters
should adopt the political stance of their employers. The observer
was clearly surprised at their failure to do so:

> It is very difficult to find a reasonable explanation of the
> strong attitude taken up by the operatives in the pottery
> industry in the latter towns. For months past the employers,
> with one or two exceptions, have been advocating a change in
> the fiscal policy of the country, which would give the local
> trade a better chance as against Germany and other foreign
> made china. The results show that no argument of the kind
> have yet influenced the rank and file of the workers.
>
> (*S. Advertizer* 20.1.1906)

The pottery manufacturers sought to use their public presence in
order to establish the dominance of their values and codes of
acceptable behaviour. But as the above comments on the 1906
election show, workers did not totally accept and adopt the judgement of their masters in the community any more than on the
potbank. Clearly the operatives were affected by the sheer weight
and traditions of employer Liberal opinion and the extent of their
activity. Yet the working potters constructed their own modes of
entry to public life. They formed their own associations and alliances with other members of the community which in turn shaped
their class awareness and political ideology (cf Dutton and King
1982: 59, 72-73). The potters' participation in the public life of the
Potteries helped explain both the form their class consciousness
took and the continual tension which existed between a spontaneous radicalism and the emergence of a pragmatic reformism.

The institutions which were set up and run by workers were seen
by many potters as a means of achieving a respectable and

independent status within their community. By 1908 it was generally thought that even the less skilled workers in the Potteries had now developed 'a sense of respectability and usefulness which ... they did not previously possess'. Trade union activity was not singled out as the vehicle for this change but was one in a list of bodies including the Pleasant Sunday Afternoon Association, the workingmen's clubs and the WEA (*S. Advertizer.* 18.1, 4.4.1908). John Ward MP was especially enthusiastic about such institutions. He believed that via these associations 'if the working men could only put their principles forward, if they were fair and reasonable ... they would always get something like decent and humane treatment'. The workingmen's clubs were a good example with seven new premises opened between 1900 and 1910. At the extension of the Stoke club in 1906 it was remarked that 'the club ought to be a centre of political and social activity and should aim at improving the status of the people in the locality' (*S. Advertizer.* 15.9.1906). The clubs became one means of asserting an independent existence, entirely separate from the employers. The Hanley club celebrated its seventh anniversary in 1908 and had become a 'necessity to the workmen of Hanley' with an income of £1,368 and 38 organisations meeting there (*S. Advertizer.* 9.5.1908). The potters' union and the local labour council allied with the clubs to develop their own education classes and later to organise the WEA activities (cf Pollard 1959: 197). The Industrial Co-operative Societies and Women's Co-operative Guild played a similar role in helping workers to enjoy a life separate from employer organisations and schemes (*Board of Trade Inquiry* 1908: 217, cf Liddington and Norris 1978: 41).

As potters endeavoured to enhance their public status and respectability they were drawn into associations which blurred their individual and collective sense of class awareness and opposition. The agitation of 1906 for the representation of Thomas Edwards and Noah Parkes on the local bench was firmly based on a sense of labour deserving representation alongside other political groups. The campaign was constructed around the rights of participation. However, in 1911 the appointment of Clowes was publicly seen as recognition for his being 'worthy and respected'. It was also said of Parkes and Edwards that their elevation was largely apolitical since 'they qualified for the position as labour representatives, but also because of their sterling worth and valuable service for the town' (*P. Gazette* 1.4.1906, 1.9.1911, 1.2.1914). The potters' union seems to have placed great store on gaining representation on local bodies. In the light of prevailing values regarding public service, the potters seem to have desired the recognition and status which membership of these institutions bestowed. They appear to have implicitly accepted the role of representatives of a sectional interest group which could influence and reform by collaborating on these bodies with the traditional leaders of the area, the employers.

The service of pottery workers and union officials on local committees and boards did not lead to a radical overhaul of the institutions concerned. The dominant image of the social relations between employers and labour from these associations was never one of class war. For example, the North Staffordshire Infirmary was a prominent concern of the potters, especially given their intimate acquaintance with industrial disease. Sam Clowes was evidently more proud of being appointed to the board of the infirmary than becoming an MP (*S. Advertizer* 21.4.1906, Interview D. Robinson). It was during his time on the board that Clowes formed a personal friendship with the Johnson brothers (CATU Coll, Annual Delegation 1916: 68, 1925: 130). In 1926 we discover the general secretary giving the prizes at the firm's whist drive in aid of the infirmary and praising Johnsons' £10,000 gift (*P. Gazette* 1.3.1926).

During the period, as manufacturers increasingly recognised union organisation at the formal levels so the union pressed for representation on more bodies. These included the Federation Committee of 1908, the war pensions and disabled boards, the development corporation of 1918 and a number of charity ventures. The potters seem to have decided that in order to make any impact on the public life of the Six Towns they had to observe and operate by the established conventions: to act outside these rules would condemn them to isolation they argued. As with collective bargaining, to the potters' officials the acceptance of the union and working potters into the public sphere as an independent force was an immense achievement given their previous exclusion. It was the strength of local conventions of public service and desire for official recognition which led the union leaders to co-operate so closely with pottery employers during the war. Fund raising was seen as a duty and opposing the government's conscription programme became a broad issue of 'the industry' against the state quite separate from the continuing conflict at the workplace (NCPI mins: 11.7.1918, CATU Coll, NEC mins: 2.1.1918).

As the potters tried to influence the administrative and legislative systems, they forged alliances which modified their class awareness. There were many contradictions in these relationships. During the potters' campaign for protective legislation regarding lead poisoning, the union joined forces with one of the richest and largest landowners in the country, the Duchess of Sutherland. The Duchess, in her local letters and speeches against lead use, disowned the politics of labour groups yet her local popularity made the union only too pleased to receive her backing against powerful employer attacks (*P. Gazette*: 2.4 and 1.8.1900, Owen 1901: 271-306). The liaison with Sarah Bennett was also ambiguous. Radical enough to chain herself to the House of Commons railings and to be put in Pentonville for suffrage agitation she was nevertheless a lady of private income who dispensed charity to pottery workers during disputes and periods of unemployment (CATU Coll, S. Clowes Scrapbook: 17.4.1907, *WTUL Quarterly Report* Jan. 1904: 40). Following the tradition of Arlidge, Drs Reid, Moody and Shufflebotham were advisers to the union on technical questions during the campaigns of the period (*Inquiry into Pottery Regulations*: Q 808). All the doctors were active progressive liberals. In each case, from the Duchess to the doctors, these individuals were held in high esteem for their practical work by ordinary working potters, as the motions to the annual delegations of 1921 and 1922 show (CATU Coll Annual Delegation mins: 113). The rhetoric of revolution and class conflict did not have a ready audience among many of the workforce who could not easily relate the actions of an Arlidge or Bennett with class oppression.

In a similar way the influence of religious feeling and attachments on the potters was curiously mixed. As Charles Shaw demonstrated, in the nineteenth century Potteries non-conformity held trade unionism in contempt and suspicion for a long time. The craft unions had therefore been assiduous in their display of respect for the dominant local faith of the workforce (Shaw 1903: 192, Warburton 1931: 73 and 123-124, cf Walker 1979: 53). The *Potteries Examiner* was careful to use religious texts in its editorials, and unionists continued to anchor their speeches on the Bible throughout our period (*P. Gazette*. 1.11.1907, 1.5.1910). Albert Stanley found it prudent to preach in Bethesda chapel as well as addressing mass meetings in the nearby Victoria Hall (*S. Advertizer*. 7.3.1908).

Around the turn of the century the constraint placed on union membership and activity by non-conformism was eroded. First, the chapel and the Sunday school provided useful training grounds for union activists. Thomas Evans, Thomas Edwards and William Machin, for example, were all active lay preachers and teachers (*P. Gazette*. 1.12.1923, *S. Advertizer*. 15.12.1906). Second, in the 1900s the so-called 'labour question' became a serious issue for the local churches and was intensely debated. One outcome of this discourse was that a significant number of non-conformists left their church to form separate labour churches, and in some cases ethical societies, because of their dissatisfaction with their fellow methodists' or baptists' views on labour (*S. Advertizer*. 17.2.1906). Even the established chapels were drawn into the disputes of the period and supported workers during, for example, the Newhall dispute of 1908 (CATU Coll letter from W. Mitchell: 1908). The ambivalent influence of non-conformity on the potters' consciousness was continued therefore even in a period of declining religious observance (cf Hobsbawm 1948: 34, Forman 1979: 176).

Lastly the need for respect and recognition within the Potteries for organised labour was largely explained by the way the ruling groups in the area defined the issue. Employers, churchmen, politicians and local leaders took great care to ensure that questions such as trade unionism were presented in their terms. Potters had to respond in similar language and employ appropriate concepts and images if they were ever to gain access to the established decision-making arenas. Unions had been depicted as irrelevant, unstable and unreliable: the first aim for the potters was to prove that the charge, and the reason for their exclusion were untrue. In 1908 a local journal carefully distanced the union in the public's eyes by describing the arguments of union officials concerning the inequality of the arbitration board as 'wild statements' (*P. Gazette*. 1.2.1908). During 1911 after a bitter dispute over wage increases (certain employers threatened the hollow-ware pressers with extinction), the trade paper saw the opportunity to state what was acceptable worker behaviour. It therefore congratulated the workers on acting 'pleasantly and quietly' and commented that 'it speaks well for the good sense and restraint of the people of the Potteries' (*P. Gazette*. 1.9.1911). A group of employers commissioned a series of articles in 1910, to make union claims regarding low pay and ill-health seem unreasonable, even absurd, under the title: 'The Workers in the Potteries. A Vindication of a Much Maligned District' (*P. Gazette*. 1.3.1910). In order even to gain a hearing from the population of the Six Towns the potters' union had to adopt the conventions of public action and debate, thereby blunting the resentment of class injustice which might have originally inspired them (cf Webb, S. and Webb, B. 1913: 565, Briggs 1980: 43-73, Stedman Jones 1983).

THE POTTERS, THE LABOUR MOVEMENT AND THE STATE

In the first decades of this century the Potteries, in common with many other areas, witnessed the appearance and growth of local political parties organised by labour. Although there was a decisive change of workers' allegiance, the changeover was neither a smooth, inevitable progression nor easily accomplished. An independent political party representing labour in the Six Towns grew not only from the potters' industrial and wider social experience but also out of their relations with other industrial and political groups. How key individuals and associations reacted to the issues raised by the economic and social changes of the time, or the actions of the state in the light of their own traditions and experience, accounts for the uneven 'rise of labour' between 1890 and 1930 (Pelling 1963: 216-228, Musson 1974: 11, Reynolds and Laybourn 1975).

A number of contending perspectives exist on the general development of the labour movement. One variant views the growth of British labour's political organisations as almost inevitable (Kynaston 1976: 155). Others have focussed on the often contradictory variety of social groups, ideologies and aspirations contained within the movement as it grew (Daunton 1977: 196). For many the evolution is regarded as the direct political manifestation of changes in the nature of the economy and work (Burgess 1980: 180, Gray 1976: 165). The Potteries' case shows how unstable and broken was labour's political development: it was a product of the inherent instability of its components. Conflict in

179

and around the workplace undoubtedly assisted the mass support of a Labour Party, but the experience of struggle was not easily politicised in the social and cultural climate of the Six Towns described. The mediation of employers' action and the intervention of local values and allegiances meant that the Potteries' labour movement could not be based only on, as Willie Gallacher put it, the 'treatment of political questions in terms of workshop economics' (cited in Reynolds and Laybourn 1975: 4).

The uneven pattern of growth for Labour in the Potteries can be demonstrated in election results. Liberals were dominant in the four parliamentary constituencies until the 1906-1910 period: thereafter Labour gradually established its supremacy. In these years incumbent Liberals moved over to labour and thereafter the new MPs were mainly Labour members (Pelling 1967: 270-275, Vincent and Stenton 1971: 110, 223 and 228, Hunt 1981: 313-317). At the council level the picture is more complicated. The non-party tradition on the councils has already been noted. The first 'independent labour representatives' were William Owen and Thomas Edwards, who were elected for Burslem East Ward in November 1891 (*Workman's: Times,* 26.12.1890, *Staffordshire Knot:* 7, 10 and 31.10.1891). Their success was seen as a reflection of the union revival of the early 1890s and coincidental with the first stages of SDF and ILP involvement in the area. However, the remainder of the 1890s demonstrated how difficult it was to field independent working men candidates in the face of depressed trade and the antagonism among both the potters' craft unions and also inside the trades council (*S. Sentinel:* 28.9.1895, *Justice:* 19.11.1897, *Labour Leader:* 18.11.1899). These were to be recurrent problems.

By 1905 Labour claimed eleven representatives (TUC 1905: 12). In 1906, Beechener lost his seat in Hanley, while Leese (president of Stoke ILP since 1895) was elected for Stoke with Sam Finney of the miners and Noah Parkes returned for Burslem. Yet in Hanley, Labour's supposed stronghold, 'there were large majorities against the labour candidates and only ten seats were even contested in Hanley and Stoke' (*S. Advertizer:* 27.10.1906). Joseph Lovatt won a seat on Hanley's council in 1907 (*P. Gazette:* 1.11.1907). The new council formations of 1910 saw Labour maintain its numerical presence yet still manufacturer representatives outnumbered Labour's by three to one (*P. Gazette:* 1.11.1908, 1.4.1910). In 1913

only six seats in the twenty-six wards of the Potteries were contested although three new Labour members were added. In 1919
Labour won fourteen seats including those of Arthur Hollins and
William Tunnicliffe, the potters' officials. In the 1920s several
employers were elected at the expense of Labour as unemployment and short time had their effect on union and party funds
(*P. Gazette.* 1.12.1913, 1.12.1919, CATU Coll, Annual Delegation
mins: 22.4.1920).

Whilst recognising that the limitations on the franchise must
qualify any interpretation of the general shift of allegiance from
liberalism to labour (in 1940 only 60% of adult males had the right
to vote), the continuity of Liberal support is noticeable. Pelling
thought the potters' loyalty to the Liberal Party down to the 1900s
'striking' (Pelling 1967: 270-274). The large manufacturer backing
of the Liberals was clearly the party's mainstay given the local
influence of the pottery owners. The traditional appeal of liberal
individualism to many of the craft potters was difficult for them to
shake off, especially when their leaders Owen and Edwards had
such lengthy ties with the party. It became even more difficult for
potters to break those traditional ties as Liberals such as Dilke
fought hard for progressive legislation designed specifically for the
pottery industry. In one sense the conservatism of the craft potter
militated against radical political change. The local constituencies
and wards did not symmetrically overlay the Six Towns, and took
in outlying rural areas, thus muting the general appeal of industrial Labour candidates (*P. Gazette.* 1.1.1911).

The relations of local industrial and political groups were basic
features of the history of the Potteries' labour movement. In
negative terms the long-running clashes between the ovenmen
and the other potters were especially divisive. The public battles
between them over the federation question in 1907 (*S. Advertizer.*
12.1., 19.10.1907) and the silicosis issue were two of the noisiest
examples. Thomas Edwards, the ovenmen's leader, had strong
connections with the local Liberal Party until his death in 1911 (*P.
Gazette.* 1.1.1911). The actions of the North Staffordshire miners
were especially relevant. Their MP, Enoch Edwards, only
reluctantly joined the Labour party as a member of the Miners'
Federation. The miners' leadership had long counselled the
workers of the Potteries to avoid conflict at all costs. The numerical
voting influence of the miners in the north-west county division

and Longton were especially strong (*Kelly's Directory* 1912: 283).

Relations with other local unions had more positive results for the development of a separate labour consciousness. On the one hand the growth of new unions and the arrival of organisers from national unions led to competition over membership, especially during 1912. Yet on the other hand, the industrial disputes of the period provided clear potential for inter-union solidarity. The bakers were very active in the early labour organisations in the 1890s and besides exchanging political theory with the potters were close allies during strikes (CATU Coll, Annual Delegation 1912: 27, NEC mins: 17.2.1923). The experience of regular organising and negotiating with the Navvies and other outside unions during the 1910-1920 period led to their joint political action and their backing John Ward and Tom Cusack, their local organiser, as candidates (*L. Gazette* 1916: 304). Moreover, as the owners had used the industry or 'the trade' in apolitical terms so the unions and labour groups learned to focus on issues common to the whole industry or area. The best example was during the 1918 reconstruction debates when the coal, iron and steel, silk and pottery unions united around the local Labour Party to fight for a Board of Trade Inquiry into the Potteries' transport system (*Times I.F.T.S.:* 7.10.1918).

The North Staffordshire Trades and Labour Council helped facilitate the growing strength of Labour in the region but at the same time gave clear expression to Labour's divisions. The trades council fits Clinton's general conclusion on the councils nationally (Clinton 1977: 4, 17, 20). It provided a training ground for trade unionists and became a means of articulating working people's interests on a wide range of issues. The council's electioneering work was doubly vital since local Labour Party organisation remained partial until after the war. As Fred Shaw of the engineers' union remarked at the time, 'trade councils assisted greatly in the changing of the struggle from the industrial to the political field' (Barker 1974: 4).

The council had been formed in 1892 as a by-product of the union revival and the potters' federation (*Workman's Times* 9.4.1892). It seems to have grown in parallel with local union strength, benefiting especially from the appearance of a number of unskilled unions between 1900-1914. As a body it was widely representative of local union power: by 1908 the council was made up of eighty-six delegates representing thirty-eight unions. The involvement of the potters was high from the outset. William Owen was the first president; Thomas Picken was treasurer from 1892 to 1905 (*S.Advertizer*. 12.1.1907, 15.2.1908); Noah Parkes held the secretary's post from 1904-1910 and Sam Clowes was treasurer from 1906 (*P. Gazette*. 1.6.1906). In return the potters were well supported by the council during strike action (*S. Advertizer*. 13.5.1907).

The potters made a clear mark on the council and were also intimately caught up and affected by its evolution, debates and disputes. In its early days the body expressed the main craft unions' attempts to win local recognition. In the council's own words:

> the friendly settlement of trade differences has always been promoted ... By the uniform discretion, moderation and good sense of its conduct with regard to public affairs, the Council has secured the approval and loyalty of the trades it represents, and also the respect and goodwill of the general public.
>
> (TUC 1905: 11)

During the 1890s the council expressly refused political allegiances. After the unemployment of that decade, the aggression of the employers in the 1899 disputes and the bitterness of the early lead campaigns, the council actively sought political alliances with the labour churches, the ILP and SDF. In 1903 they affiliated to the national Labour Party and helped to found the Potteries' Labour Representation Committee in 1906 (*S. Sentinel*. 16.1.1895, *Justice*. 30.5., 13.8.1898).

The issues which the council faced in the 1900s helped to change critically the class consciousness of the potters and other local unions. It became a public rallying point for the labour movement of the Potteries from the SDF through to the labour churches and the Clarion cyclists and field club (*S. Advertizer*. 1.5.1906, *P. Gazette*. 1.7.1910). The council and the potters worked out a joint campaign for state control of lead use in the industry; they argued for tighter regulations of workmen's compensation and the need for state medical insurance. The council publicly argued for state support of married women workers, the taxation of land values and revealed the inadequacy of old age pensions and the levels of food prices and manufacturers' profits in the First

World War (*P. Gazette* 1.11.1918). By far the keenest question was unemployment. The ravages of unemployment and poverty in the 1890s and 1900s were notorious and turned the council against the government but also called into question the very nature of capitalism for that generation of potters. The 'intimidation' and 'inquisition' of the Distress Committees and Poor Law Authorities produced bitter resentment towards local and national government and engendered a class antagonism within the workers of the Potteries in a way which no other issue could. In October 1908 potters demonstrated against unemployment when speakers 'staked their lives on the demand that there must be food' (*S. Advertizer*. 11.4.1908). In 1909 the unions and labour organisations fed 16,000 destitute children in Longton alone (*S. Advertizer*. 16.1., 6.2.1909). It was the combination of cyclical and technological unemployment that led the NAS and other unions to ally with the SDF on the Central Right to Work Committee. The potters played a leading role in the agitation with Jabez Booth for example at the head of the demonstration outside Burslem and Wolstanton Board of Guardians meeting in February 1909 (*S. Advertizer*. 6.2. 1909).

Whilst the trades council raised the level of class consciousness among the labour movement of the Potteries, the political expression of that consciousness was as disparate as the membership. A continual refrain within the council's rhetoric was the call for 'the overthrow of capitalism and its replacement by a co-operative Commonwealth'. Sam Clowes hoped that 'the potters in the future would run the potteries' (*S. Advertizer*. 11.5.1907, 16.1.1909). For the potters this was an especially daunting task since their experiments in co-operative production had failed badly in the late 1890s. Over the immediate issues which the council addressed, its solutions and policies were essentially reformist. In the short term, pressure by labour was to lead to government intervention on specific issues (*P. Gazette*. 1.11.1907, 1.9.1916). For some local unions the national Labour Party was the best vehicle for reform: others still objected violently to what they called the 'extreme socialism' of Snowden and MacDonald. The dichotomy remained between long-term idealism and the expediency of the short term throughout the period and beyond (*S. Advertizer*. 17.7.1909).

The pottery workers' relations with national labour organisations also contained conflicting elements. The potters were periodically associated with many of the main unions of the period. The potters and other national unions helped each other during disputes and campaigns. The potters' union certainly became aware of a wider labour consciousness. For example, they gave financial assistance to the railway workers in 1911, the Dublin strikers of 1913, the policemen's action of 1919 and protested vigorously at the sentence of penal servitude given to McClean in Glasgow in 1916. National unions gave aid in return. During the 1907 sanitary strike, eighteen societies gave grants to the NAS (CATU Coll, NEC mins: 15.4.1916, 25.10.1919, Annual Delegation: 29).

The Women's Trade Union League did a great deal to develop the reformist thinking and strategies of the potters' union. During the campaigns over government regulation of lead use in pottery manufacture the potters' leaders were clearly impressed by the technical knowledge of the legislation process displayed by Gertrude Tuckwell and Lady Dilke. Parkes and Clowes emulated their techniques. The WTUL were invaluable to the potters both in the organising of women and their political lobbying of the radical MPs (to whom Tuckwell and Dilke were related). Yet their aversion to 'class politics' served to reinforce the adherence of some potters to liberalism and inhibited their move towards the Labour Party. As one of the WTUL reports stated: 'we are dwelling on this earth, and are trying to make it less earthy, instead of devoting our energies to rhapsodising about heaven' (*WTUL Quarterly Report*: 24.1.1900). The potters' relationship with the TUC confirms the union's gradualism and its membership's increasing desire for independent political representation. The motions put by the union to congress, after being debated at the annual delegation, are predominantly reformist. It was the pressure within the union for more democratic organisation in 1913-15 that led to union motions to Congress in 1917 objecting to it 'taking the necessary steps to concentrate and co-ordinate political action through the TUC only' (CATU Coll, Annual Delegation 1918: 81, 84).

The international labour links of the potters were never as strong as, for example, those of the Welsh miners (Francis and Smith 1980: 28). However, the potters' union does seem to have maintained a continuous solidarity with potters in other countries. The sanitary and hollow-ware pressers were in contact with

German pottery workers over trade intelligence in the 1900s, lending financial support to the 4,000 strikers there in 1907 and 1908. The National Brotherhood of Potters in the United States co-operated throughout the period over, for example, the movement of blackleg labour and relative wage and price levels. Friendship with French and Dutch potters went back to the mid-nineteenth century (CATU Coll Fin. Ledgers Vol. 1: 2-6). It was the Potters' International which had the greatest impact on the union. The Staffordshire potters used the standards and methods of obtaining legislative protection used by foreign potters' unions. In 1906, Sam Clowes, after attending the Limoges conference, seems to have been even more convinced of the need for a wider unity of workers and the experience clearly affected his stance on the trades and labour council. The 1912 gathering of the International was in Hanley and gave a helpful boost to the growing Potteries labour movement as it unanimously carried resolutions linking the potters' opposition to capitalism and militarism (*The Times*: 27.8.1912, CATU Coll Annual Delegation 1914: 44).

The combined effect of the potters' own industrial experience in the 1900s and their relations with other labour groups, together with the growth of a local labour movement, placed immense strains on the potters' remaining ties with the Liberals (cf Emy 1973: 285, Burgess 1980: 96, 102, 133). The Liberals' 'Social Radicalism' and 'progressivism' of the 1890s and 1900s was found by the potters to be seriously wanting in terms of hard issues. Their reforms were seen as piecemeal and based on self-help with only limited assistance. The basic failure of reforms, such as old age pensions, to tackle social problems led to the final break by Labour in the Potteries. Initially, in the early 1900s the alliance of Liberals and Labour looked sound (*S. Advertizer*: 13.1., 15.12.1906, 7.12.1907). After the help of Edwards and Ward over workmen's compensation and the Trades Disputes bill, the potters and the Labour council 'pledged to do all in its power to return them in 1906'. E. Edwards in return was quick to 'acknowledge the great force of labour which had placed them in power'. In its initial phase, the Labour council thought the Liberal government 'the most aggressive this country had ever known'. The action of the local Progressives and Young Liberal League continued to attract many traditional Labour supporters of liberalism (*S. Advertizer*: 23.6.1906, 25.1.1908, 20.3.1909).

The final break with the Liberals for Labour came over the basic inadequacy of the Liberal reforms in the face of the economic and social problems of the Potteries. By May 1908 Joseph Lovatt was declaring his 'dissatisfaction with the present industrial system' and that he 'viewed with disfavour the Government's indifference to the claims of the unemployed'. The rationale of an industrial system which brought workers 'face to face with starvation' and the party which allowed it were anathema to local labour organisations (*S. Advertizer.* 9, 16.5.1908). Liberals in the Potteries saw the by-election defeat of 1909 as the result of unemployment.

By contrast it was on the issue of unemployment (which exemplified the inadequacies of the Liberal programme) that the Labour movement could unite. At a public meeting on the question in 1909 Jabez Booth spoke first. Sydney Malkin, one of the local Liberal leaders, should have followed but Booth's speech had revealed the distance which had opened up between their parties. Malkin refused to speak on the same platform as 'socialists speaking socialism' (*S. Advertizer.* 23, 30.1.1909). The Liberals themselves became deeply divided. There was considerable debate therefore over Enoch Edwards in 1909 since as they put it, he 'now takes the labour pledge' and he had criticised the party for 'moving too slowly on unemployment' (*S. Advertizer.* 30.10.1909). Unemployment diminished after 1909 but the decade had shown to Labour the limits of the Liberals' so-called 'social radicalism'.

The rise of a separate political party for labour to match the strength of the other local parties took time and faced many difficulties. Besides the retarding effects of employer construction of values and codes of behaviour the fragmentation of the potters industrially and socially slowed the development of labour's own political presence before the war. The practical problems involved in creating local organisations in the context of high unemployment during the 1900s were considerable. As the Labour Committee put it in 1908: it was 'only fighting to hold the seats they have' (*S. Advertizer.* 3.11.1906, 17.10.1908, cf Emy 1973: 287). The potters' union had to accept that the Lib-Lab incumbents of the parliamentary seats would have to remain until the potters' own candidates could be found and most of all financed. The progress of a Potteries Labour Party therefore proceeded in staccato fashion. The loose coalition of labour organisations which came together in the early 1900s over unemployment and related social issues finally formed the Hanley Labour Representation Committee in July 1906, with Joseph Lovatt as chairman. The committee's primary object was 'to secure labour representation in all local governing bodies and Parliament. A committee covering the Potteries appeared in November 1907' (*S. Advertizer.* 14.7.1906, 14.9.1907). Although leading members of the potters' union were highly active in the local labour organisation the union in general took some time to develop a common policy. The union was still debating the merits of individual affiliation to the national Labour Party in 1911 (CATU Coll, Annual Delegation 1911: 11). It was the recent legal decisions on trade unions and in particular those which made it 'illegal for trade unions' funds to be used for the purpose of Labour representation' which finally led the union to affiliate in 1912. Only in 1914 did the local coalition of labour organisations change its name to the North Staffordshire Labour Party (Labour Party Annual Report 1912: 45, 1914: 69).

The affiliation of the Staffordshire miners' union to the national Labour Party in 1908 was important for the timing of the local labour group's growth. It came just as the Hanley and North Staffordshire Labour Representation Committees had fought their first election under 'the united forces of the Labour party'. According to William Wayte, one of the joint committee's leaders, 'the miners had given their votes for labour', and so labour's opponents would now 'shake in their shoes' (*S. Advertizer.* 30.10.1909). The potters' union regularly backed members in local elections and contributed strongly to the parliamentary campaigns but it was not until the growth of union financial membership between 1916-1918 that it could consider financing its own parliamentary candidate. The pressure from the rank and file members grew as they saw the marked growth in their own political fund (CATU Coll NEC mins: 12.1.1918, 17.1.1920). Individuals played significant roles in the Labour Party's growth. At the parliamentary level it is arguable that the potters did not have a figure sufficiently well-known throughout the Potteries to replace William Owen. They had to wait until Lovatt and Clowes had spent over a decade building union structures and party bases among the Six Towns. In the wards it took a similar amount of time for Hollins and Aucock in Stoke, Coxon and Tunnicliffe in Longton and Booth in Burslem to build their reputations and credibility in both the union and the nascent Labour Party (CATU Coll NEC mins: 25.10.1919, *P. Gazette*: 1.11.1910, 1.6.1911)).

After the initial formation and growth of the local Labour Party progress was slow until the experience of the war period led to a reformation of labour. Labour leaders in the Potteries, especially those from the ranks of the potters, had their public reputations greatly enhanced by their work on the 'joint regulation' committees. The anticipation of far-reaching national reforms forced the unions and Labour Party to act on the key issues involved in the reconstruction debate. In 1918 the potters' union renewed and increased its efforts to win both municipal and parliamentary representation, with great success (*P. Gazette*: 1.5.1917, 1.7.1918). Small groups of potters in Scotland, Liverpool and Derbyshire who were participating in the growth of their local Labour Parties pressed for similar concerted action by the NAS. The levels of union and class consciousness among the potters were clearly raised at this time and sought political expression.

However, the forms of political action which emerged were completely in line with the essentially gradualist path of legislative reform which the potters and most other labour leaders had advocated. Psychologically, the return of independent Labour members was a huge goal and an immense achievement. The success in local elections and ultimately Clowes' election to Parliament in 1924 seemed to justify the way the potters had moved forward on health and compensation legislation from 1900 and also how they had used the state apparatus during the war to win tangible benefits. Political action was to be pragmatic and realistic as this resolution of the Annual Delegation in 1918 showed:

> Municipal labour representation is as important as
> Parliamentary, as many Acts of Parliament are only
> permissible and may or may not be put into operation by
> Municipal Councils. It is therefore imperative that the labour
> groups should be strong enough to enforce the adoption of
> such of these acts as are beneficial to the workers and the
> community generally.
>
> (CATU Coll Annual Delegation 1918: 84-85)

189

Lastly, the industry's relations with the state had continuous and often subtle effects on the potters' attitudes, values and actions. The potters were affected directly by government legislation which concerned the pottery industry and indirectly by the activities of the state or its agents. In terms of direct intervention by the government the potters' campaign in the early 1890s for an inquiry into the dangers of pottery manufacture set off a succession of government reports and new regulations for the industry in 1899, 1914 and 1928. In the 1890s the apparent ability to move the government to implement protective legislation provided one of the main bonds between the liberals and labour in the Potteries.

Yet, the persistent and public opposition of pottery owners, through the 1890s and into the 1900-1914 period, on the issue of employer responsibility for industrial disease and their objections to state intervention was of great significance. The owners' obstructive positions helped to dent their paternalist image (*Hansard* 1907: Col. 947, 1912: Col. 474). The Hanley Lead Reform Committee was able to focus clearly on employer pursuit of profit at the expense of labour's health as the main cause of industrial illness. While the campaigns led to periodic increases in class antagonism, the logic contained within the legislative, reforming action was based on an acceptance of capitalist society: remedial state assistance was not intended to lead to a radical restructuring of society or the economic and social relations which allowed industrial disease to exist (CATU Coll Annual Delegation 1921: 106, 121, 1922: 113). Moreover, many workers actively opposed state intervention of any kind, since they associated official regulations with unemployment and interference with basic worker control and discretion. As a result some potters were alienated from their main union and its political allies as much as from their employers. W. Milner, a dipper at Barker and Kent's, told a meeting on the new regulations of 1901, 'don't let the bread be taken out of your mouths by agitatory' (*S. Sentinel* 28.2.1901).

Conversely, while debates over the question of health legislation heightened certain differences between employers and workers, other problems which faced the industry subsumed these differences. The questions of cheap foreign imports, trade marks and freight rates were presented by manufacturers in terms of unified local industrial interest in opposition to government policy (see Cumbler 1988 on a similar phenomenon in the US pottery industry). The rationale behind the distribution of the profits, which the duties and trade marks were designed to protect, was not mentioned (CATU Coll NEC mins: 19.9.1916, Letter of Doultons to S. Clowes 10.7.1922). Government action in key instances helped develop industrial unity between employers and employed. The Munitions Act provisions of 1916 led the union and the manufacturers' federation to protest jointly to the Board of Trade. Owners and workers collaborated over government contracts for electrical ware going abroad. The language used was hardly that of the class war when potters referred to the problem 'which is in front of us, both employers and employed'.

Admittedly the action of government during the war period did lead to tension between the classes in the Potteries. Potters called for 'the conscription of wealth' as well as labour and opposed public subscription to supplement the naval and military pensions (*P. Gazette*: 10, 17.5.1917). Yet the potters' experience of direct government legislation does not bear out the thesis which identifies increased state action with the generation of class conflict: the range of responses were too diverse for that ever to be the case (cf Burgess 1980: 168-170).

The state also affected pottery in an indirect way via national legislation and the action of government departments and agents (cf Reid 1978). With regard to industrial relations and the pottery industry the government was conspicuous for its lack of direct involvement. The potters' union was alarmed by the Taff Vale case yet, as Askwith admitted, the government during the period lacked any coherent policy on industrial relations (Askwith 1920, Clegg 1979: 289). The supply of a number of arbitrators and conciliators may have assisted the spread of industry-wide collective bargaining as did the work of Dr Addison on helping to establish the National Council of the Pottery Industry. Certainly the joint lobbying of government departments by the employers' and workers' representatives on the Council must have blurred the forces of opposition and conflict which the disputes of 1916-1924 had generated. The union executive were caught between their attempt to use the Council to construct uniform and minimum standards in the industry and the need to ally with employers to press for government action to make such standard legal requirements (*L. Gazette* 1903: 95, *S. Sentinel*: 15.1.1918, CATU Coll NEC mins: 30.5.1920).

The necessary contact of the potters with other agents of the state could both strengthen and dilute the areas of conflict which arose between worker and master in the workplace. The factory inspectorate were popular with some working potters for the practical help they offered. Hilda Martindale found that many 'welcomed my visits to the works and to their homes as if I were a friend'. The inspectorate's liberal individualism was concerned with social welfare, never militancy. Miss Vines, the local inspectress in 1907, still spoke of the duties of the rich towards the poor in her model of social harmony (*HMI Factories Report* 1907: 144). The co-opting of potters' leaders such as Clowes and Hollins on to government inquiries or advisory committees to the Board of Trade and Ministry of Labour further strengthened the involvement of the potters in the consultative and legislative process and provided potent images of the system's acceptability to working potters (CATU Coll NCPI mins: 22.9.1921, 14.1.1925, *Cee on Profiteering Acts* 1921: 1).

Yet these features of the potters' relations with the state must be set against the episodes which produced antipathy and conflict. In 1910 anger was intense after the union failed to persuade the Admiralty (who had placed an order with the company) to intervene with Furnivals when the company employed three times the number of apprentices allowed by custom and refused to recognise the potters' society (CATU Coll: Lovatt to Furnivals 19.8.1910). Similarly the law was openly discredited in potters' eyes by the use made of the courts by employers. The case in 1892 when Meakins charged a group of his striking workers with conspiracy remained in the minds of potters for a long time afterwards. Pottery owners' opposition to the Trade Disputes Bill of 1906 and their backing of the Taff Vale decision increased the enmity of workers and employers during the conflict of the 1900s. This feeling was increased when pottery workers took manufacturers to court in order to recover compensation for 'dismissal without notice' and failed as in the notorious Briscoe versus Meakins case in 1896 (*S. Advertizer.* 12.4.1892, *Royal Commission on Trade Disputes* 1906: Q 4979-4980).

The increasing concern of the state with industrial life and the consequent closer involvement of labour with the machinery of government did not lead to any clear conception by labour of the separate interests of workers and the state. Although legislation and the activity of representatives of the state might engender conflict between capital and labour, master and worker, both developed their own interpretations of government action. On certain issues during the 1890s and 1900s they reached quite opposite conclusions which contributed to the growth of not only the potters' union but the local labour movement. On certain broad issues which appeared to affect the interests of employer and worker it seemed sensible for them to co-operate. Problems such as health and the government's protective legal requirements could produce diverging reactions placing potters at odds with employer and union.

CONCLUSION

The potters and their union were deeply affected by the community they lived in, the influence of the labour movement of which they were a part, and the actions of a state and political system they sought to use and reform. Not only were the social relations of the community, and the neighbourhood especially, of direct relevance to the potters' work, they also helped to form a wider social foundation for the union. These relations were of great value during disputes and periods of unemployment. It was from the social relations of the community that the distinctive class awareness of the potters grew. The codes and values of the community mediated the relations between employer and employed. Manufacturers₁ saw themselves and to a large extent were recognised by others as local leaders and figures of authority and trust, an image which they naturally exploited in industrial conflict and political debate.

The pottery workers neither uniformly accepted nor endorsed the owners' attempts to construct dominant values and codes of behaviour. The potters erected their own ideologies from their own experience, an experience that was clearly coloured by the actions of manufacturers, but never overwhelmed by their authority. The key impulse behind the potters' attempts to create their own institutions and associations, separate from employers, was the desire for independence and respectability. The intention may have been driven by an acute sense of class differentiation but the perception of those differences was reduced by the activities of many workers and unionists. In order to make an impact on the official public life of the Six Towns, working-class representatives of all kinds had to demonstrate their competence according to the prevailing rules which at first they did not control. The alliances made by the potters with other local groups and individuals also moderated their sense of class opposition.

Given the influence of the social relations within the community on the potters' class consciousness the conflict and struggle resulting from the workplace was never easily politicised. Nor was it a stable basis for the growth of an industrial or political labour movement. Traditional employer and worker allegiance to liberalism remained strong. Social and religious divisions within the workforce of the Potteries were matched by their unions' differences over industrial and political questions: both retarded the local labour movement's strength and development. It took the experience of widespread and sustained unemployment in the 1900s and the partial discrediting of employer paternalism, together with the manifest failure of the response by the Liberal administration, to compel the main unions to form their separate political party. The rhetoric and ideology of the new Labour Party appeared radical and in some cases revolutionary. In practice its political activity and immediate reformist programme was the result of: the constraints imposed by previous political strategies and the start-up costs of political organisation; the available models of action offered by their political and industrial allies; and the diverging reactions of the Potteries to the issues of the period.

CONCLUSION

Clearly there are limits to what a single industry can tell us about work and social change. Yet as each facet of work in the pottery industry has been uncovered, the connections with the experience of others seems considerable. Nor does the pottery worker emerge as some deviant (see Introduction) from the process of industrialisation. In many ways the pattern of transformation, outlined in the preceding chapters, suggests that the Potteries represent more of a scale model of British industry.

Many of the points of contact or contrast with other industrial groups have been established during this reconstruction of each main element of pottery work. However, there are three axes of comparison which can confirm the wider significance of the patterns of labour identified in the pottery industry: comparison between the British and US industries; connecting the historical development of the industry with its position in the late twentieth century; and linking the understanding of work derived from the potters to other analytical approaches. Each of the three types of comparison has been present throughout this account. Now they require separate attention in order that their full implications can be made clear.

THE ANGLO-AMERICAN CONTEXT: FROM TRENTHAM TO TRENTON

Comparisons between the US and British pottery industries are highly revealing. The similarities go much deeper than those of a common specialised trade vocabulary or the repetitions of family names as a consequence of migration. The differences are equally instructive, highlighting the distinctive character of work within the long-maturing British industry. These features are best shown by a brief examination of industrial development, production and the regulation of work.

The major difference between the North American and British pottery industries' growth in the nineteenth and twentieth centuries was the degree of concentration. In the UK the dominance of Staffordshire was well-established by the mid-nineteenth century. The vast majority of product types and output was accounted for by the Potteries – one of the sharpest examples of a region being known by the name of its principal industry. Staffordshire produced the full range of products, from fine porcelain to specialist electrical ware. The product profile remained largely untouched by economic or social change. In the 1880s and 1890s Staffordshire's dominance relied partly on inherited advantages but predominantly on the accumulated knowledge base which its potters possessed.

In the United States the pattern was quite different. Two major centres of the pottery industry developed after the Civil War boom and the influx of English potters from the mid-nineteenth century: Trenton, New Jersey and the East Liverpool area of Ohio. Unlike the UK, no single location assumed such overwhelming domination. Trenton's growth was earlier (from the 1840s), relied on immigrant English potters and resulted in production of both general earthenware and more specialised ware. The high protective US tariff sustained the trade from 1864-1894.

The so-called 'Western' industry grew out of the New Jersey trade. East Liverpool's locational advantage was derived from natural gas reserves as a power source in the Ohio river valley as opposed to Trenton's dependence on coal. East Liverpool had superior access to western and southern markets (Gates 1984). Its growth dated from the 1880s and centred on the cheaper 'five-and-dime' trade. The split location of the industry, unlike in Britain, remained into the twentieth century and in fact intensified. From 1900 Trenton progressively abandoned general ware and concentrated on specialist sanitary ware.

In the US industry from the 1920s dispersal was the rule in complete contrast to the persistent concentration of its UK counterpart. In Trenton, even the larger firms suffered irreversible decline during the late 1920s and 1930s depression.

The whole area was further weakened by a similar contraction in the rubber and iron and steel industries. At East Liverpool the problems of the trade cycle were deepened by the lack of space which new production methods required (notably continuous tunnel kilns). The result was the closure of most of the city's potteries with the survivors locating elsewhere in the US (Gates 1984: 262). By 1930 only eight firms were operating in East Liverpool. The remaining potteries of Ohio and New Jersey from the 1930s were owned by large, diversified corporations such as American Radiator and Standard Sanitary (producing the full range of construction goods). These were internationally based – in American Radiator's case in forty-two factories across the US and Canada and fourteen overseas.

In the UK the profile is very different. The industry remained highly concentrated spatially, down to the 1980s, and continued to exhibit a high level of fragmented ownership until the 1960s. In common with other traditional UK industries, the rate of change in terms of company organisation was much slower. The rapid pace of development in the early twentieth century American economy transformed the US pottery industry beyond recognition in a short space of time, just as it did a number of US industries (Houndshell 1984). As we have seen, the UK pottery industry experienced important alterations to certain aspects of its character. Yet by comparison to its US counterpart these were mere adjustments. British pottery manufacture has only witnessed such compressed, radical economic restructuring much later: in the Second World War and during the 1980s combination of contraction and the transfer of ownership to multi-product corporations from outside the region.

A closer comparison of the nature of work in both industries is revealing. Clear differences emerge, such as the opposite outcomes of major disputes in the 1920s or the degree of technological advance. Yet in spite of the accelerated rate of economic change in the US both sets of potters appear to have created similar ways of organising and regulating work. What stands out therefore is the strength of such patterns in both the British and American cases.

The fundamental complexity of the ceramic production process is amply echoed in the US industry. The US government's report on the industry (*US Report* 1915) shows over forty trades were involved at the time of the First World War. The relative lack of scientific knowledge was apparent in both. Around 1900, errors in judgement in kiln control or ware thickness could destroy a potbank's output during a single firing. As Stern (1986: 37) shows for the US case, although the division of labour was extended and modified down to the 1920s, 'the skilled pottery trades were almost never supplanted'. What was consistent therefore in both national industries was the centrality of skilled work down to the inter-war period. Moreover, both show the highly uneven impact of new technology in what was supposedly a major era of technical change (Noble 1984). In Trenton and Staffordshire alike, mechanised jiggers were only slowly introduced. Technical problems with clay recipes, worker resistance and the inability of firms to make the machinery pay in a highly unstable product market situation made for a slow and hesitant record of technological change. Only in the 1920s does the commonality break down. In Britain many of the traditional features of company organisation remained and thus casting was slowly diffused. In the US by contrast, the rise of the national corporations and the reduction of specialist ceramic production from 1930 is apparent. The consequent pressure of technological change and reduction of skill in the US was far greater.

The extensive role of workshop custom was common to both sets of potters: a logical consequence of the presence of three generations of English potters in the US pottery industry by 1900 (Montgomery 1979). Managerial control of work was broadly similar, with heavy reliance on indirect means. Piecework, the employment and supervision of day-wage assistants, group contract work in the ovens and the absence of foremen and supervisors were the rule on both sides of the Atlantic. The language of the potter's shop reflected these similar strengths of custom including the use of the 'stint': the workgroup-defined limit of production.

It was natural therefore that the union forces in the US and English potteries should have developed along similar lines. Both showed the relevance of not only industry-wide craft groups but also the importance of small-scale, localised organisation (sometimes across trades) in the workshop. The disputes of 1922 in the US and 1924 in Britain (Stern 1986, Cumbler 1988, see above Chapter 3) point to the continual tension between these two core forces of unionism and hence the persistent threat to truly national organisations in both cases.

The last broad commonality between the two national industries was the apparent routine combination of conflictual and
co-operative relations. In this respect the American and
Staffordshire potters prove equally difficult to summarise. They
exhibited no dominant single mode of owner–potter
relationships. Instead, joint attempts to regulate the inherently
unstable pottery trade were common to the masters and workers in
the US and Britain. The need to stabilise the vagaries of the
product and labour market were strong imperatives for workers
and owners alike. The drive to reach some form of accommod-
ation was reinforced by the way pottery manufacture dominated
each of the regions concerned. Yet the root cause of this tactical
'community of interest' (Cumbler 1988: 20) was also the strongest
reason for its instability. Excess capacity, the fluctuation in
demand for a consumer good and the persistence of marginal
firms and workers constantly undermined the arbitration schemes,
and national agreements of Staffordshire, Ohio and New Jersey
alike.

Comparison between the US and British pottery industry is
useful therefore in that it extends and deepens the significance of
the findings presented in the main body of this book in two main
ways. First, the dominant features of pottery work in the Potteries
are not idiosyncratic or specific only to that region. The common-
alities of a fragmented production process; the continuity of skill
in the face of industrial and technological change; the
geographical concentration of production; and the combination
of co-operation and conflict in the relations of owners and
workers, unite the two national industries. In this sense the
American and Staffordshire potters echo the conclusions of
Thompson (Thompson, P. 1983). In many ways people in certain
industries or activities, although located in different countries,
often have more in common with one another than with the
workers of other sectors in the same country.

Second, the differences which emerged in the development of
the two pottery industries in the mid-twentieth century are even
more instructive. The distinctive elements of the pattern of work
in the Potteries become clear. In the broadest sense, the
nineteenth-century forms of work in the US potteries were overwhelmed by the rise of a 'national capitalism' in the early twentieth
century. This replaced the local, 'civic capitalism' (Cumbler 1988)

of Trenton and East Liverpool. In Britain no such abrupt and powerful replacement occurred. Rather than being radically transformed between 1900 and 1930, the British pottery industry retained many of its main features of company form and organisation of work. These were only gradually changed until the enforced concentrations of the 'merger boom' of the 1960s and the high rate of company failure in the early 1980s.

The 1922 strike in the US marked the end of the traditional pottery industry. By comparison, the 1924 dispute in Staffordshire represented no more than one of a lengthy sequence of incremental adjustments (Rosenberg 1982) which would continue down to the 1939-45 period. The Staffordshire industry and many of its interior relationships persisted as a totality within the single region. In the US the differences between Ohio and New Jersey were fatal. Trenton's specialist ware disappeared. By contrast the Six Towns continued to produce the full range of ware from its mix of 'sub-industries'. The richness of its pattern of labour was maintained.

CONTINUITY AND CHANGE: POTTERY WORK IN THE TWENTIETH CENTURY

The contrasting historical portraits of the US and British pottery industries leads naturally to a second major comparison: between the forms of pottery work in the early and late twentieth century. The reading of the relations which structured work in the past (offered in the preceding chapters) provides a number of insights into the working lives of the potters of the 1980s. Even more importantly, an interplay between past and present challenges some of the received wisdom on the nature of pottery work which has developed in the last two decades. The profile which results is of a slow unfolding process of change in the industry down to the 1970s, followed by a more violent upheaval. Yet in spite of radical shifts in company form, certain fundamental aspects of the way the potters constructed their working lives endured. Indeed the values and mechanisms which the potters sustained across the century have proved vital to them during the industry's restructuring in the 1980s.

In the broadest sense, the dominant economic features of the British pottery industry and the nature of production have remained strikingly persistent. Above all, the industry's single region location and concentrated labour market have remained intact. The 1981 Census tables (*Census of Population* 1981) clearly show how only a tiny number of Potteries residents work outside the area. The population appears from the census migration tables to be predominantly native with only six per thousand Potteries residents having migrated to the region from outside. The proximity of home and work identified in the Potteries of the 1880s (see Chapter 2) is still evident today. Bellaby (1986) shows how more than three-quarters of the shopfloor workers in the firm he studied from 1983 live within three miles of their place of work. More than half had lived in the neighbourhood all their lives.

The essential character of the product market and its effect on employment has also remained unchanged. The reliance on exports has continued (see Chapter 1) with up to 60% of total output sold abroad (*The Economist* 13.10.1984). Pottery work has continued to be bedevilled by the sensitivity of its product to consumer demand both in the UK and increasingly in North America. The late 1970s and the 1980s have been wholly different though. The industry has been exceptionally vulnerable to the combined effects of the national recessions of 1974-75 and 1979-83, and the effect of the high value of the pound on ceramic exports in the 1980s. Around 20,000 jobs have been lost, almost one-third of the total industry employment in the post-war period (*The Observer* 12.4.1981).

The fragmentation of the industry has continued in two main ways. First, the 272 potbanks of Stoke-on-Trent proved resistant to concentration compared to other industries. Only by the 1970s did the top five firms (dominated by Wedgwood and Royal Doulton) account for 70% of production. By 1986 the two major firms had been purchased by industrial conglomerates from outside the industry. Royal Doulton are owned by the Pearson group, Waterford Glass controls Wedgwood (*Financial Times* 9.8.88 and 21.3.89). Second, the small scale of the potbank has been only slowly altered. In the Royal Doulton Group in 1985 the main Burslem factory employed over 1,000 people, another 500, yet the rest of the potbanks only averaged between 100-200 workers (Hart 1986: 34).

The slow pace of industrial and economic change until the late 1970s is well reflected in the pottery production process. The rate of technological change was modest: a series of piecemeal alterations rather than radical innovations. Oven technology is a prime example. The Clean Air Act of 1956 raised the need to replace the old, coal-fired bottle kilns. Yet their replacement by electric and gas ovens was slow and fitful given the constraints of small-scale potbanks and the continued existence of the smaller pottery firm (Gay and Smyth 1974).

In spite of the lack of revolutionary technological innovation or the major redefinition of its product market and location before the 1980s, the production of pottery has been influenced by developments elsewhere. The strongest indication is seen in the area of management. Although a generation later than the motor and electrical industries, the emergence of professional managers in the pottery industry is clearly evident from the 1950s. In the 1970s managers were recruited from outside as a deliberate attempt to improve efficiency. The present chief executive of Wedgwoods is an ex-director of Ford.

Allowing for such demonstrable differences between the pottery industry of the early and late twentieth century the similarities in the organisation of work are clearly evident. The robustness of the potter's work process over the decades is striking. The attempt to codify the diversity of activities of pottery work in the nineteen chapters of 'The Ceramic Industry Wages Structure' of 1977 (CATU 1977) is especially revealing if set beside the results of the wages inquiries of 1924 and 1946. (BPMF 1946). The range of 'occupational groupings' remains extensive. Over 100 separate, named groups are still in evidence in 1977 (CATU 1977: 26-33) related to the fifteen categories of product within the industry. The intricate method of wage calculation appears to be governed strongly, in all three instances, by the combination of piece and day rates, a Byzantine set of 'allowances', and the issue of 'good-from-hand' (see Chapter 2). These seem to survive, notwithstanding the abolition of formal contract work and the introduction of payment from 'the office' by 1977.

When it comes to the social relations of pottery work in the 1980s the relevance of previous social forms is even more apparent. Existing accounts of the potters and their work have drawn attention to their alleged passivity, the submissive position of women (Sarsby 1988) and the disappearance of the family as a major feature of their working lives (Bellaby 1986). However, bringing together the findings of this study with recent anthropological work on the Potteries (Hart 1986) leads to a rather different impression.

The orthodox feminist conclusions of Sarsby dwell on the disadvantageous position of women in the pottery industry. Great stress is placed on the differences between men and women as shown in official wage rates and the division of labour. Yet this is only a partial understanding. Such accounts (Sarsby 1988: 8-29) fail to recognise the wealth of relations and actions which exist around women's work. The conclusions of Hart (1986: 114-115) for the 1980s are very close to this study's view of pottery work in the earlier twentieth century. In other words, whilst certain assumptions do put women potters in a generally disadvantaged position in the industry, their everyday circumstances are never so straightforward.

The intricacy of the production process still creates opportunities for women potters in the 1980s as it did in the 1890s. Age, experience, skill and workgroup loyalties can combine to enhance individual female potters' status and earnings as the continued strength of the women decorators and paintresses shows. Participant observation on potbanks in the 1980s confirms that women potters actively constructed and shaped their work. They cannot be portrayed simply as victims of a set of patriarchal relations which somehow determines their existence. Women potters appear to have been as adept at using and reconstructing training and recruitment mechanisms, for example, to their advantage during both the depressed trading of the 1900s and the 1980s (Hart 1986:229, see above Chapter 2). In the complex division of labour and the attendant maze of workshops on any potbank, women still seem to be highly resourceful in negotiating the detailed form of their work. As Bellaby and Sidaway show (1983), female potters in a potbank in 1983 matched their male colleagues in the everyday use of joking to establish norms of behaviour and limits to managerial authority.

One of the most potent means of reshaping work which potters have maintained is the family. The extent of kin relations in the early twentieth century (see Chapters 2-4) is matched in studies of the industry in the 1970s and 1980s. The key is to recognise extended kin connections rather than restrict attention to the conjugal or nuclear family. Studies of women pottery workers have found 61% had one or more relatives employed in the industry. They have also discovered levels of over 40% of the workers on a potbank with relatives working there in the mid-1980s (Hart 1986: Ch. 9). Above all, management and potters alike still seek to use such family connections; managers as a possible means of workforce selection and discipline, potters as a way of securing employment and improving their position (Hart 1986: 284).

The vibrant unofficial culture of workgroup and occupational action in the earlier part of this century was seen in Chapters 3 and 4. Uncovering the strength of such shopfloor behaviour may be vital in developing a fuller appreciation of the control of pottery work today. Many have noted the absence of an industry-wide dispute within living memory (Burchill and Ross 1977). In some ways this is unsurprising given the fragmentation of the industry. Yet it would be wholly inaccurate to conclude that the industry is dispute-free (Williams 1958: 298). On the contrary, the strength of workgroup organisation and occupational skill levels has meant that conflict has remained a central part of shopfloor life. Just as in the early period though, such action is highly localised. In the absence of major challenges to the existence of unionism, the potters have necessarily been sectionalist (Bellaby 1986) and even individualist (Hart 1986: 227) given the intricate divisions within the industry. They have not been docile or inactive.

Bringing together detailed investigations of pottery work from the early and late twentieth century suggest two main conclusions. First, the industry's character is a composite one which includes marked changes (e.g. ownership) but also deep continuities (e.g. location and internal fragmentation). Second, taking the trouble to explore both the industry as a whole and the everyday features of work on the potbank helps dispel the myths which surround the potters. These results are of great relevance to the wider discussions on the nature of work.

PATTERNS OF LABOUR

The potters of Staffordshire represent a formidable challenge. The complexity of their industry and the high density of their social relations are not easy to penetrate. At the same time though the richness of their working lives has provided an important service. Understanding the patterns of labour in the pottery industry has required the creation of a composite analytical approach to work which is of wider relevance and potentially useful elsewhere.

Sociologists have become more aware of the way work 'occurs under definite historical circumstances' and within 'a specific economic and social context' (Edwards 1979: 15). This study of the pottery industry in the late nineteenth and early twentieth centuries has developed a framework which can help to explain the nature of such contexts. Two features of this framework stand out.

First, in order to understand the actions of industrial groups such as the potters it is imperative to examine the multiple contexts in which that activity takes place. If we are to master the problems of interpreting forms of work then we must come to terms not only with workers at the point of production but also with the full character of the industry which employs them, their homes and families and the communities which they create. Second, Moorhouse (1984: 72,4) is right to protest that our understandings of work and its meanings are still the victims of conventional analytical boundaries. He asks, for example, can work be defined by clocking in and out; can it be bounded by place? As this analysis of the potters shows, the answer must be a resounding negative. Instead, the need is to recognise the forces of production and social reproduction; the way those involved generate their own meanings of work; and above all the range of sources which fuel the process of generation.

The conclusion of this study is that the pattern of work and its meanings (Gregory 1982: 86, 179; Joyce 1988) becomes intelligible by reference to a 'grid' of influences. In other words, the nature of work cannot be deduced directly from the dominant logic of the development of a capitalist economy or the immediate needs of the market. Cross-cutting these undoubtedly major conditioning features were a range of localised definitions of what constituted work. These included the customary rules of how work was to be organised, notions of appropriate conduct and the learnt roles of employer and employed (Berg 1985: Ch. 7, Reddy 1987). The critical point to note is that these localised definitions of work originated not solely from the workshop or factory. These in turn were the product of the meanings and interpretations which workers formed outside the workplace: in their families, kin networks, neighbourhoods, union bodies, and wider regional social and political formations.

Such a grid of forces captures the full range of meanings and relationships which industries contain. It embraces not just the axes of ownership and managerial control but the pattern of intra-workforce characteristics. These included the everyday contradictions arising from skill, age, sex, family, status and locality. Each of the chapters of this book has displayed the grid of forces in detail and noted some comparisons with the conclusions of others. Drawing these findings together suggests there are five main areas of the literature on work where this study might make a contribution.

The first area concerns industrial development. The pottery industry is an example which adds further weight to the appreciation of the combined yet highly uneven process of the evolution of capitalist economies. In many ways pottery manufacture illustrates the argument of Dobb (1963/1946), Samuels (1977) and more recently Sabel (1982). Rather than growing somehow *en echelon*, industries have been shown to vary markedly in their rate of change from craft to factory and automated production. What the pottery industry (in both the US and UK) shows is that certain sectors may contain unequally developed parts, as in the case of pottery's seven sub-industries. This may be vital in understanding not merely the contrasts in technical sophistication within a sector but also the spread of work forms and their social relations. Moreover, the example of pottery challenges the notion of a single industry product life cycle (Abernathy et al. 1983) upon which the models of many management writers are founded.

Second, the potters have much to tell us on the detailed nature of work. Rather than accept the unitary typologies favoured by the occupational sociologists (Parker 1980/1967) this book has exposed the natural and enduring heterogeneity of the potters and others into the twentieth century (Reid 1980). The mix of unequal technological change and contrasting market configurations, seen elsewhere in traditional UK industries, contributed to a highly sub-divided industry structure and the complex separations within the production process and division of labour. Furthermore, the market changes and technological shifts of the period do not point to any easy model of de-skilling or the homogenisation of labour (Thompson, P. 1983). Rather it is the differential impact of such changes here and in other sectors which stands out (Penn 1985). As both Trenton USA and Staffordshire showed over casting technology, this gave rise to a demanding process of negotiation and the re-working of competences, status and reward across almost three decades.

Nor does the experience of the potters give support to those who detect the centrifugal force of labour market segmentation, be it in the form of the 'labour aristocrat' (Gray 1981) or the core and peripheral workers of Edwards (1979). Instead, a plurality of divisions, hierarchies and competing groups were sustained within the pottery industry. As other studies of UK manufacturing note (Loveridge 1983, Harrison and Zeitlin 1985), it has been the inherent instability of piece rates, product and labour markets together with the constant renegotiation of skill which has precluded the existence of any single, dominant stratum of privileged workers.

However, whilst the pottery industry was clearly divided internally this fragmentation was not left unaltered by the potters. Bases for cohesion did exist within the dense undergrowth of potbank custom, status and skill hierarchies. Association grew within the workshop and around the workgroup. As Foster (1974) showed for the nineteenth century and Sayles (1958) for the twentieth, such groupings can hold the key to understanding shopfloor life. The workgroup provided for the individual a way of interpreting and surviving the divisions and uncertainty of the factory.

These groupings protected people from irrelevance and were the vital means of creating meaning out of the vicissitudes of work. Larger groupings across the industry always appeared less stable or permanent. While relations within the workgroup were mainly cohesive, if only for survival, the relations between the array of hierarchically ordered workgroups on any one potbank were highly competitive. It was the centrality of the workgroup which ensured the paradox of a strong foundation for unofficial action and the persistent uncertainty of wider, official union organisation.

The position of women in relation to waged and non-waged work is a major concern of social scientists. The general argument presented here is that women such as the potters have not displayed the assumed female role of dependence and passivity (Hartmann 1976, Alexander 1984, Rose 1986). Instead they were active participants in the making and re-making of gender relations which took place in the home, neighbourhood and workplace. This is not to argue that patriarchal relations were reversed. Women might not overturn but they did modify key aspects of those relations. As Hewitt (1985) shows for the US, linkages between women workers can provide crucibles in which acts of rebellion may form. In spite of the negative tone of contemporary and subsequent writers on women workers, evidence from the female potters reveals a deep seam of creative women's action.

Like the women in Ross's (1983) or Yans-McGlaughlin's studies (1971), female potters were vital to the structuring of both neighbourhood and workplace culture. Recent research has highlighted the 'construction of masculinity' and the role male workers play in creating gender segregation (Coward 1983, Seccombe 1986). The experience of the potters when set beside parallel research by, for example, Angela John (1984) on mining communities would suggest this to be only a partial answer. It is the active role of women in the creation of gender relations which is equally deserving of attention.

The Potteries would seem to be an excellent example of the joint relevance of industry structure, the level of female employment and the contribution of social values to the role of the family in and around work. In particular, Chapter 3 qualifies the view that the early twentieth century saw the retreat of the family from the workplace (Tilly and Scott 1978, Hudson and Lee 1989). By going beyond the model of the nuclear family the interaction of family and work becomes more intelligible. While income and status divisions at work appear to have been generally reproduced outside the factory, family networks helped to re-shape the competitive social relations of work.

In common with Tamara Hareven's New England studies (Hareven 1982) and similar work in Britain (Grieco and Whipp 1986), this study has found that the extended kin connections of the potters were central to the organisation of their work. Through prior orientation to work, informal training and skill transmission, the family could facilitate the entry to work and the progression along career pathways. Such ties also had specialised local meanings (as shown by Segalene 1983). In the Potteries, kin connections not only strengthened workgroups and supplied the bases for action in the workshop and neighbourhood, they also became an important bridge between the workplace and the union.

The third set of insights which this study offers concerns trade unionism. Extensive evidence relating to all levels of union organisation, but especially the rank and file, is still unusual amongst students of work. Material on union structure, composition *and* action is rare (Wrigley 1986). The potters' experience suggests that the conventional distinctions between skilled and unskilled unions are not always appropriate. Rather, as the potters show, unions came to mirror their changing industrial and social settings. The National Society completed a lengthy, cumulative sequence of reconstruction from the 1890s to the 1920s. The keynote to this re-making was the acceptance of the strength of workgroup customs and shopfloor interpretations of conduct. In other words, the union's growth was a result of the way it accommodated the diverse skills of the potter, mobilised the networks of workshop and town and thereby used the abilities of both men and women. Assumptions in the literature concerning the incorporation of union officials (Flanders 1970: 35-47, Clarke and Clements 1978) simply deflect attention from the much-needed research into the social bases of collective organisation as Bodnar (1982) has shown for the USA.

The fourth aspect of the pottery industry which deserves emphasis is the nature of management and industrial relations. This study sees the competing sectional interests and ambivalent position which workers adopted in relation to their employers or co-workers as a natural outcome of their experience of work. The conclusion offers an important qualification to the recent debate over the degree of conflict or co-operation within British industry over the last hundred years (Price 1983, Joyce 1984). It would appear from the potters' evidence that the sources of spontaneous division among workers may have been sufficiently rich to preclude any simple labelling of their behaviour as independent or interdependent, conflictual or co-operative.

The potters show how workers have choices to make regarding their view of work and its regulation. Those choices will not be informed solely by attitudes originating from the market or workplace. The issue of industrial illness (see Chapter 2) is a good example. The potters do not reinforce Gersuny's view that there is 'an endemic conflict of interest between the workers at risk in manual occupations and the employers' (1981: 142). Rather, as Figlio (1978) argues, workers such as the potters developed their own rationales of work and health, in response to their immediate needs and the customary values of the home. Some workers saw ill-health as a necessary risk, others even regarded that risk as a proud hallmark of their labour. There was no direct relationship between the issue of ill-health and industrial conflict.

Furthermore the pottery industry is a strong example of how difficult British management found it to effect a shift from formal to real control (Elbaum and Lazonick 1986). Instead it was the combined use of traditional, novel and emergent managerial techniques which persisted. Although managerial control remained essentially personal and direct into the inter-war years, these features co-existed with a host of implicit means of control embedded within the potbank's employment and payment systems. As Lewchuk (1987) shows for the automobile industry, what stands out in the case of UK management in the twentieth century is its lack of direct control and the continued reliance on devolved forms of organisation through piece work and sub-contract. It is this persistent mixture of techniques which renders the labels of conflict and co-operation alone inadequate when describing the social relations of work.

Similarly, the pottery industry reinforces the view that the 1890-1930 period was decisive in the course of British industrial relations. It confirms that a more formal apparatus of industrial relations emerged. However, the potters' experience draws attention to the organic and unpredictable character of the lower, operational levels of bargaining. As with other staple industries, the industrial relations of pottery manufacture have been greatly misunderstood due to the over-concentration on national bargaining. The lower levels of bargaining in the UK have remained exceptionally strong by comparison to industries in other countries (Poole 1986: 106-9) precisely because they matched the basic organisation of work and modes of managerial control in the way we have seen in the Potteries.

The fifth way in which this account tried to deepen our knowledge of the history of work was by extending its scope way beyond the factory. The social consciousness of the potters, or other workers, is not to be 'read-off' from their workplace relations. Instead, perceptions of work must be considered within the wider ensemble of social structures which the potters created. The codes of behaviour derived from the neighbourhoods of the Six Towns help to explain how potters organised their working lives. The fragmentation of the industry, the complexity of production and the variety of responses among the potters resulted in no uniform set of industrial relations. When one adds the interests of town, religion and local traditions then it is not difficult to appreciate the fragility of union and class consciousness in the Potteries (cf Savage 1988). The compromises required of the potters as they were drawn into alliances at a local, national and international level further blurred the sense of class opposition.

The centrality of the Six Towns and its social structures to understanding work in the pottery industry leads to two observations. In the light of the continued importance of such localised patterns of economic and social activity would it not be productive to recognise the region as much as the nation state in debates over work. Historians such as Pollard (1982) and geographers such as Massey (1984) offer a way forward. At any given point it is the regional differences within a country which are as evident as the contrasts between nations. This is particularly true of work forms. The distinctive character of work and its social relations in the Potteries could be set alongside comparable regionally-based studies of, for example, Alsace, Lyon, Massachusetts (Sabel and Zeitlin 1985). Such comparisons might be as revealing as the orthodox concern with national profiles (Weiner 1981).

This account of work in its wider social settings has also something to offer to research on the community. Rather than seeing 'true' communities as existing only in pre-industrial periods, as Calhoun argues (1982), the need is to be more flexible. The social mechanisms which bind people in and outside work exist, as Raymond Williams noted (1983/1976: 75-76), to satisfy basic human needs beneath the level of society. As the potters show, these ties often develop in the interstices of legal or formal institutions. They may fall into disuse and are not necessarily harmonious. However, the community-based values and mutual understandings identified here have intermittently provided a potential resource for successive generations to interpret and use according to their needs (John 1984). These features are difficult to uncover and may lie dormant for years. Social analysts of the late twentieth century must therefore develop the skills necessary to identify both their historical and contemporary forms. Without them our understanding of the present episode of the restructuring of work will be impoverished.

This study attempts to build an appreciation of the historical forms of labour by encompassing the range of contexts in which it takes place. It has tried to take seriously the notion that the creative interactions between those involved create their own contexts. Reconstructing that interaction leads to two broad outcomes. No single discipline has established the intellectual property rights to that process. More creative interaction between subject specialisms is required, not less.

Second, exploring the values and actions of the potters has not only rescued them from their distorted stereotype, it also enlarges our understanding of the meaning of work. Work emerges therefore as an activity which occurs not on a single site but as a continuous social process involving intersecting spheres of action. Industrialisation did not impose an increasing uniformity in work; quite the reverse. Given the mix of forces which it contained, a stream of possibilities were let loose. Plurality has been the dominant motif in the pattern of labour. That pattern has not resulted from the needs of any single source. In spite of formidable attempts to appropriate it, work has always been difficult to organise, control and describe – not least because of the human act of its making.

GLOSSARY

ball clay	A clay found in Devon and Dorset, more plastic than china clay but not so white.
baller	A thrower's attendant, who weighs out balls of clay of the size required for each article, and generally takes the thrown articles and places them on a board ready for carrying to the drying stove.
biscuit or *bisque*	Ware which has been fired once only before the application of the glaze.
body	The porous substance of the ware made either of simple native clay unmixed with other ingredients, or composed of several, such as ball clay and calcined flint combined with Cornish stone and china clay in the case of earthenware.
casting	The making of articles of pottery from clay slips poured into porous moulds; the clay sets slowly on their inner surfaces owing to absorption of water by the mould, and after a time the remainder of the liquid is poured out, leaving behind the clay articles as a deposit in the mould.
china	Generally all translucent ware.
china clay or *kaolin*	The final decomposition product of Cornish stone freed from admixed impurities.
china furniture	A class of ware of great variety. Many types are pieces to be used in conjunction with other articles, e.g. heat insulators for teapot handles, eyelet rings for looms. Door knobs, electrical

fittings and ink wells are other examples. Most of this ware is made of earthenware.

crazing — The appearance of a fine network of cracks on the surface of a glazed article.

dipping — The immersion of ware in fluid glaze.

drawing of ovens — The removal of saggers of ware from the ovens after firing.

earthenware — As distinguished from china etc.: the great bulk of opaque ware, plain and decorated, made principally for domestic and general use; the body is usually made up of ball clay, china clay, flint and stone.

electrical fittings — Articles of pottery intended to be used for the insulation of electrical conductors. Frequently included in *china furniture*.

flat pressing — The shaping of dishes, plates, saucers and other articles which are technically termed 'flat', as distinct from 'hollow' ware. A 'bat' of clay is pressed down on to a mould and worked until it is in complete contact with the mould and the shape 'pressed' into the clay.

foolings — Drinking clubs in the industrial centres of the six towns.

footings — The practice of a new worker to a department being welcomed by a small celebration or tea.

gilding — Decorating with finely divided gold suspended in a suitable medium and applied to the surface of glost ware, which is afterwards fired again in a kiln.

glaze — 1. Before firing. A fluid preparation of various silicates or silico-borates, to which is added a lead compound, which is applied to the surface of ware by dipping, painting, blowing or other process.
2. After firing. The vitrified outer skin of a piece of pottery which renders a porous body impermeable by fluids.

glost oven — The oven in which ware coated with unfired glaze is fired to produce the vitrified outer skin known as glaze on finished ware.

ground laying	A method of applying colours.
hollow-ware pressing	The shaping of hollow articles, such as jugs, ewers. Two half moulds are used, a 'bat' is pressed on each and trimmed off, the two halves being finally joined together and attached to a base which has been made in a similar manner.
jet	Ware made from simple brown or red clays and coated with a glaze containing sufficient cobalt oxide to render the finished ware black.
jiggering	The shaping of an article with a hand tool on a mould rotated on the head of a jigger. (A jigger being vertical spindle carrying a revolving head which is rotated.)
jollying	The shaping of a clay article by a semi-automatic tool called a profile, on or in a mould rotated on the head of a jigger.
kiln	A furnace in which articles to be fired are placed in an inner fire-brick chamber which can be heated to the required temperature without flame or gases from the fire entering the inner chamber or muffle.
oven	A furnace for the firing of ware enclosed in saggars.
painting	The application to ware, by means of a brush, of colours or glaze.
phthisis	Fibroid phthisis or lung disease, locally known as 'potter's rot'.
potbank	Local name for any china or earthenware factory.
potter's rot	See *phthisis*.
potter's shop	Workshops where clay articles are fashioned.
pressing	1. The moulding of clay articles from plastic clay. 2. The moulding of articles from powdered clay in mechanical presses.
printing	The decoration of ware by transferring to its surface patterns which have first been impressed on paper by means of an engraved roller or plate.

rockingham Ware made from simple brown or red clay and coated with a glaze containing sufficient manganese to give the finished ware a rich brown hue.

saggar A fireclay box used to hold ware during its firing in an oven. A corruption of safeguard.

sanitary ware Baths, closets, urinals, operating tables, lavatory basins etc., whether made with a fireclay body, or one similar to that used for general earthenware.

throwing The shaping of a clay article by hand on a potter's wheel.

towing The smoothing of the surface and edges of a clay article by pressing a wad of tow on it as it revolves on a jigger head.

NOTES

INTRODUCTION

1. The Potteries is the name given to the region of the 'Six Towns' of North Staffordshire, viz.: Tunstall, Burslem, Hanley, Stoke, Fenton and Longton. A 'potbank' is the local term for a pottery factory.

CHAPTER ONE: THE POTTERY INDUSTRY

1. The traditional recipe or mixture for an earthenware body was: ball clay, 25 parts by weight; china clay, 25 p.b.w.; flint, 35 p.b.w.; stone, 15 p.b.w. Ball clay provided strength and plasticity. China clay adds whiteness as does flint which also helps the body to cloy. Earthenware had a robust body suitable for everyday use and was opaque. Majolica was made of the same body as earthenware but before glaze was applied it was mixed with colouring oxides. Stoneware had a small quantity of china clay but a high percentage of ball clay. It was less porous and much tougher than earthenware. Jet and rockingham were made from simple brown clays. If the glaze contained cobalt, 'jet' was the outcome, if manganese was added 'rockingham' was the result.
2. Lomax's index appears in K.S. Lomax 'Growth and productivity in the United Kingdom', in D.H. Aldcroft and P. Fearson (eds) (1969) *Economic Growth in Twentieth Century Britain*, CUP, Ch. 2, Table 3. It is worth noting that B. Mitchell and P. Deane's (1962) *Abstract of British Historical Statistics*, CUP, Table 14 compared with pottery's output in the *National Census of Production* in 1907, 1912 and 1924 indicates that the pottery industry at least paralleled the UK pattern of output growth.

CHAPTER TWO: WORK AND HOME

1. In the 1900s the mortality rate of potters in the 25-55 age range was equal to that of the coal and lead miners. Insurance companies in 1919 informed potters that they would have to be considered seven years older than their true age in any insurance contract. The causes

of such ill-health were related directly to working conditions. Temperatures on the potbank varied from 70°-80°F in the potting shops up to 100°F when drawing the ovens. Physical exertion was marked in the work of clay carriers and other assistants, and notably among the placers who carried full saggars weighing up to 100 lbs. Fifty-eight per cent of the total mortality of pottery workers was accounted for by dust-related diseases. The siliceous particles in the clay and flint dust of the potbank damaged respiratory organs. 'Phthisis' or 'potter's rot' led to asthmatic and consumptive conditions. One in ten of all potters were in some way affected in the inter-war years. Lead poisoning arose from the use of lead-based glazes. There were 106 recorded cases in 1901 but the figure fell to 14 in the late 1920s as leadless glazes were more generally adopted. For a more detailed account see Whipp (1984).

CHAPTER THREE: TRADE UNIONISM IN THE POTTERY INDUSTRY

1. The membership registers of the lodges are by no means complete. The entries regarding name, marital status, and residence are generally sound: those for age and trade are imperfect. In comparing the Hanley lodge entries for 1920 and 1930 there was no statistically significant change in the occupation or skill structure of the union for men and women. The Chi^2 test gave values of 7.26 for occupation and 5.49 for skill with 3 degrees of freedom.
2. This almost certainly is an under-estimate since the recording of family groups was strictly limited to those who were co-resident and shared common surnames. Higher figures would have been obtained for family and kin membership had the apparently co-residing in-laws and relatives been included.

CHAPTER FOUR: POTTERS, MASTERS AND UNION

1. The CATU Coll letter archive shows 116 firms (29%) recognised the union in this period out of 400 pottery firms (excluding brick companies).
2. Out of a sample of 393 clearly recorded bargaining episodes from the CATU Coll, 313 (79.6%) involved only a single firm; 78 (20.4%) concerned manufacturers' associations or groups of companies. Of a sample of 288 recorded disputes 102 (35.4%) related to individual workers; 138 (47.9%) to workgroups; 17 (5.99%) to a whole factory; 25 (8.7%) to a collection of workers across a sub-industry; and 6 (2%) related to an entire sub-industry.

BIBLIOGRAPHY

PRIMARY SOURCES

Manuscripts and documents

Horace Barks Library	– G. Carpentier, *Reminiscences of Life in the Potteries* (nd) – F. Parkin, *Autobiography of a Trade Unionist* (nd) – Rules and Regulations of the British Earthenware Manufacturers Association (30 Oct. 1916) – The Minton Manuscripts, compiled A. Gibbs-Jones (1973)
Modern Records Centre	– The Great Potters' Strike Handbill (16 Dec. 1881) – Reports of the Committee of the London Society of Compositors – Minute Book of the Amalgamated Society of Lithographers – Lucy Deane Streatfield Collection
Staffordshire Record Office	– Lord Hatherton Papers – Wolstanton and Burslem Poor Law Union Minute Books – Records of a Ceramic Engineer (1904-1914) – Plans of the Eastwood Works
Public Records Office	– Home Office Papers on the Lead Poisoning Campaign, HO 45/9933 B26610; HO 45/9988 X74420; HO 45/1018/B12393 P and Friendly Societies and Trade Unions FS12/24, S1503 1574.

BIBLIOGRAPHY

Webb Trade Union Collection in the British Library of Political and
Economic Science. Section A, Vol. XLIV correspondence and notes on
trade unionism in the Potteries; Vol. XLVII, the difficulties of organising
women; Vol. CIX wages of hollow ware pressers and handbill, 'An Appeal
to Hollow Ware Pressers'. Section C, Vol. 72, Rules of the China and
Earthenware Gilders Union 1890; Rules of the North Staffordshire
Potters Federation (nd); Rules of the Staffordshire Potteries Board of
Conciliation and Arbitration (nd); Vol. 73, Rules of the Operative
Cratemakers Society 1890; Rules of the United Firemen, Dippers, Placers,
Saggar makers and Kilnmens Protection Association 1891; Rules of the
Amalgamated Society of Hollow-ware Pressers and Clay Potters 1890;
Rules of the National Order of Potters Trade Association 1891; Rules of
the Printers and Transferrers Amalgamaged Trades Protection Society
1885.
Worcester Royal Porcelain Company Limited, Scheme for Employees
Benefit Fund and Members Register and Ledger of Awards. The Royal
Porcelain Works Institute Company Minute Books.

Ceramic and Allied Trade Union Collection includes:

- Letter collection (786 pieces classified)
- Document collection
- Count and Price Ledgers
- Sam Clowes Scrapbook
- Annual Delegation Minute Book
- National Executive Committee (NEC)
  Minutes
- Emergency and Joint Committees
  Minutes
- Financial Ledgers and Accounts
- TUC 1905 Meeting and Potteries
  History
- Report of a Conference of Operatives
  and Manufacturers on the Pottery
  Industry (1917)
- Reports and Minutes of the
  Proceedings of the National Council of
  the Pottery Industry
- The National Council of the Pottery
  Industry (reprinted from the *S. Sentinel*
  1918)
- Address to Managers by J. Booth
  (1918)
- Preservation of Health of Pottery
  Workers, A. Hollins (nd)
- Memo on Works Committees
  (1 Jan. 1919)
- Training Department of Ministry of

Labour, Apprentices in the Pottery
Industry
– NCPI, Dermatitis (1920)
– NSPW, Memo on Labour Policy (1920)
– BPMF Terms of Settlement of Notices
given on Behalf of Manufacturers and
Operatives (25 March 1920)
– Minutes of Proceedings before Judge
Ruegg of an Inquiry into the Draft
Regulations for the Manufacture and
Decoration of Pottery (1911 and 1912)
– 1920 wage negotiations and
appendices on apprentice regulations
and female wages
– NCPI, Henry Clay, The Wages Problem
– Welfare Work and Industry, R.G. Hyde
– Lighting in Factories and Workshops,
D. Wilson and E. Werner
(12 April 1923)
– E. Werner, Pottery Regulations
(7 April 1924)
– Wage negotiations 1924, Minutes,
Report and Appendices
– Accountant's Report to a Special
Committee of Inquiry into Wages in
the Pottery Industry (1924)
– A. Hollins, Improperly Pugged Clay
(1924)
– E. Werner, Leadless and Low
Solubility Glazes (1925)
– China Trade, Handbook of
Agreements (1926)
– Collectors Credentials and
Instructions (nd)
– 1931 Wage Negotiations, Operatives
Statement and Wages Inquiry
– Silicosis, A. Meiklejohn (1933)
– Newsletter
– Census of Employees (1 Feb. 1922)
– Lodge Membership Registers
– Reconstruction in the Pottery Industry
(Manchester, NSPW 1945)

Parliamentary Papers and Government Publications

Annual Statement of the Trade of the United Kingdom (1898-1929)
Abstracts of Statistics of the Board of Trade (1900-1933)
Census of Staffordshire (1891, 1901, 1911, 1921)

BIBLIOGRAPHY

Census of England and Wales, Occupation Tables (1924)

Ministry of Labour, *A Dictionary of Occupational Terms based on the Classification of Occupations used in the Census of Population 1921* (1927)

Hansard. Parliamentary Debates

HM Inspectorate of Factories and Workshops Reports

Labour Gazette of the Board of Trade

Reports on Trade Unions 1888-1910

Reports on Strikes and Lock-outs (1900)

Royal Commission on the Depression of Trade and Industry, C4621 (1884)

Royal Commission on Labour, 1893, Vol. III Group C and C. Collet, the Employment of Women, the Staffordshire Potteries Fifth and Final Report and Appendix III

Report on the Conditions of Labour in the Potteries (1893)

Report on the Statistics of Employment of Women and Girls (1894)

Report on Lead Compounds in Pottery (1899)

Report of the Inter-departmental Committee on Physical Deterioration, M. Garnett, A. Anderson, Appendix V (1903)

Royal Commission on Trade Disputes and Trade Combinations, Cd. 2826 (1906)

Report of the Board of Trade on Earnings and Hours (1906)

Report of the Departmental Committee on the Truck Acts (1906)

Final Report on the Census of Production (1907 and 1924)

Departmental Committee on Compensation for Industrial Diseases (Samuel Report) Cd. 3496 (1907)

Cost of Living of the Working Classes. Report of an Inquiry by the Board of Trade into Working Class Rents and Retail Prices with the Standard Rates of Wages, Cd. 3864 (1908) and Cd. 6955 (1912)

Royal Commission on the Poor Laws and Relief of Distress, Vols. XVI, XLIV (1909)

Report of the Departmental Committee on the Employment of Children Act 1903 Cd. 5229 (1910)

Report of the Departmental Committee on the Use of Lead in the Manufacture of Earthenware and China (1910)

Report of the Departmental Committee on Sickness Benefit Claims under the National Insurance Act, Cd. 7687 (1914)

Central Committee on Women's Employment, Interim Report, Cd. 7848 (1915)

Commission of Inquiry into Industrial Unrest. Report of the Commission for the West Midlands Area, Cd. 8665 (1917)

Reconstruction Committee. Sub-Committee on Relations between Employers and Employed, Cd. 8606 (1917)

Report of the War Cabinet Committee on Women in Industry, Cd. 1135 (1919)

Report of the Committee on Women in Industry, Cd. 187 (1919)

Report on Profit-sharing and Labour Co-partnership in the UK (1920)

Departmental Committee on Workmen's Compensation, Vol. I Cd. 908 (1920)

Departmental Committee on the Employment of Women and Young Persons on the Two-shift System, Cd. 1038 (1920)

Central Committee Report on the Profiteering Acts. Report on Pottery (1921)

Report to the Ministry of Labour of the Committee of Inquiry into the Working and Effects of the Trade Boards Acts, Cd. 1645 (1922)

Report on the Evidence of Silicosis in the Pottery Industry (1926)

Board of Trade Merchandise Marks Act, Report of the Standing Committee respecting Pottery, Cd. 3028 (1928)

Balfour Committee on Industry and Trade, 1926, Volumes on Survey of Industrial Relations and Factors in Industrial and Commercial Efficiency

A Study of the Factors which have Operated in the past and those which are now operating to Determine the Distribution of Women in Industry, Cd. 3508

Board of Trade Working Party Reports. Pottery (1946)

Department of Commerce Bureau of Foreign and Domestic Commerce Misc Series No. 21

The Pottery Industry (Washington 1915)

Newspapers and Periodicals

Staffordshire Advertizer
Daily Chronicle
Potteries Examiner
Pottery Gazette
Potteries Free Press and Staffordshire Knot
Staffordshire Sentinel
Times, Times Imperial and Foreign Trade Supplement, Times Engineering Supplement
Workman's Times
Christian Commonwealth
Daily News
Morning Leader
Spectator
Westminster Gazette
British Medical Journal
Cassells Magazine
Fortnightly Review
Justice
Labour Leader
Nineteenth Century
Women's Trade Union League Quarterly Review and Annual Reports
Young Oxford

SECONDARY SOURCES

Abercrombie, N. (1980) *Class Structure and Knowledge*, Oxford: Basil Blackwell.

Abernathy, W. (1978) *The Productivity Dilemma*, Baltimore: Johns Hopkins University Press.

Abernathy, W., Clark, K. and Kantrow, A. (1983) *Industrial Renaissance*, New York: Basic Books.

Abrams, P. (1980) 'History, sociology and historical sociology', *Past and Present*, 87, 2.

Aldcroft, D.H. (ed.) (1968) *The Development of British Industry and Foreign Competition 1875-1914*, London: Allen & Unwin.

Alexander, S. (1984) 'Women, class and sexual differences in the 1830s and 1840s: some reflections on the writing of a feminist history', *History Workshop*, 17.

Allen, G.C. (1937) *British Industries and their Organization*, London: Longman.

Allen, V. (1954) *Power in Trade Unions: A Study of their Organization in Great Britain*, London: Longman.

Allen, V. (1964) 'The origins of industrial conciliation and arbitration', *International Review of Social History*, IX.

Amsden, A. (1980) *The Economics of Women and Work*, Harmondsworth: Penguin.

Anderson, M. (1980) *Family Structure in Nineteenth-century Lancashire*, Cambridge: Cambridge University Press.

Anderson, M. (1976) 'Sociological history and the working class family: Smelser revisited', *Social History*, 3, Oct.

Anderson, M. (ed.) (1980 edn 1971) *Sociology of the Family*, Harmondsworth: Penguin.

Anderson, M. (1980) *Approaches to the History of the Western Family 1500-1914*, London: Macmillan.

Anderton, P. (1974) 'The Liberal Party of Stoke-on-Trent', unpublished Ph.D. thesis, University of Keele.

Askwith, G. (1920) *Industrial Problems and Disputes*, London: John Murray.

Astor, J.J. (1922) *The Third Winter of Unemployment*, London: King.

Bain, G. (1970) *The Growth of White Collar Unionism*, Oxford: Basil Blackwell.

Bain, G. and Price, R. (1980) *Profiles of Union Growth: A Comparative Statistical Portrait of Eight Countries*, Oxford: Basil Blackwell.

Barker, B. (1974) 'Anatomy of reformism: the social and political ideas of the labour leadership in Yorkshire', *International Review of Social History*, XIX, 2.

Barrett-Greene, H. (1905) *The Hanley TUC*, the author.

Batstone, E. (1988), *The Reform of Workplace Industrial Relations: Theory, Myth and Evidence*, Oxford: Clarendon.

Batstone, E., Boraston, I. and Frenkel, S. (1978) *The Social Organization of Strikes*, Oxford: Basil Blackwell.

Bealey, F. (1965) 'Politics in Newcastle', *North Staffordshire Journal of Field Studies*, 5.

Beaver, S. (1964) 'The Potteries: a study in the evolution of a cultural landscape', *Institute of British Geographers Transactions and Papers*, 34, June.

Bell, Lady (1911) *At the Works*, London: Nelson.

Bellaby, P. (1986) 'Personal biography, the household cycle and the myth of family work in a potbank', mimeo, Sociology and Social

Anthropology Dept., University of Keele.

Bellaby, P. and Sidaway, J. (1983) 'Sexual joking on a potbank: affirmation and challenge in gender, age and class relations', mimeo, Sociology and Social Anthropology Dept., University of Keele.

Bendix, R. (1956) *Work and Authority in Industry*, New York: Wiley.

Bennett, A. (1902) *Anna of the Five Towns*, London: Methuen.

Bennett, A. (1907) *The Grim Smile of the Five Towns*, London: Chapman and Hall.

Bennett, A. (1912) *The Matador of the Five Towns*, London: Methuen.

Bennett, A. (1916) *Those Twain*, London: Methuen.

Berg, M. (1985) *The Age of Arts and Manufacture*, London: Fontana.

Berg, M. (ed.) (1979) *Technology and Toil in Nineteenth Century Britain*, London: CSE Books.

Beynon, H. and Blackburn, R. (1972) *Perceptions of Work*, Cambridge: Cambridge University Press.

Bienefeld, M.A. (1972) *Working Hours in British Industry: An Economic History*, London: Weidenfeld & Nicolson.

Blaxall, M. and Reagan, B. (eds) (1976) *Women in the Workplace*, Chicago: Chicago University Press.

Bodnar, J. (1982) *Workers' World: Kinship, Community and Protest in an Industrial Society, 1900-1940*, Baltimore: Johns Hopkins University Press.

Boraston, I., Clegg, H. and Rimmer, M. (1975) *Workplace and Unions*, Oxford: Basil Blackwell.

Bornat, J. (1977) 'Home and work: a new context for trade union history', *Radical America*, 12, 5.

Boston, S. (1980) *Women Workers and the Trade Unions*, London: Davis-Poynter.

Bowley, A.L. (1921) *Prices and Wages in the United Kingdom 1914-1920*, Oxford: Clarendon.

Braverman, H. (1974) *Labour and Monopoly Capital*, New York: Monthly Review Press.

Bray, R. (1911) *Boy Labour and Apprenticeship*, London: Constable.

Braybon, G. and Summerfield, P. (1987) *Out of the Cage: Women's Experience in Two World Wars*, London: Pandora.

Briggs, A. (1980) *Iron Bridge to Crystal Palace*, London: Thames & Hudson.

Brown, K. (ed.) (1985) *The First Labour Party 1906-1914*, London: Croom Helm.

Burawoy, M. (1978) 'Towards a Marxist theory of the labour process: Braverman and beyond', *Politics and Society*, 8.

Burawoy, M. (1985) *The Politics of Production*, London: Verso.

Burchill, F. and Ross, R. (1977) *A History of the Potters' Union*, Hanley: CATU.

Burgess, K. (1975) *The Origins of British Industrial Relations*, London: Croom Helm.

Burgess, K. (1980) *The Challenge of Labour*, London: Croom Helm.

Cadbury, E., Matheson, M. and Shann, G. (1906) *Women's Work and Wages*, London: Fisher Unwin.

Calhoun, C. (1980) 'Community: toward a variable conceptualization for comparative research', *Social History*, 5,1, Jan.

Calhoun, C. (1982) *The Question of Class Struggle: Social Foundations of Popular Radicalism during the Industrial Revolution*, Oxford: Basil Blackwell.

Cannadine, D. (1982) 'The transformation of civic ritual in modern Britain: the Colchester oyster feast', *Past and Present*, 94, Feb.

Cannadine, D. (1984) 'The past and the present in the English industrial revolution 1880-1980', *Past and Present*, 103.

CATU (1977) *The Ceramic Industry. Wages Structure*, Hanley, CATU.

Celoria, F. (1973) 'Ceramic machinery of the nineteenth century in the Potteries', *Staffordshire Archaeology*, 2.

Chapman, S.J. (1908) *Work and Wages*, London: Longman.

Charles, R. (1963) *The Development of Industrial Relations in Britain, 1911-1939*, London: Hutchinson.

Child, J., Loveridge, R. and Warner, M. (1973) 'Towards an organizational study of trade unions', *Sociology*, 7.

Church, R. (1971) 'Profit sharing and labour relations in England in the nineteenth century', *International Review of Social History*, XVI, 1.

Clapham, J.H. (1938) *An Economic History of Modern Britain: Machines and National Rivalries, 1887-1914*, Cambridge: Cambridge University Press.

Clay, H. (1929) *The Problem of Industrial Relations*, London: Macmillan.

Clarke, J. and Clements, L. (1978) *Trade Unions Under Capitalism*, Brighton: Harvester.

Clegg, H. (1954) *General Union*, Oxford: Basil Blackwell.

Clegg, H. (1979) *The Changing System of Industrial Relations in Great Britain*, Oxford: Basil Blackwell.

Clegg, H., Fox, A. and Thompson, R. (1964) *A History of British Trade Unions since 1889. Vol. 1, 1889-1910*, Oxford: Oxford University Press.

Clinton, A. (1977) *The Trade Union Rank and File*, Manchester: Manchester University Press.

Coates, K. and Topham, T. (1970 edn 1968) *Workers' Control*, London: Panther Books.

Coates, K. and Topham, T. (1988 edn) *Trade Unions in Britain*, London: Fontana.

Cole, G.D.H. (1918) *The Payment of Wages*, London: Fabian Research Dept.

Cole, G.D.H. (1923) *Workshop Organisation*, Oxford: Oxford University Press.

Cole, G.D.H. (1924) *Organised Labour*, London: Allen & Unwin.

Cole, G.D.H. (1939) *British Trade Unionism Today. A Survey*, London: Gollancz.

Cole, G.D.H. (1955) *Studies in Class Structure*, London: Routledge & Kegan Paul.

Cooper, P. (1987) *Once a Cigar Maker: Men, Women and Work Culture in the American Cigar Factories, 1900-1919,* Chicago: University of Illinois Press.

Coward, R. (1983) *Patriarchal Precedents: Sexuality and Social Relations,* London: Routledge & Kegan Paul.

Cronin, J. (1979) *Industrial Conflict in Modern Britain,* London: Croom Helm.

Crossman, R. (1975) *The Diaries of a Cabinet Minister, Vol. I,* London: Hamish Hamilton & Jonathan Cape.

Cumbler, J. (1988) 'Civic capitalism to national capitalism', mimeo, Dept. of History, University of Louisville.

Daunton, M. (1977) *Coal Metropolis: Cardiff 1870-1914,* Leicester University Press.

Davin, A. (1978) 'Imperialism and motherhood', *History Workshop Journal,* 5.

Davidson, R. (1985), *Whitehall and the Labour Problem in Late Victorian and Edwardian Britain,* London: Croom Helm.

Davis, H. (1941) 'The theory of union growth', *Quarterly Journal of Economics,* 55.

Dawley, A. (1976) *Class and Community,* Boston: Harvard University Press.

Dearle, N. (1914) *Industrial Training,* London: P.S. King.

Dobb, M. (1963 edn 1946) *Studies in the Development of Capitalism,* London: Routledge & Kegan Paul.

Drake, B. (1920) *Women in Trade Unions,* London: Allen & Unwin.

Dublin, T. (1979) *Women at Work,* New York, Columbia University Press.

Dutton, H. and King, J. (1982) 'The limits of paternalism', *Social History,* 7, 1.

The Economist (1984) 'Living off American tables', 13 October.

Edwards, P. and Scullion, H. (1982) *The Social Organization of Industrial Conflict,* Oxford: Basil Blackwell.

Edwards, R. (1979) *Contested Terrain: The Transformation of the Workplace in the Twentieth Century,* London: Heinemann.

Eisenstein, S. (1983) *Give us Bread but Give us Roses: Working Women's Consciousness in the United States, 1890 to the First World War,* London: Routledge & Kegan Paul.

Elbaum, B. and Lazonick, W. (1986) 'An institutional perspective on British decline', in Elbaum and Lazonick (eds) *The Decline of the British Economy,* Oxford: Clarendon.

Emy, H. (1973) *Liberals, Radicals and Social Politics 1892-1914,* Cambridge: Cambridge University Press.

Figlio, K. (1978) 'Chlorosis and chronic disease in nineteenth century Britain', *Social History,* III.

Flanders, A. and Clegg, H. (eds) (1967) *The System of Industrial Relations in Great Britain,* Oxford: Basil Blackwell.

Flanders, A. and Clegg, H. (1970) *Management and Unions,* London: Faber.

Flinn, M. and Smout, T. (1974) *Essays in Social History,* Oxford:

Clarendon Press.

Fogarty, M. (1945) *Nuffield Reconstruction Survey of Britain*, London: Methuen.

Forman, C. (1979) *Industrial Town*, London: David & Charles.

Foster, J. (1974) *Class Struggle and the Industrial Revolution*, London: Weidenfeld & Nicolson.

Fox, A. (1958) *A History of the National Union of Boot and Shoe Operatives, 1874-1957*, Oxford: Basil Blackwell.

Fox, A. (1971) *A Sociology of Work in Industry*, London: Collier Macmillan.

Francis, H. and Smith, D. (1980) *The Fed. A History of the South Wales Miners in the Twentieth Century*, London: Lawrence & Wishart.

Frankenberg, R. (1966) *Communities in Britain*, Harmondsworth: Penguin.

Freeman, C. (1982) *The Economics of Industrial Innovation*, London: Frances Pinter.

Gates, W. (1984) *The City of Hills and Kilns*, East Liverpool Ohio: E. Liverpool Historical Society.

Gattrell, U. (1977) 'Labour, power, and the size of the firm in the Lancashire cotton industry in the second quarter of the nineteenth century', *Economic History Review*, XXX, 1.

Gay, P. and Smyth, R. (1974) *The British Pottery Industry*, London: Butterworth.

Gersuny, G. (1981) *Work Hazards and Industrial Conflict*, London: University Press of New England.

Giddens, A. (1984) *The Constitution of Society, Outline of the Theory of Structuration*, Cambridge: Polity Press.

Godelier, M. (1980) 'Work and its representations: a research proposal', *History Workshop Journal*, 10, Autumn.

Goodrich, C.L. (1975 edn 1920) *The Frontier of Control: A Study in British Workshop Politics*, London: Pluto Press.

Gordon, D., Edwards, R. and Reich, M. (1982) *Segmented Work, Divided Workers*, Cambridge: Cambridge University Press.

Gorz, A. (1976) *The Division of Labour*, Brighton: Harvester.

Graham, M. (nd 1908?) *Cup and Saucer Land*, the author.

Grant, L. (1989) 'Women in a car town: Coventry 1920-45', in Hudson, P. and Lee, W. (eds), *Women's Work, Family Income and the Structure of the Family in Historical Perspective*, Manchester: Manchester University Press.

Gray, R. (1976) *The Labour Aristocracy in Victorian Edinburgh*, Oxford: Clarendon Press.

Gray, R. (1981) *The Aristocracy of Labour in Nineteenth-Century Britain*, London: Macmillan.

Gregory, D. (1982) *Regional Transformation and Industrial Revolution: A Geography of the Yorkshire Woollen Industry*, London: Heinemann.

Grieco, M. (1987) *Keeping it in the Family: Social Networks and Employment Chance*, London: Tavistock.

Grieco, M. and Whipp, R. (1986) 'Women and the workplace: gender and control in the labour process', in Knights, D. and Willmott, H.

(eds) *Gender and the Labour Process*, Aldershot: Gower.

Gutman, H. (1976) *Work, Culture and Society in Industrializing America*, New York: Knopf.

Hamilton, M. (1941) *Women at Work*, London; Labour Book Service.

Hamnett, C. (1984) 'The family', *New Society*, 14 June.

Hareven, T. (1982) *Family Time and Industrial Time: The Relationship between the Family and Work in a New England Community*, Cambridge: Cambridge University Press.

Harrison, R. and Zeitlin, J. (1985) *Divisions of Labour: Skilled Workers and Technological Change in Nineteenth-century Britain*, Brighton: Harvester.

Hart, E. (1986) 'Paintresses and potters: work skill and social relations in a potbank in Stoke-on-Trent 1981-84', unpublished Ph.D. thesis, L.S.E.

Hartmann, H. (1976) 'Capitalism, patriarchy and job segregation by sex', in Blaxall, M. and Reagen, B. (eds) *Women in the Workplace*, Chicago: Chicago University Press.

Hewitt, M. (1958) *Wives and Mothers in Victorian Industry*, London: Rockliff.

Hewitt, N. (1985) 'Beyond the search for sisterhood: American women's history in the 1980s', *Social History*, X.

Hobsbawm, E. (1948) *Labour's Turning Point*, London: Lawrence & Wishart

Hobsbawm, E. (1964) 'Trade union historiography', *Bulletin of the Society for the Study of Labour History*, 8, Spring.

Hobsbawm, E. (1968) *Industry and Empire*, London: Weidenfeld & Nicolson.

Hobsbawm, E. (1974) *Labouring Men*, London: Weidenfeld & Nicolson.

Hobsbawm, E. (1987) *The Age of Empire*, London: Weidenfeld.

Hobsbawm, E. and Ranger, T. (eds.) (1983) *The Invention of Tradition*, Cambridge: Cambridge University Press.

Hodgson, G. (1988) *Economics and Institutions*, Cambridge: Polity Press.

Honig, E. (1986) *Sisters and Strangers: Women in the Shanghai Cotton Mills 1919-1949*, Palo Alto: Stanford University Press.

Houndshell, D. (1984) *From the American System to Mass Production, 1800-1932*, Baltimore: Johns Hopkins University Press.

Hudson, P. and Lee, R. (eds) (1989) *Women's Work, Family Income and the Structure of the Family in Historical Perspective*, Manchester: Manchester University Press.

Humphries, J. (1977) 'Class struggle and the persistence of the working class family', *Cambridge Journal of Economics*, 1, Sept.

Hunt, E. (1973) *Regional Wage Variations in Britain 1850-1914*, Oxford: Clarendon Press.

Hunt, E. (1981) *British Labour History, 1815-1914*, London: Weidenfeld & Nicolson.

Hutchins, B.L. (1915) *Women in Modern Industry*, London: Bell.

Hutchins, B.L. and Harrison, A. (1911) *A History of Factory Legislation*, London: P.S. King.

Hyman, R. (1972) *Strikes*, London: Fontana.

Ingham, G. (1970) *Size of Industrial Organization and Worker Behaviour*, Cambridge: Cambridge University Press.

Jackson, B. (1968) *Working Class Community*, London: Routledge & Kegan Paul.

John, A. (1980) *By the Sweat of their Brow*, London: Croom Helm.

John, A. (1984) 'A miner struggle? Women's protest in Welsh mining history', *Llafur*, iv.

John, A. (ed.) (1986) *Unequal Opportunities: Women's Employment in England 1800-1918*, Oxford: Basil Blackwell.

Joyce, P. (1980) *Work, Society and Politics: The Culture of the Factory in Later Victorian England*, Brighton, Harvester.

Joyce, P. (1984) 'Labour, capital and compromise: a response to Richard Price', *Social History*, IX, Jan.

Joyce, P. (ed.) (1987) *The Historical Meanings of Work*, Cambridge: Cambridge University Press.

Joyce, P. (1988) 'Work' in Thompson, F.M.L. (ed.) *Cambridge Social History of Great Britain 1750-1950, Vol. II*, Cambridge: Cambridge University Press.

Kaplan, S. and Koepp, C. (eds) (1986) *Work in France: Representations, Meaning, Organisation and Practice*, New York: Cornell University Press.

Kaplinsky, R. (1984) *Automation: The Technology and Society*, London: Longman.

Kennedy, S. (1979) *If All We Did Was to Weep at Home: A History of White Working-Class Women in America*, Indianapolis: Indiana University Press.

Kessler-Harris, A. (1975) 'Where are the organized women workers?' *Feminist Studies*, 3.

Kessler-Harris, A. (1982) *Out to Work: A History of Wage Earning Women in the United States*, New York: Oxford University Press.

Khan, S.V. (1979) 'Work and network' in Wallman, S.(ed.) *Studies in Ethnicity: Ethnicity at Work*, London: Macmillan.

Knights, D. and Willmott, H. (eds) (1986) *Gender and the Labour Process*, Aldershot: Gower.

Kochan, T., Katz, H. and McKersie, R. (1987) *The Transformation of American Industrial Relations*, New York: Basic Books.

Kynaston, D. (1976) *King Labour*, London: Allen & Unwin.

Lamb, A. (1971) 'Machinery and the application of steam power in the North Staffordshire pottery industry 1793-1914', *North Staffordshire Journal of Field Studies*, 17.

Landes, D. (1969) *The Unbound Prometheus*, Cambridge: Cambridge University Press.

Langlois, R.N. (1983) 'Systems theory, knowledge and the social sciences', in Machlup, F. and Mansfield, U. (eds) *The Study of Information*, New York: Wiley.

Laybourn, K. and Reynolds, J. (1984) *Liberalism and the Rise of Labour 1890-1918*, London: Croom Helm.

Lewchuk, W. (1987) *American Technology and the British Vehicle Industry*, Cambridge: Cambridge University Press.

Lewenhak, S. (1977) *Women and Trade Unions*, London: Benn.

Liddington, J. and Norris, J. (1978) *One Hand Tied Behind Us*, London: Virago.

Loveridge, R. (1983) 'Sources of diversity in internal labour markets', *Sociology*, 17, 1, Feb.

Lowe, R. (1986) *Adjusting to Democracy: The Role of the Ministry of Labour in British Politics, 1916-1939*, Oxford: Clarendon.

Lummis, T. (1985) *Occupation and Society: The East Anglian Fishermen, 1800-1914*, Cambridge: Cambridge University Press.

McCabe, D. (1932) *National Collective Bargaining in the Pottery Industry*, Baltimore: Johns Hopkins University Press.

McCarthy, L. (1977) 'Women in trade unions today' in Middleton, L. (ed.) *Women in the Labour Movement*, London: Allen & Unwin.

MacDonald, J.R. (ed.) (1904) *Women in the Printing Trades*, London: P.S. King.

McDougall, L. (1978) 'Consciousness and community: the workers of Lynn, 1830-1850', *Journal of Social History*, 12, 1, Fall.

MacFarlane, A. (1977) 'History, anthropology and the study of communities', *Social History*, 5, May.

McKendrick, N. (1961) 'Josiah Wedgwood and factory discipline', *Historical Journal*, iv.

Machin, D. (1973) 'The economics of technical change in the British pottery industry', unpublished M.A. thesis, University of Keele.

Manners, G. (1980) *Regional Development in Britain*, Chichester: Wiley.

Marglin, S. (1974) 'What do bosses do? The origins and functions of hierarchy in capitalistic production', *Review of Radical Political Economics*, 6.

Marsden, D. (1986) *The End of Economic Man? Custom and Competition in Labour Markets*, Brighton: Wheatsheaf.

Marshall, A. (1919) *Industry and Trade*, London: Macmillan.

Martin, B. (1981) *A Sociology of Contemporary Cultural Change*, Oxford: Basil Blackwell.

Martin, R. (1968) 'Union democracy, an explanatory framework', *Sociology*, 2, 2.

Marx, K. (1938 edn 1889) *Capital*, trans. Moore, B. and Aveling, B., London: Allen & Unwin.

Massey, D. (1984) *Spatial Divisions of Labour: Social Structures and the Geography of Production*, London: Macmillan.

Matsumura, T. (1983) *The Victorian Flint Glass Makers 1850-1880*, Manchester: Manchester University Press.

Matthews, R.C., Feinstein, C.H. and Odling-Smee, J.C. (1982) *British Economic Growth 1856-1973*, Oxford: Clarendon.

Meacham, S. (1977) *A Life Apart: The English Working Class 1890-1914*, London: Thames & Hudson.

Melling, J. (1980) 'Non-commissioned officers: British employers and their supervisory workers 1880-1920', *Social History*, 5, 2, Autumn.

Merkle, J. (1980) *Management and Ideology*, London: University of California Press.

Merritt, J. (1986) *The Making of the Australian Workers' Union 1886-1911*, Oxford: Oxford University Press.

Mess, H.A. (1924) *Factory Legislation and its Administration*, London: P.S. King.

Messenger, B. (1975) *Picking Up the Linen Threads*, Austin, University of Texas.

Middleton, L. (1977) *Women in the Labour Movement*, London: Croom Helm.

Milkman, R. (1980) 'Organizing the sexual division of labour: historical perspectives on "women's work" and the American labour movement', *Socialist Review*, 10.

Milkman, R. (1987) *Gender at Work: The Dynamics of Job Segregation by Sex During World War II*, Urbana: University of Illinois Press.

Moisley, H. (1950) 'The Potteries coalfield: a regional analysis', unpublished M.Sc. thesis, University of Leeds.

Montgomery, D. (1979) *Workers' Control in America*, Cambridge: Cambridge University Press.

Moorhouse, H. (1984) 'Labouring', *Bulletin of the Society for the Study of Labour History*, 49, Autumn.

Morgan, A. (1942) 'Regional consciousness in the North Staffordshire Potteries', *Geography*, March.

More, C. (1980) *Skill and the English Working Class 1870-1914*, London: Croom Helm.

Mulvey, C. (1978) *The Economic Analysis of Trade Unions*, London: Martin Robertson.

Musson, A.E. (1974) *Trade Union and Social History*, London: Cass.

Musson, A.E. (1978) *The Growth of British Industry*, London: Cass.

Nicholls, D. (1988) 'Fractions of capital: the aristocracy, the city and industry in the development of modern British capitalism', *Social History*, 13, 1, Jan.

Nixon, M. (1976) 'The emergence of the factory system in the Staffordshire pottery industry', unpublished Ph.D. thesis, University of Aston.

Noble, D. (1984) *Forces of Automation: A Social History of Production*, New York: Knopf.

The Observer (1981) 12 April, p. 4.

Orton, W. (1921) *Labour in Transition*, London: Philip Allan.

Owen, H. (1901) *The Staffordshire Potter*, London: Grant Richards.

Pahl, R. (1984) *Divisions of Labour*, Oxford: Basil Blackwell.

Palmer, B. (1979) *A Culture in Conflict*, Montreal: McGill University Press.

Pankhurst, R. (1979) *Sylvia Pankhurst: Artist and Crusader*, London: Cass.

Parker, S.R. (1980 edn 1967) 'Industry and Social stratification' in Parker, S.R., Brown, R., Child, J. and Smith, M., *The Sociology of Industry*, London: Allen & Unwin.

Payne, P. (1974) *British Entrepreneurship in the Nineteenth Century*,
London: Macmillan.

Pelling, H. (1971 edn 1963) *A History of British Trade Unions*,
Harmondsworth: Penguin.

Pelling, H. (1967) *A Social Geography of British Elections 1885-1910*,
London: Macmillan.

Penn, R. (1985) *Skilled Workers in the Class Structure*, Cambridge:
Cambridge University Press.

Perrot, M. (1987) *Workers on Strike: France 1871-1890*, Leamington Spa,
Berg.

Pfeffer, J. (1987) 'Bringing the environment back in: the social context
of business strategy', in Teece, D. (ed.), *The Competitive Challenge*,
Cambridge, Mass.: Ballinger.

Phelps-Brown, E. (1959) *The Growth of British Industrial Relations*,
London: Macmillan.

Pleck, E. (1976) 'Two worlds in one', *Journal of Social History*, 10, 2,
Winter.

Pollard, S. (1959) *A History of Labour in Sheffield*, Liverpool: Liverpool
University Press.

Pollard, S. (1962) *The Development of the British Economy 1914-1950*,
London: Arnold.

Pollard, S. (1965) *The Genesis of Modern Management*, London: Arnold.

Pollard, S. (1982) *Peaceful Conquest: The Industrialisation of Europe
1760-1970*, Oxford: Clarendon.

Poole, M. (1980) 'Managerial strategies and industrial relations', in
Poole, M. and Mansfield, R. (eds) *Managerial Roles in Industrial
Relations*, Aldershot: Gower.

Poole, M. (1986) *Industrial Relations: Origins and Patterns of National
Diversity*, London, Routledge & Kegan Paul.

Price, R. (1980) *Master, Unions and Men*, Cambridge: Cambridge
University Press.

Price, R. (1983) 'The labour process and labour history', *Social History*,
8, 1, Jan.

Price, R. (1984) 'Conflict and co-operation: a reply to Patrick Joyce',
Social History, 9, 2, May.

Price, R. and Bain, G. (1976) 'Union growth revisited', *British Journal of
Industrial Relations*, XIV, Nov.

Priestley, J.B. (1934) *English Journey*, Harmondsworth: Penguin.

Randall, A.J. (1987) 'Commerce, morals, markets and the English
crowd', *Past and Present*, 114, Feb.

Reddy, W. (1987) *Money and Liberty in Modern Europe: A Critique of
Historical Understanding*, Cambridge: Cambridge University Press.

Reich, M., Gordon, D. and Edwards, R. (1973) 'A theory of labour
market segmentation', *American Economic Review*, 63, 2, May.

Reid, A. (1978) 'Politics and economy in the formation of the British
working class: a response to H.F. Moorhouse', *Social History*, 3, 3.

Reid, A. (1980) 'The division of labour in the shipbuilding industry,
1880-1920 with special reference to Clydeside', unpublished Ph.D.

thesis, University of Cambridge.

Reid, D. (1986) 'Putting social reform into practice: labour inspectors in France 1892-1914', *Journal of Social History*, XX.

Reynolds, J. and Laybourn, K. (1975) 'The emergence of the Independent Labour Party in Bradford', *International Review of Social History*, XX, 3.

Roberts, D. (1979) *Paternalism in Early Victorian England*, London: Croom Helm.

Roberts, R. (1971) *The Classic Slum*, Manchester: Manchester University Press.

Robertson, J. (1985) *Future Work*, Aldershot: Gower.

Rose, S. (1986) 'Gender at work: sex, class and industrial capitalism', *History Workshop Journal*, 21.

Rosenberg, N. (1982) *Inside the Black Box: Technology and Economics*, Cambridge: Cambridge University Press.

Ross, E. (1983) 'Survival networks: women's neighbourhood sharing in London before World War 1', *History Workshop Journal*, 15.

Rowe, J.W. (1928) *Wages in Practice and Theory*, London: Routledge.

Routh, G. (1965) *Occupation and Pay in Great Britain 1906-1960*, Cambridge: Cambridge University Press.

Rubery, J. (1978) 'Structured labour markets, worker organisation and low pay', *Cambridge Journal of Economics*, 2, 1, March.

Sabel, C. (1982) *Work and Politics: The Division of Labour in Industry*,, Cambridge: Cambridge University Press.

Sabel, C. and Zeitlin, J. (1985) 'Historical alternatives to mass production', *Past and Present*, 108.

Samuels, R. (1977) 'The workshop of the world', *History Workshop Journal*, 3, Spring.

Sarsby, J. (1988) *Missuses and Mouldrunners: An Oral History of Women Pottery Workers at Work and Home*, Milton Keynes: Open University Press.

Savage, M. (1988) *The Dynamics of Working-Class Politics: The Labour Movement in Preston 1880-1940*, Cambridge: Cambridge University Press.

Sayles, L. (1958) *Behaviour of Industrial Work Groups. Prediction and Control*, New York: Wiley.

Schloss, D. (1907), *Methods of Industrial Remuneration*, London: Williams & Northgate.

Seccombe, W. (1986) 'Patriarchy stabilised: the construction of the male bread winner wage norm in nineteenth-century Britain', *Social History*, XI.

Segalene, M. (1983) *Love and Power in the Peasant Family*, Oxford: Basil Blackwell.

Segalene, M. (1987) *Historical Anthropology of the Family*, Cambridge: Cambridge University Press.

Shadwell, A. (1906) *Industrial Efficiency*, London: Longman.

Shaw, C. (1903) *When I was a Child by an Old Potter*, London: Methuen.

Simmons, P. (1988) 'Women in frames: the eye, the gaze, the profile in Renaissance portraiture', *History Workshop Journal*, 25, Spring.

Sisson, K. (ed.) (1989) *Personnel Management in Britain*, Oxford: Basil Blackwell.

Skocpol, T. (1984) *Vision and Method in Historical Sociology*, Cambridge: Cambridge University Press.

Smith, D. (1965) 'Industrial architecture in the Potteries', *North Staffordshire Journal of Field Studies*, 5.

Smith, D. (ed.) (1980) *A People and Proletariat*, London: Pluto Press.

Smith, H. (1976) 'Feminism and the methodology of women's history', in Carroll, R.A. (ed.) *Liberating Women's History*, Chicago: Chicago University Press.

Spaven, P. (1978) 'Main gates of protest' in Harrison, R. (ed.), *The Independent Collier*, Brighton: Harvester.

Stearns, P. (1974) 'Measuring the evolution of strike movements', *International Review of Social History*, XIX, 1.

Stedman Jones, G. (1975) Review of Foster, *Class Struggle in the Industrial Revolution*, *New Left Review*, 89.

Stedman Jones, G. (1977) 'Class expression versus social control', *History Workshop Journal*, 12.

Stedman Jones, G. (1983) *Languages of Class*, Cambridge: Cambridge University Press.

Steed, P. (1980) 'The language of Edwardian politics', in Smith, D. (ed.) *A People and Proletariat*, London: Pluto Press.

Stern, M. (1986) 'The potters of Trenton, New Jersey, 1850-1902: a study in the industrialization of skilled trades', unpublished Ph.D. thesis, State University of New York.

Surrey-Dane, E. (1950) 'The economic history of the Staffordshire pottery industry to 1850', unpublished M.A. thesis, University of Sheffield.

Thistlethwaite, F. (1958) 'The Atlantic migration of the pottery industry', *Economic History Review*, XI, 2.

Thomas, J. (1971) *The Rise of the Staffordshire Potteries*, Bath: Adams & Dart.

Thompson, E.P. (1968 edn 1963) *The Making of the English Working Class*, Harmondsworth: Penguin.

Thompson, E.P. (1978) 'Eighteenth-century society: class struggle without class', *Social History*, 3,2, May.

Thompson, P. (1983) *The Nature of Work*, London: Macmillan.

Thompson, P. (1987) 'Living the fishing: a study in working together', *New Society*, 8 Sept.

Thompson, P. (1988) 'Playing at being skilled men: factory culture and pride in work skills among Coventry car workers', *Social History*, 13, 1, Jan.

Tilly, C. (1981) *As Sociology Meets History*, New York: Academic Press.

Tilly, L. and Scott, J. (1978) *Women, Work and Family*, London: Holt, Rinehart & Winston.

Tolliday, S. (1986) 'High tide and after: Coventry's engineering
   workers and shopfloor bargaining 1945-80', in Lancaster, W. and
   Mason, A. (eds) *Life and Labour in a Twentieth-century City: The
   Experience of Coventry*, Coventry: Cryfield Press.
Turner, H. (1962) *Trade Union Growth, Structure and Policy*, London:
   Allen & Unwin.
Turner, H., Clack, G. and Roberts, G. (1967) *Industrial Relations in the
   Motor Industry: A Study of Industrial Unrest and an International
   Comparison*, London: Allen & Unwin.
Vicinus, M. (1972) *Suffer and be Still*, Indiana University Press.
Vincent, J. and Stenton, M. (1971) *McCalmont's Parliamentary Poll Book:
   British Election Results 1832-1918*, Brighton: Harvester.
Walker, W. (1979) *Juteopolis. Dundee and its Textile Workers 1885-1923*,
   Edinburgh: Edinburgh University Press.
Warburton, W.H. (1931) *The History of Trade Union Organization in the
   North Staffordshire Potteries*, London: Allen & Unwin.
Webb, S. and Webb, B. (1902) *Problems of Modern Industry*, London:
   Longman Green.
Webb, S. and Webb, B. (1913) *Industrial Democracy*, London: the authors.
Webb, S. and Webb, B. (1920) *The History of Trade Unionism*, London:
   WEA.
Wedgwood, J.C. (1913) *Staffordshire Pottery and its History*, London:
   Sampson Low.
Weiner, M. (1981) *English Culture and the Decline of the Industrial Spirit
   1850-1980*, Cambridge: Cambridge University Press.
Westwood, S. (1984) *All Day Every Day*, London: Pluto.
Whipp, R. (1984) '"The art of good management": managerial control
   of work in the British pottery industry 1900-1925', *International Review
   of Social History*, XXIX, 3.
Whipp, R. (1985a) '"The stamp of futility": the Staffordshire potters
   and trade unionism', in Harrison, R. and Zeitlin, J. (eds) *Divisions of
   Labour: Studies in Craft Unionism 1850-1914*, Brighton: Harvester.
Whipp, R. (1985b) 'Labour markets and communities: an historical
   view', *Sociological Review*, 33, 4, Nov.
Whipp, R. (1987a) 'Women and the social organisation of work',
   Midland History, XII, 1.
Whipp, R. (1987b) '"A time to every purpose": An essay on time and
   work', in Joyce, P. (ed.) *The Historical Meanings of Work*, Cambridge:
   Cambridge University Press.
Whipp, R. (1988) 'Work and social consciousness', *Past and Present*, 119,
   May.
Whipp, R. and Clark, P. (1986) *Innovation and the Auto Industry: Product,
   Process and Work Organisation*, London: Frances Pinter.
White, J. (1986) *The Worst Street in North London: Campbell Bank, Islington
   between the Wars*, London: Routledge & Kegan Paul.
Williams, B. (1958) 'The pottery industry', in Burn, D. (ed.) *The
   Structure of British Industry*, Cambridge: Cambridge University
   Press.

Williams, L. (1980) 'The coalowners' in Smith, D. (ed.) *A People and a Proletariat*, London: Pluto Press.

Williams, R. (1983 edn 1976) *Keywords: A Vocabulary of Culture and Society*, London: Fontana.

Wood, S. (ed.) (1982) *The Degradation of Work? Skill, De-Skilling and the Labour Process*, London: Hutchinson.

Wrigley, C. (ed.) (1986) *A History of British Industrial Relations vol. 1, 1914-39*, Brighton: Harvester.

Yans-McGlaughlin, V. (1971) 'Patterns of work and family organization', *Journal of Interdisciplinary History*, 2.

Yeaman, W. (1968) 'The geographical factors influencing the major changes in the pottery industry of North Staffordshire 1945-1965', unpublished M.A. thesis, University of London.

Young, M. and Willmott, P. (1957) *Family and Kinship in East London*, London: Routledge & Kegan Paul.

Zeitlin, J. (1980) 'The emergence of shop steward organization and job control in the British car industry', *History Workshop Journal*, 10, Autumn.

Zimbalist, A. (ed.) (1979) *Case Studies in the Labor Process*, New York: Monthly Review Press.

Zuboff, S. (1988) *In the Age of the Smart Machine*, New York: Basic Books.

INDEX

Printed in the United States
by Baker & Taylor Publisher Services

Printed in the United States
by Baker & Taylor Publisher Services